Elephant Mountain

Also by Debbie Ethell

The Will of Heaven:
An Inspiring True Story About Elephants, Alcoholism, and Hope (Book One)

Elephant Mountain

A Remarkable True Story
About Elephants, Fate,
and Echoes from the Past

- Book Two of *The Will of Heaven* series -

Debbie Ethell

ELEPHANT MOUNTAIN
A Remarkable True Story About Elephants, Fate, and Echoes from the Past
Book Two of *The Will of Heaven* series
Copyright © 2025 by Debbie Ethell

Alberta Pearl Publishing

To contact the author please email authors@albertapearl.com.

For information about foreign translation rights, permissions, or other inquiries regarding this book, please email info@albertapearl.com.

All Rights Reserved. No part of this publication may be reproduced, distributed, or transmitted in any form or by any means, including photocopying, recording, digital scanning, or other electronic or mechanical methods, without prior written permission of the publisher, except in the case of brief quotations embodied in critical reviews and certain other noncommercial uses permitted by copyright law.

ISBN: 978-17335887-6-8 (softcover)
ISBN: 978-17335887-7-5 (jacketed hardback)
ISBN: 978-173-35887-3-7 (printed case hardback)
ISBN: 978-17335887-8-2 (ebook)
Audio version also available everywhere audiobooks are sold.
Library of Congress Control Number: 2025810931

Publisher's Cataloging-In-Publication Data

Names: Ethell, Debbie, author.

Title: Elephant mountain : a remarkable true story about elephants , fate , and echoes from the past / Debbie Ethell.

Series: The Will of Heaven

Description: Includes bibliographical references. | Portland, OR: Alberta Pearl Publishing, 2025.

Identifiers: LCCN: 2025810931 | ISBN: : 978-17335887-7-5 (hardcover) | 978-17335887-6-8 (paperback) | 978-17335887-8-2 (ebook) | 978-17335887-9-9 (audio) Subjects: LCSH Ethell, Debbie. | Berry, Morgan. | Berchtold, Eloise. | Elephants--Conservation.| Elephant trainers--United States--Biography. | Human-animal relationships. | BISAC BIOGRAPHY & AUTOBIOGRAPHY / Personal Memoirs | NATURE / Animals / Mammals | NATURE / Environmental Conservation and Protection

Classification: LCC GV1831.E4 .E74 2025 | DDC 636.08/88--dc23

Cover watercolor by Sandra Ethell / Drawing by Debbie Ethell
Cover and interior design and typeset by Katherine Lloyd, The DESK

SOME OF THE NAMES OF THE PEOPLE AND THE PLACES IN THIS BOOK HAVE BEEN CHANGED TO PROTECT THE IDENTITY AND ANONYMITY OF BOTH. WHILE THE EVENTS IN THIS STORY ARE TRUE TO THE BEST OF MY KNOWLEDGE, CERTAIN DIALOGUE HAS BEEN RECONSTRUCTED FOR NARRATIVE CLARITY AND EMOTIONAL AUTHENTICITY.

This book is dedicated to Jason Reynolds,
my guiding star in both this world and the next.

PROLOGUE

"You better watch yourself," the strange voice said. "Stay out of places you don't belong, or you might find yourself ... strung up."

The computerized voice shattered the peaceful silence of my darkened living room. Alert, I sat up, realizing that my life had just veered in a dangerous, unexpected direction. The frozen screen on my television emitted a haunting glow, while outside, a raging storm paled in comparison to the one brewing within.

The unknown number rang through to voicemail, dismissed as yet another sales call. Turns out, I was wrong. I took a deep breath to steady myself before listening to the message again.

Strung up? What the fuck does that mean? I wondered if the caller meant to say 'strung out,' as in relapsed since I was sixteen years sober, or 'strung up' as in hanging from a tree. I supposed the intent mattered little when the consequence of either was the same.

My hands trembled as I dialed the police, and the dark night closed in. I struggled with the idea that my work at the zoo was related to the threat, even though I'd been warned to keep my head down. I was told that some of the people there could be volatile. Unfortunately, the advice I was given lacked specifics.

An officer arrived and listened to the message, but due to its ambiguity, there was little he could do. His kind eyes were laced with concern. After he asked me a series of questions, I shared a recent, strange encounter I'd had with one of the elephant keepers. Though peculiar, neither of us considered it serious enough to warrant a threat.

The officer stepped outside to look around, and I watched him disappear into a swirling cloud of rain. He returned a few minutes later.

"Your apartment is awfully exposed here. It wouldn't be difficult for someone to monitor you from anywhere in the vicinity. Perhaps you should think about moving somewhere safer," he said.

I told him I would consider it, as water from his jacket collected in shimmering pools at his feet. Before he left, he scribbled a note and handed me a wet piece of paper.

"This is a friend of mine. Why don't you call her in the morning. If you think this could involve the zoo, she might be worth talking to."

And then he was gone. I paced across my living room, wondering how the name in my hand could help. I set the note on my table to dry without smudging further. Perhaps this was all a sick joke or maybe someone dialed the wrong number.

Of course, I'd heard of people who worked around elephants that had faced similar threats, but I was careful. I followed the advice of my peers and kept my head down. In the fall of 2012, I transferred to Portland State University to finish my bachelor's degree. It was there that a fellow researcher asked me to join him in the most extensive study on captive elephant welfare ever conducted in the United States. I jumped at the chance to use my research skills, grateful that it was only temporary. Working in a zoo wasn't something I intended to do for long.

I had always considered the possibility of future threats, but receiving one now, without knowing why, was both confusing and terrifying. I wondered how I'd made such a deadly mistake.

My mind wandered back to Kenya. *What would David do?* He had received numerous threats over the course of his life from both the poachers he hunted and from those wanting to sell their precious ivory. Memories of his past emerged as I searched for inspiration or a clue.

David Sheldrick was a pioneer as the first game warden of Tsavo, the largest national park in Kenya. He and his wife Daphne tirelessly rescued the youngest victims of the poaching plague in the 1950s: orphaned baby elephants that never would have survived without their help. They were also at the forefront of elephant research, in a unique position to study them like no one ever had. And the discoveries they made were astonishing.

They realized how every member of their makeshift herd relied on each other *emotionally* for their survival, something never observed before. Bull elephants formed strong, lifelong bonds with each other, challenging the prior belief that they lived a solitary existence. The Sheldricks sensed they were using a silent form of communication long before the scientific community identified it as infrasound. These low-frequency sound waves, below the threshold of human hearing, are vital to how they relay information.

When I was eight years old, I began documenting the life history of every elephant the Sheldricks' rescued (and there were hundreds). But it all began with one: Eleanor. She was the first elephant I ever met—not in person, of course—we were far too poor to travel to Kenya from our rural home in Oregon. Initially, I was introduced to her in a documentary, and later, I explored her story through books, films, and research papers.

I'd witnessed Eleanor's profound grief when she lost an orphan too far gone to save, and her elation when another, deemed hopeless by everyone else, made an unexpected recovery due her unwavering dedication. It reminded me of the way recovering alcoholics worked with each other, how we too showed up on death's doorstep and were brought back to life by the survivors.

Eleanor transformed the idea of what elephants were capable of and played a crucial role in the Sheldricks' operation. Soon they couldn't imagine saving any baby elephants without her. Fortunately, for the next three decades, they didn't have to. Just when they thought she would never return to the wild, Eleanor surprised everyone by doing exactly that. There she gave birth to three wild-born calves of her own and, apart from a few visits to introduce them to Daphne and her former keepers, remained free of all human contact for the rest of her life.

Elephant poaching spread across the country David loved, and it was there that he made his final stand, departing too soon and too young. He succumbed to a fatal heart attack at fifty-seven, just as his efforts showed the first signs of success, turning former poachers into the elephants' most ardent protectors. Daphne and her daughters carried on his work by founding the David Sheldrick Wildlife Trust in 1977, ensuring the lasting impact of his legacy.

Inspired by figures like David, as well as women scientists and conservationists, I took a leap of faith at thirty-five. I gave up everything to pursue my own dream of sharing the stories of wild elephants like Eleanor and the discoveries being made about them. Deep down, I knew that a science degree would put me in the best position to help, but I had never learned math. It took several years longer than the average person to become the scientist of my dreams, but at forty-one, I finally achieved that goal.

Lightning flashed, illuminating my apartment. One-one-thousand, two-one-thousand, three-one-thousand—thunder. David and Daphne had faced worse storms, but it was the elephants who showed unparalleled bravery. When confronted with an imminent threat—guns pointed directly at them or their loved ones—they charged, protected, and defended each other in displays so shocking, so courageous, they brought grown men to their knees.

That evening, as I lay in bed, I reflected on their remarkable character. If they could confront the dangers they faced, then so could I. It was a mantra I'd recited for most of my life.

Another sheet of lightning lit up my room, followed by an immediate thunderous boom. Nightmares visited often, and I already knew the moment I closed my eyes, they would not forgive this opportunity.

The next morning, still jittery from the night before, I picked up the wrinkled piece of paper from the table where I'd left it. The rain was nothing more than a calm, wistful pitter-patter, and I hoped it was a sign. I dialed the number, and a secretary answered announcing the name of a law firm, which caught me off guard. Why would the officer refer me to an attorney?

Intrigued, I asked to speak to the person whose smudged name was barely legible. She picked up on the first ring. After I explained the reason for my call, we talked about my work on the research project and the strange behavior of the elephant keeper, but nothing seemed to raise any red flags, at least not to the level of being threatened.

"Is there anything else unusual or out of the ordinary that happened at the zoo?" she asked.

I thought about it for a moment before I remembered something. A few days earlier, I'd witnessed a heated discussion between two men in the back of the elephant barn. I recognized one as the zoo director, but the other was a stranger. They noticed me, and although I was behind a solid piece of glass and unable to hear what they said, the strange man's piercing look left an impression. At the time, I found it disturbing and out of proportion regarding the situation. I mentioned it to the lawyer, though it felt trivial, as if I were reading too much into it. But as soon as I provided a physical description of that man, her quiet demeanor suddenly shifted.

"Debbie, we have to stop this conversation *now*. Anything else we say has to be in person. Do you understand? I will text you with an address. And bring five dollars."

I automatically gave her my number. "I don't get it. What—what just happened?"

"Not. One. More. Word. Just meet me at the location I send you."

And then the line went dead. Somehow, I had indeed crossed paths with danger. This was no accident. It wasn't a wrong number or a sick joke. This was fucking real. I had no idea what I'd gotten myself into, though it was clear she did.

The buzz of my phone made me jump. I placed a hand over my pounding heart as I glanced at the screen: a text with an address. My mind swirled with unanswered questions, as a growing sense of panic tightened in my chest. I fought to stay calm, inhaling deeply to steady myself, but it was no use.

Without another thought, I grabbed a coat, my keys, and then I ran.

INTRODUCTION

*T*homas Jefferson once said, "For here we are not afraid to follow truth wherever it may lead."

These words have lingered with me throughout the writing of this book. There is a certain luck I've come to recognize, simply by being in the right place at the right time, that leads to inspiration when I let go, get quiet, and listen. It's how I discovered these events and the elephants who led me there.

I didn't know just how dangerous it was to keep male elephants in captivity, had no idea how hard they fought back until I was pursued by a teenage ghost who begged me to learn his story. It was while working in a secret museum full of elephant bones that I stumbled across a legend.

At the top of a small mountain in the Pacific Northwest, surrounded by cascading hills of old-growth forests, Morgan Berry collected hundreds of exotic animals. But like me, it was elephants that changed his life. He achieved unprecedented acclaim when two of his herd produced one of the most famous babies that ever lived: Packy, the first elephant born in captivity in nearly half a century.

The birth at the Oregon Zoo, catapulted Morgan into fame and fortune, and he quickly became known as the man who cracked the breeding code. Some considered him a hero, while others—*let's just say*—didn't. Rightly or wrongly, one thing was certain: Morgan sparked a ruthless desire across the globe to replicate his success. Everyone, it seemed, wanted a baby elephant of their own.

The craving mirrored that of a powerful drug—intoxicating, unshakable, and potent enough to drive desperate men to even more desperate measures. It reminded me of my own disease of addiction. Both shared an insatiable hunger and held us by the throat in a white-knuckled grip until we learned how to break the devil's spell.

In 1962, among the 264 elephants in U.S. zoos, just thirteen were males. Then Morgan came along and began transporting them by the hundreds, both male and female, out of every Southeast Asian country that had them. They were taken to his farm, near Woodland, Washington, where they were traded like stocks on the exchange.

The relentless capture of elephants by men like Morgan, combined with poaching for ivory, led to the collapse of the entire wild Asian population by 1976. Ironically, three years later, Morgan was killed by an elephant he had raised. Just one year earlier—nearly to the day—Eloise Berchtold, the great circus performer and his life partner, encountered a similar fate, falling victim to another elephant they had cherished since birth.

I first learned of their tragic love story while working at the Oregon Zoo. The front page of a local newspaper detailing the gruesome tragedy was tacked to a wall just outside the main research office. Although I never truly understood what happened until now. What I discovered was shocking and, in many ways, surreal. The circumstances surrounding their deaths, including those of the elephants in their care, appeared to have been altered, and I was determined to find out why.

While unraveling this mystery, I found solace in the inspiring journey of one wild bull in particular. His courage became my pillar of strength when it felt like this story would consume me whole. He challenged much of what scientists once believed about male elephants—revelations they're only just beginning to grasp. Woven into these pages, his extraordinary life is more than mere storytelling; it documents real events.

Throughout this experience, I was forced to confront difficult truths, not only about myself, but the individuals you are about to meet. If parts of it feel challenging, as they certainly were for me, I urge you to consider: to look away is as if the lives of these elephants never existed. But this happened. It's real. And they matter.

In my first book, *The Will of Heaven,* I wrote something that bears repeating here: What you are about to read is based on my experiences in life and with the elephants I have come to know. Their stories, as well as my own, are told to the best of my ability as nothing more and nothing less than an educated observer of both.

History—like the truth—is neutral by nature. It just is what it is. So I ask that you trust me as your guide down this somewhat tumultuous river. I won't lead you anywhere that isn't necessary for the journey to come, and I know where this story ends: calmer, peaceful waters lie ahead. The way sunlight breaks through a storm, butterflies emerge from a cocoon, or how a flower rises from the burnt ash of a forest floor—there is *always* hope.

For the elephants.

And for alcoholics like me.

CHAPTER 1

I traced the raggedy edge with my finger—the entry point of the bullet. It was the only elephant skull I had ever seen up close, or even touched. Although I would handle hundreds in the years to come, my first made the strongest impression. Perhaps that's why it was so difficult to let go or the reason I was so eager to learn its story. But sometimes ghosts have a way of finding me, as if they've heard somehow I'm looking for them.

Violet appeared from behind a bookshelf as the museum's curator and a biologist.

"How did you know?" I was always impressed when she had it waiting for me.

"Because even when you don't ask," she raised a playful eyebrow, "I know you want to see it again."

I smiled—it was true. That skull fascinated me. She'd placed it on a stainless-steel cart, allowing me to walk around it freely, examining and admiring every intricate detail. It was also the first bone where I could see the obvious sign of death, as if someone had stood back and taken careful aim to get it just right, to lodge that bullet square between the elephant's eyes.

A research colleague at the Oregon Zoo told me about this place: a closed-off, windowless building lined with rows of elephant bones. I called it the "secret museum" because it was off-limits to the public and known only to a select few. The large room carried a distinct aroma—a chemical bouquet laced with a hint of decay—an acquired taste, one that admirers like us grew accustomed to over time.

I don't know why I went there as often as I did, maybe to search for clues, maybe to pay my respects, but that museum intrigued me as much as performing necropsies did. In my last year of school, I worked part time with the Marine Mammal Stranding Network, an organization that collects and studies the bodies of sea creatures to determine their cause of death.

Each necropsy (or animal autopsy) I conducted revealed secrets of the life that animal lived. I didn't realize I could learn so much by studying death, but tiny clues left behind surprised me every time. Many shared harrowing escapes, bearing scars of old wounds that should have killed them but didn't. There was starvation, multiple births, shiny coats indicating health, and poor ones signaling malnutrition. And more bullets than I could count, some lodged deep within, but not enough to kill. Even the smallest details provided insight into their world and that, by itself, captivated me more than if I'd simply read about it in some book.

The elephant skull before me wasn't white like the others, but a rich, earthy brown. While I continued examining it, Violet disclosed parts of its story.

"Supposedly, some students found it buried along a riverbank, which is why it's a darker color due to water exposure and in such poor condition."

I imagined a group of college kids on a random nature hike when a half-submerged elephant skeleton suddenly appeared out of nowhere, dangling from the water's edge—though that seemed unlikely.

ELEPHANT MOUNTAIN

"Rumor has it this elephant killed his trainer, so that's why they shot him," Violet said, sharing the last of what she knew.

My heart sank. *Of course.* It used to be common practice to kill elephants known as 'man-killers' or 'rogues,' and it certainly explained the marksmanship of the bullet. The elephant would have had its legs chained to the ground, therefore making it an easy shot.

She didn't think it was one from the Oregon Zoo, but plenty of circuses had passed through the Pacific Northwest over the years. It could have been from any number of them. My hand rested on the skull. Whatever happened, its secrets were likely buried along the riverbank wherever it was found.

Violet was as passionate about bones as I was about necropsies; both of us loved unraveling a good mystery. There were two obvious bulbs on top, revealing it was an Asian elephant, and not African, whose heads were smooth. We also knew it was a male because of the large openings that once held his tusks, which are smaller and less pronounced in females. The teeth gave us our final clue—he couldn't have been much older than thirteen when he died.

The elephant is the only mammal whose lifespan mimics our own in terms of age and understanding. The sixth and final set of teeth comes in when an elephant is around forty years old and lasts for the rest of their life, until the age of sixty or so. A thirteen-year-old elephant comprehends its surroundings in much the same way as a thirteen-year-old boy. Both were too young to have been shot point blank in the head.

It was late by the time I left. The night air embraced me, a stark contrast to the cool, sterile environment of the museum. My arm hung out the car window, skimming the warm breeze as

I drove. I stared at the road ahead consumed by thoughts of my future.

Days after graduation, in June 2014, I traveled to Kenya, to pursue my childhood dream and search for any sign of the elephants I had always imagined. Since returning just weeks ago, one thing was clear: I was broke—*dead broke*. That trip cost me every last dime I had and with rent due, I took the first job anyone offered. I hadn't planned on staying there for long, but I spent most nights answering phones in a darkened cubicle, sending help to stranded drivers on the freeway. In my free time, I continued to visit the secret museum and the ghosts who occupied it.

Now that I had a science degree and had been to Kenya, the next step would not materialize. I wished to find work I loved, but that also paid the bills. The secret museum was my top choice, but nobody got paid for working there. Unraveling the mystery of dead marine life was also high on my list, but no one got paid to do that either.

For weeks, I'd asked for a sign. Why would I be given a dream I couldn't fulfill? How could I get myself into a position to help my wild friends—the same elephants who had saved me all those years ago.

Whenever my world spun out of control in my childhood, and I felt scared, overwhelmed, sad, or depressed, I read about them. Their stories quieted even my darkest thoughts. As I learned how they overcame insurmountable challenges, their resilience inspired me to do the same. Their life histories gave me hope when nothing else did. If they could heal from the wounds of their past, then so could I.

What struck me, though, now that I had finally graduated, was my sheer lack of foresight at what to do next. I had been so focused on living one day at a time that "the future," as unbelievable as it sounds, hadn't really crossed my mind.

The first ten years of my sobriety were consumed with simply learning how to live life sober: something incomprehensible to anyone not afflicted with addiction. But for an addict, an alcoholic in recovery like me, few things are more difficult. I had to relearn skills most people take for granted like how often to brush my teeth, pay bills, or how to ride a city bus.

Before that time, when a car was my home, my primary concern was finding the drugs and alcohol I needed to survive. Nothing else mattered. When the prospect of making it through the day felt uncertain, dreaming or looking ahead—even just to tomorrow—became a luxury I couldn't afford.

After being expelled from multiple colleges for repeated drinking offenses, I gave it another try. Only this time I was thirty-five with nearly a decade sober. I began with a fifth-grade math education, hired a rather small seventh grader as my tutor, and was eventually allowed to enroll in classes at a local community college.

For six long years, I worked toward getting my science degree and took each challenge as it came, *one class at a time,* careful not to look further into the eyes of a false future. And I took a math class every single semester until I understood how numbers communicated with each other, like pretty words on a page.

Before our final showdown, I bowed to my adversaries—statistics and calculus—as a sign of respect for the warriors we both were. My sword was nothing more than the prick of a pencil, but during our last battle, I had a secret weapon. Because by then, I had finally learned the most important lesson of all: how to ask for help. I faced my foes with an army of tutors who trained me in the art of war, and I slayed those dragons.

∞

"You should start a nonprofit," Jason said thoughtfully.

His gaze wandered across the cozy coffee shop we frequented on rainy afternoons. He was more than a friend; Jason was my mentor. For over an hour, he listened patiently, as I rattled off my fears about the uncertainty ahead.

"As a way to teach people about elephants," he added with a gentle smile.

I took a deep breath. "I wouldn't even know how to do something like that."

"Oh, come on," he said. "You made it through calculus, I think you can handle this. Besides, nonprofits are my specialty."

Jason had founded one of the largest public service organizations in Oregon. He worked tirelessly for the underdog: the poor, disenfranchised, homeless, mentally ill, and the forgotten. Even though I didn't know where or how to begin, he did, and I trusted him.

Throughout the years, he shared bits of his past with me, and each time I listened in stunned silence. His childhood was full of unspeakable torture, and one he likely wouldn't have survived had fate not dropped the only person into his life that could save him.

While living in Queens, New York as a teenager, a stranger approached him one day in a synagogue, not far from where he grew up. The older gentleman with a long white beard recognized Jason by the pain he wore on his sleeve—not as a numbered tattoo as the man had, a remnant from the notorious Auschwitz concentration camp—but in the way one trauma survivor recognizes another. It was the first time Jason talked to anyone with a past more awful than his. And it was through their shared experience that he finally began to heal.

ELEPHANT MOUNTAIN

It was my parents who introduced us when he secretly guided them on how best to deal with me in my final months as a practicing alcoholic nightmare. He suggested they cut me off until I got sober, which they did—something I deeply resented him for. I devised various plans for all the horrible things I would say when, and if, we ever met in person. The universe, however, had other ideas.

One morning, I arrived late to a recovery-based meditation meeting. I stood outside the crowded room so as not to disrupt the gentleman's opening comments as he led the group. My heart stopped the moment I recognized Jason's voice. Having only heard it on the phone, his tone was unmistakable. Weeks earlier, I celebrated one year of sobriety and was determined to stay that way. I had also learned all the ways my alcoholism hurt those closest to me, and was no longer offended by his intrusion on my family, but deeply grateful. Instead of punching him, as I'd imagined a million times, I gave him a hug, and we've remained close friends ever since.

Jason had lived in Oregon for more than a decade by that time, celebrated over twenty years of sobriety, and embraced life as a proud gay man. If I had to guess, he'd helped hundreds if not thousands of alcoholics like me. Our friendship was a unique, transformative example of what can happen when recovery takes hold. We also shared a second passion—elephants, but that is something I take complete credit for.

Finishing his coffee, Jason stood and unzipped the main compartment of his large backpack.

"Congratulations," he said. "You've made me love elephants." He stopped for a moment and looked at me.

I could never tell with him if he was being sarcastic or serious. His straightforward New York-style bluntness made it difficult for me to decipher. Sensing my confusion, he continued.

"Don't worry, it's a good thing. It means, however, that it's time to get to work."

I stared at him with an unspoken question as he dropped a massive book onto the tiny coffee table, nearly tipping it over.

"This is considered the Bible of nonprofits. It will tell you everything you need to know. Make *this* your next class and read every word." He tapped the cover with his finger. It wasn't a suggestion.

During the night shift, between calls when it was slow, we could do whatever we pleased. While others played video games or streamed the latest hit series, I followed Jason's direct order. Over the following months, I studied every inch of that book building something I could not yet see. When I finally reached the end, I realized his demand, pointing me in that direction, was the right one for me to follow.

Researchers around the world were uncovering groundbreaking discoveries about elephants, but that information remained largely hidden—though not intentionally, of course. It was published inside scientific journals, inaccessible to the average person, or included in long, boring books that nobody but other scientists read. I wanted to bridge that gap. My dream is to educate the public—the non-scientists. I wondered if a deeper understanding might encourage people to see them as more than just mammals, but as highly intelligent beings deserving of our respect.

Little could I have known how much my life was about to change, how daunting the task ahead would be, and how a voice I didn't even know I had would emerge. A seed had been planted, and an idea took root. I was reminded that every beautiful flower's story begins the same, deep underground, in a place no light can reach. Over time, its burden grows accustomed to the darkness.

There is no escape, and it does not wish to be disturbed. It is a necessary process to discover who it is and what it's made of. It cannot be rushed or forced, and although the lesson may seem arduous, it is essential. Only then is the flower able to reveal its brilliance to the world and become exactly who she was always meant to be.

CHAPTER 2

Keepers of the Ark was a daunting read. Not only did it reveal the inner workings of zoos in a way that was both surprising and new, but it was self-published and unedited, which made it all the more—a hidden gem.

In his book, R.J. Ryan, a former elephant keeper at the San Diego Wild Animal Park (now known as the Zoo Safari Park), shared his experiences from the 1980s. Though the events took place long ago, I found his perspective unique. He highlighted a dangerous combination: the lack of a formal education among zoo keepers in charge of elephants combined with the male ego. He exposed the devastating impact this had on the elephants in their care.

Most elephant keepers were recruited from other lower-paying jobs at the park or from local farms, due to the physical demands of the role. Even though several books on elephant behavior were available then, the men in charge chose to 'learn as they go' with a hands-on approach. Their sheer incompetence, combined with an utter lack of curiosity was a mistake for which the elephants paid dearly.

The troubling account described the events leading up to one of the largest and most significant animal welfare cases in California's history, centered on a tragic event involving a female African elephant named Dunda. The case was so riveting and grotesque that it triggered statewide Senate hearings, lawsuits, and ultimately legislation aimed at protecting other elephants from what happened to her. Although the elephant keepers* beat Dunda within an inch of her life, she survived. That disturbing episode underscored Mr. Ryan's point with undeniable clarity.

    I devoured *Keepers of the Ark* in one sitting. Then I read it again. Unable to locate a copy outside of a library, I photocopied it cover to cover to remember every awful detail. When it was time to name my nonprofit, there was only one choice: the title of that book.

    After multiple failed attempts to track down R.J. Ryan and ask his permission, I decided on KOTA, using the first letter of each word in the title as a hat tip to his inspiring body of work. Thanks partly to him, in February 2015, *The KOTA Foundation for Elephants* was born.

    However, there was another aspect of R.J.'s book that struck me nearly as much as Dunda's court case. He pointed out the ways to tell if the system had changed since then and why he doubted it ever would. Still, with all we've learned about elephants over the past forty years, things *must* have improved. But I was stunned to learn, in some respects, just how little they had.

    The answers lay hidden in other court cases. In the four decades since the tragic incident involving Dunda, testimonies from various keepers supported R.J.'s claims. Their accounts illustrated the ongoing harm the lack of education continued to have on the elephants in their care.

    In one case, a keeper testified that striking an elephant with a bullhook caused no harm, that it could barely feel it. The claim

---

* R.J. Ryan was on disability leave due to an injury when the beating occurred, and later became a defendant for Dunda in the case against the San Diego Wild Animal Park.

was absurd, considering the bullhook is essentially a long-handled tool—similar to a baseball bat—fitted with a sharp hook and spike at the tip. Yet, it was a defense I'd heard countless times, with the earliest dating back to 1912 at the Bronx Zoo in New York.

Visitors became outraged after witnessing a keeper repeatedly beating Gunda, the zoo's only elephant. To calm the crowd, which grew larger by the day, the zoo's director, Dr. William Hornaday, posted a sign in front of Gunda's exhibit insisting that the public was mistaken. Even though Gunda *appeared* to be in pain, Hornaday explained, he wasn't. Gunda merely *thought* it was suffering but, really it was all fine.

Hornaday, of all people, would know. After all, he was a "Doctor" and considered a "worldwide expert." But the public didn't buy his defense, as evidenced by an outpouring of letters from concerned citizens published in the New York Times.

It turned out, Hornaday was a doctor in name only—he held no academic degrees. There was, however, one area in which he could claim true expertise: taxidermy. He was also the same guy who came up with the idea of putting a Congolese slave, a man named Ota Benga, on display in the Monkey House to attract larger crowds.

It's long been recognized that elephants can feel something as light as a fly landing on their skin. Similar to ours, it's highly receptive and able to sense the slightest touch, although tougher and less prone to tearing. When an elephant gets hit, it also bruises, even if the discoloration isn't always clear to the naked eye against its grayish surface. Yet, bruising on the underlayer is just as visible as it is on human tissue. It reflects trauma and trauma hurts. This information had been in the public realm for decades, so whoever was teaching those keepers clearly wasn't keeping up.

By the early 1990s, a safer approach to elephant training called "protected contact" began gaining traction. It introduced a barrier to separate handlers from elephants, ensuring the safety of both. When the Association of Zoos and Aquariums (AZA) officially endorsed it as an alternative training method in 1995, it seemed the tide was finally shifting.

It was especially significant since breaking elephants, I'd learned, is not so different from the traditional, yet brutal manner once used to break horses. Adopting "protected contact" required zoos to remodel their structures and enclosures. But, even among those that underwent major renovations in the following two decades—including Portland—most failed to implement the necessary changes.

Fewer than a third of all AZA-accredited facilities housing elephants had adopted it by 2011. Modern cowboys realized that positive reinforcement and kindness are far more effective than inflicting pain—even they have abandoned the idea. Why, I wondered, hadn't zoos?

There was a knee-jerk reaction by some in the animal rights community to condemn all zoo elephant keepers, but I disagreed. They are also the last line of defense. Nearly every court case in the United States involving harm to elephants was brought forth by current or former elephant keepers wanting to do the right thing.

Across Europe and the United States, all four legitimate elephant sanctuaries—offering hundreds to thousands of acres for elephants to roam—were founded by former keepers and trainers. These were the very people who had witnessed the brutality of their professions firsthand. They are not the enemy, but part of a system-wide breakdown spanning the entire industry that was beyond their control or ability to change.

Jason and I decided that KOTA's mission was to focus on the one thing we could: education. I believe we are Keepers of the Ark, with the power to either let elephants go extinct or to save them. In the end, that decision is up to us, and I'm also convinced that education (at every level) is the key.

Once we established the foundation, Jason and I began seeking board members with industry experience, and the response was overwhelming as scientists, scholars, and business leaders eagerly volunteered. But then we faced an obstacle we never saw coming. Each new trustee asked the same question:

"Where did KOTA stand on elephants in captivity? Were we for it or against it?"

From the outside, it seems so simple—but from where I stood, from where I had just been, I knew that answering it one way or the other would create enemies. Even worse, if not handled appropriately, it could also be … *dangerous*. According to everyone I spoke with, however, it was a question we needed to answer and it had to be done publicly.

"There is no middle road," they said.

I wondered why, when our mission—*KOTA's mission*—was to 'educate' about elephants. Besides, I'd learned in sobriety that things are seldom black and white; there were always shades of gray. I was taught to look for and find the similarities, not the differences, not the divide. But there was another reason I was not prepared to answer that question: it would require an act of faith I wasn't sure I had.

The truth is, I was still reeling from an event I didn't fully understand. It wasn't just the threat … it was what happened next that shifted my entire perspective.

ELEPHANT MOUNTAIN

∞

The "Great Portland Elephant Watch" had begun. It was a famous tradition at the Oregon Zoo, which has seen more births than anywhere else in the world. Rose-Tu was in labor, preparing for the arrival of her second baby. The local press was full of updates as the public flocked to see the pregnant Asian elephant for themselves.

Sizable crowds of children and tourists lined up outside the small cement barn, eager for any sign of the delivery. The news caused the predicted frenzy that had become a hallmark of the city whenever one of the elephants gave birth.

Another researcher had called in sick, and I was asked to take her place. Armed with a clipboard, I sat at the back of the main observation area, waiting to record a list of specific behaviors, though there weren't many. It always appeared the same: restless discontent. Locked in a stall smaller than my living room, Rose walked in a circular pattern for hours.

Her aunt, an elephant named Shine (originally Sung-Surin), was kept inside with her. She had taken the place of Rose's mother, Me-Tu, after she died of severe foot disease when Rose was just two. Now, at fourteen, she was fortunate to have her closest family member by her side.

A door opened in the back of her enclosure and several men stepped through. That's when I realized the zoo must have closed and why there were no more visitors. I'd lost track of time sitting alone in the dark. After escorting Shine out of the cramped room, the keepers, armed with bullhooks, made Rose perform what appeared to be circus tricks. I had asked one of them before why they did this, since it was so unnatural compared to wild elephant behavior.

"It's for their own good," he said. "It's just exercise."

It didn't look like exercise. It looked like a circus trick, and it was embarrassing. This was an *endangered species*—pregnant, no less. If exercise were the motive, I wondered what exactly they thought labor was. Instead, Rose appeared stressed and agitated, having lost the comfort and company of Shine.

In the wild, elephant females are seldom, if ever, alone during labor. They're surrounded by trusted members of their herd, who support and guide them through the birthing process. Removing Shine caused Rose more stress, not less—even I could see that.

No one noticed me sitting in the dark as a door to the back room opened, revealing two men in a heated conversation. I recognized the zoo director, Mike Keele, but the other was a stranger.

I was not a fan of Mr. Keele and had met him only once, on my first day when I joined the elephant conservation project, as one of the many researchers. His office walls were lined, from floor to ceiling, with plaques given to him by the AZA, the organization that grants zoo accreditation.

He began working at the zoo in 1971, fresh out of high school. Hired to clean animal cages, Mr. Keele was soon promoted to security guard. Before long, he was recruited as an elephant keeper—the most prestigious role in the city at the time. Due to the large number of elephants born at the Oregon Zoo over the years, elephant keepers were treated more like local celebrities.

Eventually, he became the zoo director, earning a salary in the hundreds of thousands—a remarkable achievement for someone without a formal education. But Mr. Keele's most notable accomplishment was creating the first Asian Elephant North American

Regional Studbook, which tracked the sperm used for impregnating captive females. The nefarious business of inbreeding Oregon's elephants had been exposed by various reporters over the years; the studbook was a way to ensure offspring remained genetically pure and unrelated.

In 2009, Mr. Keele had drawn an onslaught of media attention when he appeared as an "expert witness" for Feld Entertainment, the largest circus corporation in the world. Apparently, I wasn't the only one who found it strange that a zoo director would testify in such a case. Local newspapers were full of opinion pieces laced with rage.

Mr. Keele explained to the Court during the ASPCA v. Feld Entertainment case that, although he was hired as an "expert," he had no formal education beyond classes taught by his employer, the AZA. And worse, he had never even seen a wild elephant. His expertise relied solely on "practical experience and discussions with others," which seemed to shock the courtroom as much as it did me.

Just then, one of the keepers noticed I was sitting in the viewing room. He rapped his bullhook on the window, startling me.

"Hey! What are you doing here?" Everyone stopped and stared.

"Oh, sorry," I said, gathering my things. "I'm filling in for Lindsay ... collecting data."

It was clear he wasn't interested, and I was not welcome, though I was confused as to why. When I tried to leave, the strap of my bag got caught on the doorknob. I struggled for a moment until I was finally able to free it. When I looked up, Mr. Keele and the man he was speaking with had stopped talking and were fixated on me. The stranger locked eyes with mine. His dark, piercing gaze cut like a knife as he stepped forward. The metal door slammed shut with such force that I jumped, my heart racing as I was left alone and shaken.

The next day I followed my usual path to the research office, located just steps from the outdoor elephant exhibit. I always took a few moments to observe whichever bull was held in the yard before heading inside.

While watching Rama, an unfamiliar sound caught my attention. I looked around and discovered a camera I hadn't noticed before nestled in the bushes. It rotated until it was pointed directly at me before it stopped. I smiled and waved, since I was the only one there assuming that whoever was behind it was focused on something else. Then an unmarked door opened in the back of the exhibit and the same mean keeper from the day before walked into the yard. Without even looking at Rama, he squared his stance, and glared at me.

After a long uncomfortable silence, I said, "Hi, I'm Debbie."

He stayed quiet, tapping his bullhook into his hand like a mobster with a bat.

"I'm one of the researchers—"

"Maybe you should get to work," he interrupted in a most unfriendly tone.

I immediately turned and left. The whole ordeal felt creepy as fuck. Later, a co-worker filled me in on what she knew about him. Apparently, he'd been recruited as a keeper from a restaurant at a different zoo, a common theme mentioned in R.J.'s book. He wasn't some educated elephant guru—some bigshot scientist with a stick up his ass. Instead, he was nothing more than a thug holding a tiny baseball bat, highly trained on how to deliver fast food.

For the next several days, each time I walked past the back elephant yard on my way to the research office, I heard the camera, and the same intimidating keeper appeared as if he knew the exact moment I would be there. None of the researchers, including myself, followed a fixed routine. We showed up between university classes whenever our schedules allowed, making his continued presence that much more unsettling.

Then I received the threat—*a disguised voice on the other end of the phone*—and my entire world turned upside down.

CHAPTER 3

"Did you bring it?" The unmarked door cracked open revealing half of a woman's face.

I stared at her with a blank look. "Bring what?"

"The five dollars."

"Oh ... yeah. I almost forgot," I said, as my fingers fumbled against the fabric of my coat.

After handing it to her, she swung the door open to let me in. I followed her up a steep staircase into a small office, where she gave me a document and explained nothing more could be said until I signed it. I quickly realized it was a contract. In order to speak, we needed attorney/client privilege to protect us both. The five dollars sealed the deal. Otherwise, anything we said could be held against us in the court of law—a script I had long memorized due to my countless arrests.

My lower lip throbbed, tender and swollen from the relentless gnawing. Once the document had both our signatures, she tossed it onto a desk and gave a subtle nod, motioning for me to follow. I trailed behind her like a shadow down a dark hallway, illuminated by a single light at the far end. It reminded me of a wormhole leading to another dimension.

We stepped into a back room, where two other attorneys stood and introduced themselves. Perplexed by the unfolding events, I took a seat at a modest table, its surface cluttered with reams of paper, surrounded by mismatched chairs.

I sat still and listened as they began. First one, then the next, shared parts of a story that was so shocking it hardly seemed real. It involved millionaires and billionaires, government officials at fantastically high levels, espionage, and illegal wire-tapping by ex-CIA officers who fell from grace under less-than-appealing circumstances. There was one theme, though, that stood out: a small group of very wealthy individuals appeared desperate to silence anyone from speaking out about the welfare of captive elephants. I don't feel comfortable going into further detail, except to say that some of those who traded elephants as a commodity were among the most dangerous.

Although what they shared was deeply disturbing, I failed to make the connection between its relevance and the threat against me. It seemed impossible that the two were related. Then my lawyer sifted through a large stack of documents, scanning for something specific.

"I'm sure you're well aware, the zoo has been under fire for the past couple of years, getting caught in multiple lies and taking hits publicly for each," she said.

I nodded. My work on the research project had coincided with one of the biggest firestorms in the zoo's history.

"If they thought you were in that room as an animal activist or trying to 'catch them' doing something wrong ..." she hesitated, looking at the other lawyers, "we think that would be enough."

Based on the description I'd provided, they believed the man I saw in the heated conversation with the zoo director was not only someone they recognized, but the most likely reason I received the threat.

"But I didn't see anything," I argued. "What do they possibly think I saw?"

"You saw him, and he saw you," said another attorney.

I took a deep breath, still struggling to make sense of everything.

"Take some time and read these," my lawyer said, pushing a sizable stack of papers across the table. "What we shared should become a lot clearer once you do."

She stood and opened the door, signaling the end of our meeting. We retraced our footsteps down the long hallway and steep staircase until we reached the entrance. Then she turned and paused, resting her hand on the documents I was holding.

"This should give you all the information you need to know. In the meantime, keep your eyes open and call me right away if anything else happens."

I nodded as she closed the door behind me. As I stepped onto the sidewalk, I hesitated, trying to process what had just happened. A coffee shop across the street caught my attention. Instead of going home, I went there, intent on staying for as long as it took to sort through this strange new reality.

No one could have prepared me for what those materials revealed. The articles, court transcripts, and reports were in all honesty the most sordid—most fucked up—thing I have ever read. Each source proved the attorneys' story was true, no matter how astonishing it seemed. However, there was one part I knew better than most: the controversy that erupted at the zoo when I worked there.

In 2008, in the middle of the Great Recession, Portlanders voted to increase their own property taxes by passing a $125 million bond measure to remodel the Oregon Zoo. But what truly captured their heart—and became the emotional centerpiece for the entire campaign—was the plan to build an off-site elephant preserve, offering the seven-member herd over one hundred acres to roam. This was an astonishing upgrade from the single acre they were currently squeezed into. And it was the main reason so many people and animal rights organizations supported it.

Six years passed, and by 2014 (while I was on staff) almost nothing had changed. Construction on the promised projects had barely even begun, and the much-anticipated elephant preserve was still just a hopeful wish on paper. The public grew suspicious, wondering exactly what they had done with the taxpayer funds.

A previous audit revealed zoo personnel had provided false information to the board that governs them. And not just once. The entire operation was plagued by gross mismanagement, and there were whispers of corruption. Every major investigative reporter in the city pounced on the story as zoo officials ducked and dodged another onslaught of negative publicity.

When pressed, they finally admitted there would be no off-site preserve. They insisted voters had simply "misunderstood" the original bond measure—that the elephant range wasn't even mentioned in the fine print of the initiative filed with the state. Technically, they were right; it wasn't. Yet, it was the crown jewel of a relentless media blitz, dominating television commercials and campaign materials for months. The public was outraged at the egregious bait and switch.

One project, meanwhile, quietly moved forward while the rest stalled. They constructed a state-of-the-art fertility lab. It was so rare, expensive, and advanced that few like it existed anywhere. The lab's sophisticated technology eliminated all the guesswork. It could pinpoint the moment a female elephant was fertile. And it could detect a pregnancy within weeks. This level of accuracy had never been possible before.

The original bond measure paperwork and campaign materials made no mention of that lab. Its existence remained largely overshadowed by the uproar that followed. When news of it finally broke, zoo officials insisted it would revolutionize *all* captive breeding programs for *every* zoo. And they claimed it would restore the Oregon Zoo's reputation as the "elephant breeding capital of the world."

A police siren wailed as two squad cars flashed by the coffee shop. I stood to stretch, rolling the tension from my shoulders, then walked to the counter to refill my cup. Suddenly, I stopped, recalling something I had just read. I returned to my table, set my coffee down, and quickly sifted through a stack of court transcripts. My finger traced the pages, scanning each witness testimony until I found it.

"Unless zoos made significant changes to their breeding strategies," said Mike Keele, when he testified in the Feld Entertainment case, "then there would be no elephants in captivity left."

He admitted that the long-term prognosis of captive elephants was grim unless they updated, modernized, and transformed the entire elephant breeding process. They were dying faster than they were being born.

I leaned back in my chair and looked out the window, wondering if that had always been the true mission of that bond measure in the first place—to build that lab. With so much money originally set aside for the off-site preserve and other projects that never came to fruition, I couldn't help but question whether some of those resources found their way into the lab's construction without anyone realizing it. The timing was certainly ironic, considering it was built shortly after Mr. Keele's 2009 testimony, just a few months after the zoo received its first round of funding.

A fellow researcher told me that he (meaning Keele) was awarded a large cash bonus for every successful elephant birth as a result of using his studbook, but I didn't know if that was true. I wouldn't be surprised, though. Their new high-tech lab would have certainly increased those odds, along with the bank account of whoever was cashing in. There was no dispute, however, that nothing made a zoo more money than a baby elephant. Period. And when you have that kind of cash flowing in, there are always people willing to do whatever it takes to keep it from going out. Even if it goes against science. Even if it goes against all human decency.

With so much money involved, I couldn't shake the attorney's words, that just being seen in that room after the zoo had closed could be enough to make me a target.

Apparently, circuses and zoos weren't technically supposed to be in business together anymore, at least not as they once were. Elephants could no longer be traded—quietly in the dead of night—as they had been for years. If the creep I'd seen through that half-open door at the elephant exhibit was the man my lawyers suspected, he was not only prominent in the circus world, but if his prison record was any indication, he was also dangerous. His presence at the zoo suggested that the relationship between the two was cozier than anyone cared to admit.

For reasons I still couldn't fully grasp, my having seen him stirred controversy. However, the documents and court cases detailing the treatment of elephants in captivity—and the fates of those who spoke out against it—were both crystal clear and terrifying.

As I drove home that evening, shocked and disturbed, I tried to process everything that had happened. If the zoo wasn't doing anything wrong, then why was I being threatened for something I didn't even know I'd seen? That is, if they were the ones who issued the threat in the first place, though nothing made sense anymore.

For weeks after that meeting, I felt as if I was being followed. I woke at the slightest sound, and life as I knew it shrank. I grew suspicious of new people in recovery, strangers who held my gaze a second too long, and each time my phone rang with an unknown number, I froze. Even regular visits to a therapist failed to alleviate my growing anxiety. Instead, I ramped up my meetings, picked up more service commitments, and worked with women struggling to stay sober—searching for anything to distract my attention in a positive way.

My constant worry blinded me to the fact that the solution rested on a bookshelf within feet of where I made my morning coffee. As usual, the answer lay buried in those wild elephant stories, but the deafening noise surrounding me swallowed their voices whole.

CHAPTER 4

I sprang up, my eyes frantically searching for light. It took a moment to recognize my surroundings and the source of my terror: another nightmare. The clock on the bedside table revealed it was the middle of the night. I placed my hand over my heart to calm my breathing, realizing my t-shirt was soaked.

A noise off the balcony caught my attention and I reached for a hammer hidden under my pillow. I listened for any sign of an intruder, but determined it was nothing more than the usual sounds of a large apartment building. Besides, the walls were so thin, if anyone screamed, everyone could hear.

Nightmares had plagued me for most of my life. Once I learned what wild elephants had to endure to survive, they became full-blown night terrors—visions so vivid it felt like I was there witnessing their slaughter. After receiving the threat, the bad dreams intensified.

I got up to change out of my wet clothes and make some tea, since going back to sleep was no longer an option. As I waited for the water to boil, a darkness crept. Perhaps it was a remnant from the nightmare, though I remembered nothing but fear.

My therapist taught me an exercise to overcome the lingering effects of my worst dreams: to place myself inside a specific memory that brought me happiness then see if the dark feeling remained.

The scent of mint wafted through the air, reminding me of a dear friend. I got out a second mug, for old time's sake, and placed it on the counter next to mine. Whenever I used to set my tea down, my cat (a calico named Amelia) would dip her paw in for a little taste, ruining the cup I'd prepared for myself. It wasn't just any type she loved—mint was her favorite, too. If I wanted to have any peace, I also had to make some for her. My friends thought it was hilarious that I made Amelia her own cup of tea, but it was the only way she would leave us alone. I smiled as I thought about her strange quirks.

Amelia's ghost faded with the rising steam, yet the shadow of dread remained. Whatever it was wouldn't let me go. Meditation, especially if I allowed my mind to dive deep, was my sole hope for peace. For me, meditating was like exercise. It took practice to stay in the abyss of the unconscious for long stretches of time and though it had been a while since I'd reached that far; it was my last option. I wondered what would reveal itself when I focused my attention directly on it, while present and listening.

I settled into my couch, grabbed a blanket, and lit a candle. Then I began my usual routine of taking deep breaths while I waited for that sliver of peace and weightlessness, where my conscious self merged with the unknown. It didn't take long to realize what stalked me: plain, unadulterated fear. Every move I made was motivated by that very thing. I couldn't be present—truly present—for anyone or anything. Fear had become my master.

My breathing slowed as I dove deeper, looking for a solution. Memories floated overhead, most too high for me to reach. Then a picture appeared, like a projection on the wall right in front of me. It was a snapshot from a time when terror and anxiety controlled my every move, just as it did now. I had fallen into this hole before, but I'd forgotten how I got myself out.

The image was of someone who had taught me a valuable lesson: how to turn the fear that held me back into a powerful source of strength. She helped me not just overcome it, but use it as my own personal weapon—as a means to move forward. There was only one person who recognized how terrified I was so many years ago, and she showed me how to transform that liability into a most useful asset.

∞

A good catcher knows you better than you know yourself. In a fierce competition on the softball field, no one else mattered. She could read my mind, and I hers. We were the guts of the machine. If we made a mistake, then everything around us fell apart. But if we were in sync, like twins who unconsciously chose the same outfits, then we were *unstoppable*. The connection we shared was one that gave me a sense of being part of something I'd never experienced—a capital I that becomes a capital H—forming an unbreakable bond when both sides come together.

A few months before the beginning of my freshman year in high school, I met Deana. The varsity softball pitcher had just graduated, leaving no one to fill her place. A team without a pitcher was like a ship without a captain. The coach heard about me because I had earned a coveted spot on one of the most celebrated fast-pitch teams in Oregon and had studied pitching since I was ten.

In the summer league, fierce tryouts separated the most talented athletes. During the school season, however, we had no choice who to play with. If we were lucky, our team was good. If not, we had to wait until the break, when the competition was steep.

The varsity coach requested a private meeting—an audition—and he wanted his star catcher, Deana, to join us. I already knew who she was. She had a reputation for her tenacity, and apparently, wasn't afraid to tell off anyone, no matter who they were. Though I'd played with tough athletes before, she was by far the most intimidating.

Once I learned about the meeting, I did my best to hold it together and understood how important it was for the two of us to get along. My dad and my pitching coach, Wayne (who was like a second father), were so excited they could hardly contain themselves. This was the break we had been waiting for and, if I played my cards right, it was also my ticket to college, which my parents had made clear they couldn't afford.

Wayne insisted we meet him at the gym an hour before everyone else.

"You're like a racehorse that gets jittery before the big event," he said. "We need to work you out first to get you calm."

I complained but did it, anyway. By the time everyone arrived, I was already dripping in sweat. The coach stepped in and caught a few pitches. With a satisfied look on his face, he handed the mitt off to Deana, who knelt in her catching position without saying a word to me.

"What do you want me to throw?" I asked.

"Throw whatever you want," she barked.

I threw fast balls as hard as I could—*heat*, which she caught easily. Instead of tossing the ball gently, as I expected, she stood up and threw it like she was aiming for left field. It struck my mitt with a sharp *pop*, and I flinched before the sting shot through my palm. Initially, I thought it was a mistake since there was no reason to throw that hard at someone standing so close. I looked at her with a *What the fuck?* expression, but she simply smirked. When she threw it the second time, she stood up and paused, then reared back and zapped me again. I felt a wave of anger flush across my face.

Then I threw my specialty—*junk*. I pitched curve balls, rise balls, drop curves, trying every which way to throw her off. Without knowing what was coming next, she easily caught each one, which was impressive. Yet each time she threw the ball back, it hit me like a shot from a cannon. We went back and forth until I was convinced—I didn't like her at all.

In the middle of a pitch, Deana got up and walked to the group waiting anxiously on the sidelines, as the ball slammed into the empty wall.

"Not bad," she said to my dad and Wayne, ignoring me. "She'll do," she told the coach. Then she grabbed her bag and left.

I was stunned by her arrogance and didn't see her again until our first practice, having made the team. When she called me "Barbie," I wanted to punch her in the face but instead we played the same game as we had in the gym. I threw harder, then she threw harder—until the palms of both our hands went numb.

"You can always tell what the batter wants by looking at their feet," she said. "That's how you know what they can hit, so you throw the opposite."

She was the first catcher to point this out, though I was already aware. Usually, I was doing the teaching. Batters were quite easy to read when you knew what to look for. The direction of their feet always gave their real motives away. They took the same stance each time they stepped into the box, secretly hoping I would throw the one ball they could smash out of the park.

Deana and I worked out what our "signs" would be for each type of pitch, and I was struck by her ability to call exactly what I was thinking—we were in sync.

Our team quickly climbed the ranks from the worst team in the league to the most formidable, and we became a pitching/catching duo I'd heard about but never experienced. Deana's reputation didn't do her justice. I found her even more daunting than the rumors suggested. She never hesitated to confront umpires, opposing players, or coaches, and her ability to throw runners out on every base was unmatched by anyone. She was an unstoppable force that nothing seemed to shake. Secretly, it was what I admired most about her.

Halfway through our first season, during a difficult game, I got flustered. My pitches weren't working the way I wanted, and people were everywhere. A considerable crowd surrounded the softball field, drawn by our team's impressive winning streak. Reporters and photographers were staked out behind the backstop lined up over the top of Deana's head, with their cameras pointed at me, hoping for another great action shot. The sight of so many spectators increased my fear and frustration—not just of failing in front of a live audience, but doing so on camera for the world to see. I shook off every sign until Deana lost her patience and called a time-out.

"What the fuck is your problem?" She snapped before she'd made it halfway to the mound.

"What's your fucking problem?" I hissed back.

Coach hated it when we cussed, but he had long given up on me. Trying to control Deana was also hopeless. Out of the corner of my eye, I saw him drop his shaking head. The infield jogged in for a huddle but quickly gave a signal for everyone to fall back, as our swearing intensified.

I tried to explain that none of my pitches were working. I felt it safer, in situations like this, to just throw fast balls and hope the other team wouldn't launch them into the stratosphere. Deana made it clear that I had no choice in the matter. If we were ever going to get out of this game, I had better pitch what she called. I rolled my eyes and went back to the mound.

Once the batter returned to the box and the umpire took his position, I leaned into my starting stance and waited for her sign. And there it was—a middle finger. A silent *Fuck You*. My anger ignited like a match to gasoline. Rage blurred my vision. All the stress I'd felt moments earlier evaporated, replaced by a single, sharp focus on her. I threw every tricky pitch I had with only one desire: to see Deana falter and drop the ball just once. Everything around us disappeared—the game was now a personal duel between only her and me. It didn't matter if she dropped everything I threw, and the other team scored ten times. I was so angry; I wished for it.

But that isn't what happened.

Instead, I struck out one batter after the next. Suddenly, all of my pitches started working, including my deadly drop curve. Deana never even so much as flinched. Each time she got into her catching position, she gave me the *Fuck You* sign, and I threw whatever I felt like. And to my surprise, the two of us played an absolutely perfect game.

"I don't know what happened to you two, but do more of that please!" Coach said after we won.

I looked at Deana and she smiled, wider than I'd seen before. From that point forward, our connection was unshakable. I never questioned her again, and she quit flipping me off between pitches … most of the time, anyway. Sometimes she still flashed it, but it wasn't out of frustration. She used it as a sign for me to get my head in the game. And it worked. The two of us have remained close friends ever since.

Deana had figured something out about me long before I did: anger was the fuel to move through my fear. She understood that rage distracted and focused me in a way nothing else could. It was the perfect catalyst when I felt cornered with nowhere to go.

My mind unexpectedly drifted back to the threat and the dots began to connect. I opened my eyes and paced across my living room. The darkness lifted, and a sense of clarity washed over me. I reviewed everything that had happened again, this time through a new lens, and finally—I could see.

What if the threat is a sign?

I thought about it for a moment and froze. What if it wasn't something to hide from but a glaring signal that I was headed in the right direction. What if I stopped trying to play it safe, stopped pitching fastballs praying for a miracle, and faced whatever was coming for me head-on. God knows, I'd seen the elephants do that very thing: turn and directly face danger. I owed it to myself to try. I owed it to them.

I walked over to my bookshelf and ran my hand across the spine of each massive notebook that held the hundreds of elephant stories. Then it stopped. Something in there was trying to get my attention. Carefully, I set a large volume on the floor and opened it to a random section, revealing the identity of one extraordinary individual. He'd learned over time how to trust his instincts, just as I needed to trust mine. And he had faced life-threatening obstacles with unparalleled bravery. Without a doubt, I knew that this—*his story*—was the key to unlocking the answer I had been searching for all along.

CHAPTER 5

*M*ishak sat up the instant he heard the faint sound ringing in the distance. The orphanage was unusually quiet until the stillness of early morning was broken by a soft whisper. He looked at the dark outlines of his men sleeping in their bunks, their chests rising and falling with the familiar rhythm of exhaustion. Each breath was a testament to their tireless dedication, devoid of the gentle symphony of snoring or the stirrings of dreams.

Most of the rescue team remained fully dressed. They slept in their uniforms, including boots, which allowed them to steal a few extra moments of sleep before peace was violated once again. With a soft sigh, Mishak gathered his things and went outside, knowing their well-deserved rest would be short-lived. He listened as one hushed voice turned into several until he heard the unmistakable sound of someone jogging toward him in the dark: a man sent to raise the alarm. Elephants were under siege across Kenya.

"*Amka! Okoa!*" He rushed back inside and whispered urgently to his men. *Get up! Rescue!*

Mishak woke them as quietly as possible, careful not to disturb the orphaned elephants and their keepers on the other side of the compound. The men, adept in their routines, sprang from their bunks rushing outside to the waiting vehicles, as rescuers one moment and keepers the next.

While they raced toward a region beyond Mount Kenya, Mishak relayed the information he'd received—and it wasn't good. A female elephant had been shot several times while giving birth at the edge of a forest that could no longer sustain the small herd living inside. Their migration corridors had been cut off by human settlement, driving the elephants to search for food in the farmers' fields nearby.

The thought of that location was enough to send shivers down Mishak's spine. Years earlier, it had been the scene of his very first rescue with two young elephants, Ndume and Malaika, who had barely escaped with their lives. It took hours for the men to calm the angry villagers, intent on killing the last two survivors. When the keepers finally reached the babies, Ndume had been beaten unconscious and Malaika's legs were cut to the bone by machetes. Yet, despite a long recovery, both elephants miraculously survived.

To Mishak's relief, there was no angry mob waiting for them this time. Instead, a small group of brave locals stood next to the dead female elephant, guarding a tiny mound at her feet. A poacher had snuck into their territory during the night and shot the young mother while she was giving birth and unable to flee. Before he collected what he came for—her long white tusks—several men, alerted to the unwelcome intrusion, chased him away.

Mishak wondered if the villagers' protection of the baby was the result of their outreach in the local communities following the tragic events involving Ndume and Malaika. The keepers had worked hard to teach the people (those who hated and feared elephants) everything they knew, hoping to turn wolves into shepherds. Whatever the reason, it was a relief to be welcomed by those wanting nothing more than to help.

The small mass wiggled, still wrapped inside its protective amniotic sac. Mishak grabbed a stick and pierced it, while the tiny elephant kicked itself free. The men gathered round and watched him take his very first breath. Mishak lightly touched his head.

"Huyu ni mshindi." This one is a survivor.

"What should we call him?" asked a member of the rescue team.

Mishak paused before looking back toward the forest.

"Imenti," he said. They all agreed that he should be named after the place he came from.

At the elephant orphanage in Nairobi, Daphne Sheldrick had never received an elephant so small or so new to life. Fortunately, a few years earlier, she had identified the missing ingredient for the ideal milk formula—coconut fat. Her recipe enabled her to keep baby elephants under the age of two alive, given that cow's milk poses a deadly threat. As herbivores, an elephant's digestive system is adapted to processing plant matter. They cannot easily break down animal proteins, including the high fat content in dairy milk. Ingesting it often leads to fatal consequences.

Since Imenti had no fear of humans, he adjusted faster than most, consuming every bottle the keepers offered. But instead of thriving over the following days, he took on the sunken appearance of starvation. It became clear they had to come up with a new strategy—and fast—if they were to have any chance of saving him.

After an examination, the veterinarian paused, weighing the implication of his findings. Then he turned to Daphne.

"He has had no colostrum. I believe this is why he is not thriving as he should."

Colostrum is a unique type of milk produced in the first few days after birth by all new mothers, including humans. It's rich with nutrients and antibodies to boost a newborn's immune system. The vet had witnessed the decline of many young animals without it. Deprived of the milk's life-saving properties, it seemed a hopeless outcome for Imenti, unless an alternative could be found in time.

"We could try a blood transfusion from another baby elephant," the vet proposed.

"Would that work?" asked Daphne.

"I haven't tried it for this specific problem, but a transfusion is fairly straightforward. Plasma is introduced from an elephant who already has the antibodies. I can't think of any other solution," he said.

Daphne thought about it for a moment. Imenti's condition had worsened faster than they anticipated. Without intervention, she knew from experience that there wasn't much time. If this was their only chance, they owed it to him to try. She nodded in agreement.

"We need to decide on which elephant," the vet said.

This presented another problem. Days earlier, all the orphans except for one had been relocated to Voi, a rehabilitation center located deep in the heart of Tsavo, just outside the town of the same name. There, the young elephants (those beyond the age of two) would spend the next several years bonding with the older orphans and the wild herds, all under the watchful eye of their matriarch, Eleanor. The only remaining elephant in the compound was a tiny, four-month-old female—too young and weak to be transferred.

In the short time since her rescue, she'd struggled to connect with the others. They kept her behind, knowing that due to the uptick in poaching, she would have more company soon.

Mishak's tall frame appeared out of the shadows in the adjoining stall.

"*Tumlete pamoja naye,*" Mishak nodded toward the open door. *Let's bring her in with him.*

The little elephant stood a few feet away, draped in a brightly colored quilt. She twisted her tiny trunk in the dirt, oblivious to the discussion centered around her. Daphne looked back at Mishak and smiled. *Of course.* It was a risk; this they knew. If the young elephant bonded with Imenti and he died, it might be enough to send her over the edge. But if he lived, it could be the one thing that saved her.

Three months earlier, she had fallen into a neglected privy (an abandoned pit filled with human waste) next to the Manyani Prison in Tsavo. During the night, a herd of elephants alerted the guards to trouble. At sunrise, the men ventured out to investigate and found the elephants clustered around a small area. As they drew closer, the herd moved a short distance away.

At first, the prison guards saw nothing unusual until one man almost fell into an unmarked, uncovered hole. Far below, they discovered a tiny baby elephant treading water, out of reach for the adult elephants to attempt a rescue. Although, judging by the deep ruts in the ground, it was clear they had tried.

The guards rushed to pull the baby out as the distressed herd rumbled in the distance, but made no move to approach, perhaps recognizing the men were not a threat. They were shocked when they realized it had struggled for hours waiting for a miracle.

Once the young female was on dry land, Daphne instructed them to cover the calf in elephant dung to mask the stench of human waste, hoping to reunite her with her family. From behind the safety of the prison walls, the guards watched as the matriarch cautiously approached. Just as the baby stood and reached with her trunk, the large elephant shoved her to the ground, and ran away. Perplexed by the matriarch's strange reaction, the men shared surprised looks.

Then another elephant walked toward the crumpled gray heap, ears spread wide, as if sensing a threat. The baby lay motionless, too exhausted to rise. The adult female stopped within a few feet, assessing the situation. Suddenly, she kicked up a plume of dust, engulfing the young elephant before she trumpeted and ran back to the herd.

A short time later, the matriarch gave a silent signal, and the entire group turned and left, leaving the calf behind. The way they moved, purposeful and coordinated, suggested they weren't coming back. The guards called Daphne again, hoping that she and her team could coordinate a rescue in time to save the newborn elephant.

At the height of the dry season in Tsavo, water is scarce for everyone. It is trucked in from afar and is a precious and expensive commodity. Deliveries are infrequent and unreliable, meant only for human consumption. Washing excrement off a baby elephant was considered not just wasteful, but it could also be deadly. If they ran out of water before the next delivery, it would jeopardize the survival of every man in the prison.

The matriarch holds the responsibility to make decisions that protect the group as a whole, even when her own personal sacrifice is required. An exhausted baby elephant, drenched in human waste, was likely to attract predators far and wide. She knew they still had a long walk ahead to reach a waterhole. Their chances of making it with the vulnerable calf would not just slow them down, but put all their lives at risk.

After her rescue and arrival at the orphanage, the tiny elephant was named Emily to commemorate the birth of Daphne's first granddaughter, and Mishak was assigned as one of her keepers. To his relief, Emily accepted the milk he offered, but within hours, she became visibly distressed. The vet suspected a serious stomach ache from ingesting dirt and human waste. Many young elephants rescued from disused water pits or abandoned latrines also developed severe, often fatal, digestive ailments. After trying various remedies, they found one that eased Emily's discomfort, and she finally settled.

As soon as that crisis was averted, a more deadly threat emerged—*depression*. So many orphans overcame life-threatening injuries and harrowing rescues, only to succumb to the one thing they couldn't see. If Emily was unable to bond with another elephant, there was little hope of saving her.

Mishak stayed by her side and prayed for a miracle. Each night Emily woke screaming from nightmares, a common manifestation of trauma shared between elephants and humans. It often took hours to calm her down, yet Emily continued her retreat, sinking ever deeper into the dark shadows of her mind. Even though she ate normally and joined the other young elephants on their daily walks, she preferred to stay by herself—alone and apart. It seemed the sudden loss and rejection by her family was an emotional mountain too high for her to climb.

Despite having shown no interest in any of the elephants recently transferred to Voi, Mishak walked over and guided Emily into Imenti's stall hoping this time would be different. At first, she stood behind her keeper's long legs, as if waiting for guidance. He touched Emily's tiny head, offering reassurance as everyone watched quietly. Then a small, wobbly trunk appeared, reaching toward the newcomer sleeping peacefully a few feet away. Mishak took a step back, but Emily hardly seemed to notice as she remained fixated, watching the tiny mound snuggled under a quilt similar to hers.

Edwin, the head keeper, tapped Mishak on the shoulder as he handed him another small cushion from an adjoining stall. After it was placed on the ground next to Imenti, Emily inched closer. She inspected the baby lightly with her trunk. Imenti opened an eye, watching her, too weak to do anything more. While Mishak coaxed Emily to lie down, Imenti had her full, undivided attention.

Daphne leaned in and whispered to the vet that Malaika should be the one chosen for Imenti's blood transfusion. It was possible the two were related since both were from the same area. After a quick discussion, he was dispatched by plane to Voi, returning a short time later with the valuable specimen in hand.

A thin tube was inserted into Imenti's ear to begin the procedure, though the fragile elephant showed little reaction. Still lying next to Emily—face-to-face, trunk-to-tiny-trunk—the two appeared mesmerized with each other. Most female elephants are captivated by the smallest babies, but until that moment, Emily had shown no interest.

Once the transfusion was complete and Imenti was fast asleep, Mishak lifted Emily to her feet and walked a few paces outside of the stall, expecting her to follow. When he turned, she remained glued to Imenti's side.

Edwin looked at Mishak and they smiled. If she wanted to stay, they would not interfere. They both knew an elephant connection when they saw one. They'd seen first-hand how precious an elephant bond was, and understood its importance was so great it would likely save both their lives. Nothing heals an elephant's wounds faster—those we can see or those we cannot—than being loved by its own kind. Now all they could do was wait.

A few hours later Imenti stood up on his own, and a small crowd of keepers gathered outside his stall. A man slapped Mishak on the back, grinning from ear to ear.

"*Inafanya kazi!*" *It's working!*

Mishak grinned, but recognized that Emily and Imenti were far from being out of danger. No one knew what hidden hazards might still be lurking. And he had seen depression kill more elephants than he could count. It was best to be cautiously optimistic about both.

"*Tutaona,*" *We'll see*, he said.

Later that evening, when Mishak came to collect Emily once more, Imenti followed close behind. When another keeper tried to intervene, he squealed in protest, insisting on following his new friend. It was clear the two would not tolerate being separated again. From that point forward—he became *hers*.

Mishak's concern softened as Imenti's health visibly improved each day. While it was unusual for orphans to share a stall, exceptions were made for special cases. The bond between Emily and Imenti reminded everyone of a similar connection between Ndume and Malaika, who had also refused to be separated.

Over the following year, the two elephants flourished in each other's company. But, for reasons no one fully understood, they remained apart from all the others that came in after them. Until the day a new rescue arrived, unveiling another great mystery of elephant behavior when she became the third spoke in their wheel. Why they chose her is a question no human could answer. Why the duo suddenly transformed into a trio is still a secret not yet revealed.

CHAPTER 6

I first noticed Leslie before I even entered the fellowship hall. She sat alone on a bench, facing the large crowd. Though I could only see her from behind, something about her drew me in. Perhaps it was because she was all by herself—an outlier—in a sea full of familiar faces.

As I opened the sliding glass door, I was struck by the stark contrast between the bright, jovial mood inside and the dark, moonless night outside. Immediately, I found myself surrounded by a group of old friends. The scent of pine from the wood-covered walls, combined with the energetic sound of laughter, created a warm atmosphere. To a casual observer, it might have seemed like a long-awaited reunion, rather than a weekly meeting. But it was this sense of community and conviviality that kept me coming back.

Sunset was on fire that night. I had experienced its magic for the first time several years earlier, as it was the meeting that marked the beginning of my own sobriety. I'd felt about as overwhelmed as Leslie looked. I hugged my way across the room, where she clung to a bench like a life raft in the middle of the ocean. Blonde hair swirled around her shoulders, and perfectly well-cut bangs framed her face. She was older than I was, and had an impressive sense of style, even at her worst. Her beautifully-manicured fingernails immediately caught my attention as I slid into the seat beside her and introduced myself. She glanced at me over the top of her bright red glasses, her eyes filled with a mixture of fear and shyness.

Like everyone in that room, she'd found herself in a world—a new reality—she never could have imagined. I wanted to make her feel less alone, just as other women had done for me. How could I have known that one simple act would change my life in such a profound way?

But it did.

Over the next several years, Leslie emerged from her cocoon and spread her brilliant wings, like the stunning butterfly she was. Her remarkable transformation reflected the experience of so many in early sobriety, when they rediscovered their will to live after separating from the one thing that gave them life.

As our friendship deepened, Leslie became a kindred spirit I couldn't imagine living without. Her sharp wit and sense of humor made us quick to laugh or poke fun at ourselves. And it was through that shared laughter that we moved past our pain.

One afternoon, we met for lunch, excited to finally see each other in person. My busy work schedule made it difficult to meet, but we kept in touch by phone every few days. She knew all about the threat and the circumstances surrounding it. We were both relieved that nothing more had happened in the weeks since.

During a pause in our conversation, she leaned forward.

"I thought about what you said the other day, about your fear. Perhaps it isn't there to hold you back but to lift you up."

"What do you mean?" I asked.

"Well, consider all the things that have fallen into place to get you here … all the times you wanted to quit but didn't because another direction became clear. All I'm saying is to keep your eyes open and look for the signs. They're there. You just have to trust. Have faith that whatever it is," she gestured toward the ceiling, "the road you're supposed to take will be revealed at the right time."

Her words made me shiver. I was struck by the uncanny resemblance to what she said and the awakening I'd experienced a few nights earlier. The combination of the two convinced me that the threat was definitely a sign, not something to avoid—but to confront, even if I wasn't sure yet how.

I loved how confident Leslie was in my ability to keep moving forward and get things done, as if there were no question from her perspective. From where I stood, everything felt like a struggle, as though I was climbing a ladder with a giant boulder strapped to one shoulder.

Without her, I never would have made it to Kenya, or even graduated, for that matter. Her encouragement of my dreams was astounding. She had never been to college but always dreamed of earning a degree. Perhaps it was why she wouldn't let me quit, despite how much I may have wanted to.

After Leslie excused herself to wash her hands, I settled into our familiar booth, it's polished dark wood—a witness to countless shared memories. Seasons and Regions was known for its decadent seafood and casual, yet chic ambiance. We'd discovered a Caesar salad that made our mouths water at the very mention of it.

The restaurant was empty except for us; we had purposefully selected a quieter time to enjoy a longer, uninterrupted visit. In the silence, my mind wandered.

During my last year of school, before a difficult final exam in a zoology class, I broke down, overwhelmed by the sheer volume of material I just couldn't seem to memorize. Defeated and ready to abandon my dream, I made the mistake of calling her.

"It's a beautiful afternoon," Leslie said. "Why don't you meet me in the park by your house at our regular spot where we can talk more about it. Bring that big red blanket and your note cards."

Reluctantly, I agreed. Even though my mind was set, school was just too hard, and the idea of finishing a science degree felt nearly impossible.

"Are you Debbie?" A strange man approached, as I waited for her in the park.

"Ah ... yes." I stiffened, wondering who the fuck he was.

"It's my shift. I'm the one o'clock," he said.

"What do you mean ... what?" I was totally confused.

"Leslie called Brian, and he called me. He told me to meet you here for some service. Are those your note cards?"

I stared at him blankly, unable to compute what was happening. Before I could respond, he reached over my shoulder and grabbed a large stack lying next to me. He leafed through them before he paused.

"The Northern Spotted Owl," he said, looking at me.

Without thinking, I rattled off the taxonomy—the domain, kingdom, phylum, class, order, family, and finally the genus of each species he quizzed me on. A half hour later, an older woman arrived. Apparently, she was my one-thirty. I handed her a stack of cards, and we continued. All afternoon, complete strangers showed up.

Leslie wasn't interested in hearing me whine about giving up, especially after I'd received the opportunity of a lifetime to go back to school and earn the degree both of us had dreamed of, regardless of how long it took. She'd called several of her friends in recovery and asked them to send their newly sober men and women—newcomers—who needed something constructive to do between meetings. "Look for the girl on the red blanket," she said when I wondered how they all knew where to find me.

As my last appointment of the day, Leslie arrived with a picnic basket filled with sandwiches and snacks, knowing I'd be starving after memorizing the material. I received the third-highest score on that test in one of the hardest classes I ever took, and none of it would have happened without her.

The sound of footsteps pulled me back to the present. I looked up to see her and our server approaching the table at the same time.

"How are you feeling?" Leslie asked, once we'd placed our order.

I instinctively laid a hand across my scarred stomach, where it still felt as though half my guts had been ripped out.

"Pretty good," I said. "I'm not as tired as I was."

The surgery had been brutal, much worse and far longer than my doctors anticipated. Although it had happened months earlier, a full recovery was expected to take about a year, and I was only halfway there. Leslie, along with several devoted friends, had kept a watchful eye on me.

"Have you heard anything about him?" she asked.

For a moment, I wondered if she meant the guy who'd made the threat, but the kindness in her eyes and gentleness in her voice suggested otherwise. Besides, she wouldn't refer to that guy with anything other than "that motherfucker."

"No," I said, playing with the straw in my glass. "I mean, not directly. But I ran into one of his friends at the grocery store the other day and I guess ... he met someone." Leslie took a deep breath as I continued, "And she's pregnant. So there it is. I know I made the right choice."

"Oh, sweetie," she whispered.

"Honestly, I feel pretty good about it. I mean, it was always what he wanted. It was the best decision."

"It is," she nodded. "And it was. The love of your life is still out there. You'll see."

I smiled, but found it difficult to mask my doubt. While I was sure that ending the relationship was the right decision, it still felt as raw as my surgical wounds. As I struggled to heal, my friends stayed close while I learned how to breathe again. They took me to meetings, brought me food, and did everything possible to keep me from feeling alone, even though without him, I did anyway. I yearned for the peace and serenity a quiet room once offered. Instead, it only magnified the crushing weight of my loneliness. Every day, I woke up repeating the slogan *This Too Shall Pass,* praying for the moment it finally did.

∞

He led me to his heart with a trail of wildflowers. I had recently ended a relationship with a very wealthy man, who'd reminded me again how manipulative and cunning those kinds could be. No matter how hard I tried to avoid men with a false sense of entitlement and superiority, they kept showing up—appearing as a rose, only to reveal themselves as a thorn.

The first time he asked me out, I politely declined, convinced he was another player, and I'd had enough of those, too. The second time, I said no again. Instead of looking frustrated, he stepped back and smiled, as if this were simply a battle of patience over will.

Days later, I found a purple wildflower sitting on top of my duffle bag at the gym, where he worked, and we'd first noticed each other. The flowers showed up consistently after that, nothing store-bought or fancy, just something he'd picked out in the parking lot—yet no sign of him. Patience was winning.

Finally, when he asked again, I agreed, but *only* for a cup of coffee down the street. Instead of selecting the perfect outfit and doing my hair and makeup, as I normally would, I showed up after one of my hard workouts, still in my sweaty clothes wearing a baseball hat. I wanted him to see how uninvested I was, so we could both move on.

When I arrived at the busy coffee shop, he wasn't there. I smiled to myself and knew I was right. Players always make you wait. Men who are genuinely interested are always waiting. When I turned to leave, I heard someone call my name from behind the coffee steamer. I walked closer to see who it was when I realized it was him.

"Do you work here, too?" I asked, puzzled.

"No," he smiled brightly, without explaining. "I've set us a table over there," he pointed. "Go have a seat, and I'll bring you something delicious."

In the corner, surrounded by windows, stood a round table, distinguished from the rest by a delicate linen tablecloth decorated with miniature vases full of marigolds and dandelions. A small box, wrapped in parchment paper and tied with a white silk bow, was placed in front of one of the wooden chairs. I slowly walked across the room, intrigued by the presentation. It was quaint and simple, beautiful and unexpected.

Before I sat down, he approached from behind and set two steaming cups on the table. It was then that I noticed he was in a three-piece suit, while I was still dressed in my sweaty gym clothes. The situation became even more amusing when I opened his gift to find a delicate bar of soap. Embarrassed, he desperately tried to clarify that it had nothing to do with my current appearance. It was just his favorite, bought during a recent visit to his home country.

It was touching, and I giggled. "What's going on?"

A hint of cinnamon hung in the air as I struggled to comprehend the surprising turn of events.

"Oh, they're my friends here." He nodded toward the coffee station. "They can't make chai the way I like it, so they let me do it myself. Try it and see what you think."

I didn't have the heart to tell him I hated chai tea. But his smoky eyes were locked on mine while I took a small sip. It was overwhelmingly delicious. I had never tasted chai like that before.

"Wow," I gasped, honestly impressed. "This is amazing!"

It turned out that I was wrong about everything. On the outside, he was a beautiful man with long, dark curly hair, a warm olive-toned complexion, well-defined muscles, and a huge smile filled with perfect teeth, yet he wasn't the player I'd pegged him to be. He spoke multiple languages, had two degrees, and made a good living for many years as a prominent artist who owned his own gallery.

However, he'd become disillusioned along the way. Some of his paintings were commissioned for thousands of dollars, but as he explained, money like that changed him. His discomfort grew until he sold all of his possessions, gave away most of his wealth, and quit. He craved a simpler life, so he took a job at the gym. He hoped to reconnect with all the things that had sparked his inspiration in the first place.

We spent every day together after that, and he understood my need to move slowly. I wasn't the type who could dive into relationships, especially not sober. I soon learned that he could paint like Picasso, cook like Wolfgang, and write like a Sultan.

After I transferred to the university, he kept up the tradition of leaving wildflowers on my regular route between classes. Just a tiny blossom here or there dotting my way. Often he would settle on a bench along my usual path that, by the time I arrived, would be stacked with home-cooked food, deliciously prepared and already laid out, complete with a small tablecloth, napkins and his most delicious chai tea steeping hot in a thermos.

"You need to keep up your strength, Ten. Come, share some food with me. Then go and conquer." He called me Ten because it means "honey" in his native language, and because I reminded him of Farah Fawcett, who was also a Ten.

We slept on a futon mattress on the floor that moved nightly under one of his many skylights according to the position of the moon, something we both loved watching before falling asleep. I knew then that this was no ordinary man. He appreciated things in the same way I did: things money can't buy.

Our relationship was built on passion and on comfort, an experience I never realized was even possible with the same man. We talked about the simplest things for hours. He recited his favorite poetry and shared stories of growing up in a Muslim country across the world. He spoke in a language I'd never heard before, and sang me the same songs his aunties sang to him when he was just a boy, years before his homeland became engulfed in war and his family was forced to flee. His passion for art mirrored my own for elephants, and for a long time we felt like one.

Things unraveled during my last year of school, and I couldn't figure out how to return to where we started. The flowers disappeared. Our conversations turned sharp and focused on the idea of having children—something I did not want. It was a point of shame I'd carried for most of my adult life: that I *should* want the one thing everyone else did, but knew deep down I absolutely didn't.

Perhaps it was because addiction took hold of me so early, or that I saw what happened to some of the children born to those suffering from the same disease I shared. I don't know why I had such a strong maternal instinct for animals, but none whatsoever for humans. It was clear it was a dream he needed to fulfill and one I couldn't stand in the way of.

The pain of ending that relationship was almost more than I could bear. It was a strange feeling to have such a deep ache, yet know he was not the right man for me. Despite everything, I was thankful for having experienced a love and passion so profound—a rare gift that many seek but few ever find.

Shortly after we broke it off, I went for a routine exam and received devastating news—my abdomen was full of tumors. The shock didn't set in right away; I was still numb, unable to process the weight of it all. Not even the concerned look on the doctor's face could shake me. An emergency surgery was scheduled, fortunately on the last day of the fall semester, giving me several weeks to recover before the winter term began. They suspected it was cancer, though couldn't be sure until the affected organs could be biopsied once I was cut wide open.

One thing was certain: my uterus would not survive. It was so ironic, after all that had happened, where for so long every conversation seemed focused on the very organ I did not want. Now she was fighting back.

My surgeons were identical twin sisters who tag-teamed each other during a surgery that was more complicated than my scans suggested and lasted hours longer than they anticipated. And just like that, a series of strategically placed scars across my abdomen became my signatures of freedom. Freedom from worry that I would accidentally get trapped by a baby I didn't want. Freedom from living someone else's dream. Freedom to go to Kenya to follow my heart and search for the elephants that captured it in the first place.

Luckily, there was no sign of cancer, but the complexity of the surgery meant that healing would take longer than expected. My parents brought me to their home, so that I could recover. Each day, I pushed myself a little further.

"Once you can walk the length of the farm and back," my dad said, "you should be able to make it on your own."

It took over a month before I managed to do so by myself. My classes had to be switched to online until I gained enough strength to attend again in person. The physical discomfort of healing became a most welcome distraction from the torture of ending that relationship.

Once I was back in my apartment, Leslie and my friends took over. They understood that a roller coaster of emotions loomed. It wasn't the pain of losing my reproductive organs—I was thrilled about that—but from the pain of losing him.

Finally, at the beginning of the spring semester, I was able to attend classes on campus again. And in June 2014, I graduated with my science degree, five long months after my surgery. A few days later, I boarded a plane—body and heart less wounded—headed for Kenya, to the place where my dreams began as a young girl. And where I discovered full moons are as common as wild elephants roaming beneath them.

∞

"Have you thought about putting together a talk on elephants?" Leslie asked after we'd finished lunch. "I can't help but think people would be moved."

I was grateful for the shift in conversation to KOTA. Leslie and I had spent countless hours discussing the various ways I could educate others about elephants through the foundation.

"That's funny," I said. "A friend just asked me to speak at his Rotary Club, but I told him I'd have to think about it."

"Why?"

I took a deep breath. "Well, how do I condense the vast topic of elephants into a fifteen-minute presentation? I wouldn't even know where to begin."

"Why don't you see if Jason has any ideas? Every time you speak about elephants your passion shines through. That could be a powerful tool if you can find a way to harness it. Reread the elephant stories, gain your strength through them like you always have. I know you'll find the answers you're looking for."

I knew she was right and went home to do just that.

CHAPTER 7

"Naki ng'ole—Enkai!" We must go—NOW! One of the men shouted, kicking dirt to smother the flames.

Moments earlier, a small group of warriors on patrol along the western edge of the Maasai Mara gathered around an early morning fire, before the demands of the sun dictated their day. Draped in their traditional red-and-black striped *shukas*—a single piece of brightly colored fabric—they spoke in hushed tones until the sound of gunshots disrupted peace. Grabbing their spears, they stood alert, straining to listen for any sign of the lurking intruder. A faint, slow roar echoed across the plains, and their hearts began to race as they realized they were directly in the path of danger.

The Maasai ran to higher ground along the edges of Aitong Crater, and the noise increased to a deafening level. The gunshots had sparked a stampede of buffalo. As soon as the men reached a safe distance above the chaos, they waited while the glowing horizon turned into a murky haze. A poacher had slipped into their community-managed reserve, but they could do nothing until the dust settled.

By the time they climbed down from the crater's edge, the first rays of sunlight cut through the eerie fog. They noticed several small, unmoving mounds—unfortunate victims caught in the panic. It took them a moment to find what they were looking for.

A man called out. "*Enkiyio!*" *It's here!*

Soon the group surrounded the body of a dead female elephant: the target of the poacher's intrusion. Like the tribesmen, he fled after triggering the stampede, with no time to take the elephant's tusks.

"*Oloiboni enkai.*" The young warrior pointed to the engorged mammary glands. *She is a new mother.* When full of milk, they looked eerily similar to a woman's breasts.

"*Nakai enkiteng' epaata.*" *You two guard the elephant*, the patrol leader instructed.

He divided the rest of the men into groups: one to stay behind in case the poacher returned, and the other to fan out across the desert floor to find the missing baby.

Moments later, a voice permeated the landscape. *"Naki kiltir!" I've found it!*

The others followed the man's call until they located the tiny elephant. It had been carried a considerable distance from its dead mother. As the warriors gathered around its lifeless body, one poked it with the tip of his spear. The baby lifted its head, causing the men to jump back in surprise. Its survival after the stampede was nothing short of miraculous.

Elephants are highly respected across most Maasai tribes. They hold a significant place in their culture, where they are seen as reincarnated humans or the spirits of dead relatives. A runner sprinted to a nearby ranger station to report the poacher and call Daphne to initiate a rescue. The baby elephant had no chance of survival without intervention, but the Maasai could at least give it that.

When the keepers arrived at the orphanage later that afternoon, the veterinarian determined the calf was a female and just a few months old. Aside from a bump on her head, she appeared to have no significant injuries: a remarkable outcome, considering how few animals emerge unscathed from a deadly stampede.

Their elation, however, was short-lived. The true extent of her injuries became apparent when she tried to walk for the first time. Instead of walking straight, the baby twisted in a circle like a dog chasing its tail. A keeper gently lifted the young elephant and placed her on flatter ground, a few feet outside the stall, where they could observe her more clearly. She remained still until the man stepped away. When she attempted to follow, the twisting resumed.

A quiet hush fell across the keepers. Mishak sat down on the hard earth, crestfallen, while they watched the young elephant spinning in circles. She hadn't made it out unscathed, after all. The hope and triumph they had experienced moments earlier was replaced by dread and dismay as they realized what her fate would be. Her injuries weren't the kind they were used to—those they could see on the outside—but equally devastating just the same. An elephant with a brain injury as severe as hers had no chance of survival.

No one noticed the two little elephants standing quietly in the background. Emily and Imenti hadn't joined the other orphans on their walk that day. Instead, they stayed behind at the orphanage and were there to witness the arrival of the injured baby.

Without warning, the pair stepped forward, moving between the group of distraught men. As Emily passed, she brushed against Mishak, startling him, before she and Imenti stood on either side of the newcomer, preventing her from twisting further. For a moment, the young calf rested as everyone looked on in silence.

Emily laid her trunk across the little female's back, while Imenti inspected her head as if trying to find the reason. The small elephant wobbled and then collapsed. Imenti let out a screech as two keepers rushed to gather Aitong (named after the crater near where she was rescued) and gently carried her back to her stall, where they placed her on a cushion. The vet determined her collapse was due to exhaustion and instructed them to let her rest. A decision would have to be made, but for now, there was nothing left to do but wait.

The following morning, when Aitong's keeper opened the door of her stall, Emily and Imenti were already waiting for her on the other side. Once again, he carried her to flatter ground. If she didn't try to move, the twisting stopped. But when she tried to take a step, Aitong veered hard to the left.

The two elephants surrounded her, just as they had done the day before. While Aitong stayed motionless, they ran their trunks across her body. Then Emily and Imenti went completely still.

"*Kitatokea nini?*" *What's going to happen?* asked one of the keepers, nodding in Aitong's direction.

"*Sina uhakika,*" *I'm not sure,* Mishak said quietly.

The truth was that he had no idea. Despite having witnessed remarkable things when it came to elephant behavior, he was still a student in their classroom.

Aitong remained still while Emily moved slowly around her. Imenti stood just off to one side, watching. Then Emily went to Aitong's left side, and positioned herself as close as she could without knocking her over. Meanwhile, Imenti walked in front and stopped.

The keepers were confused and looked to Mishak for guidance, but he was so focused on the unfolding scene he didn't seem to notice.

Emily let out a soft rumble and leaned into Aitong. To avoid being completely knocked over, she latched onto Imenti's tail. Her keeper jumped to catch her, but Mishak grabbed his sleeve, signaling for him to wait and see what would happen.

Emily rumbled again, this time louder. After a few moments, Aitong lifted her front foot as if to take a step forward, but veered sharply into Emily's side. At the same time, Emily leaned into her with even greater force, preventing the little elephant from twisting further. Aitong quickly dropped her wobbly foot, but after a few minutes, tried again. They continued for over an hour until Aitong was too exhausted to go on. Mishak tapped her keeper as they carried her back to her stall for some much-needed rest. The lesson was over for the day.

News about the elephants' strange behavior spread across the compound, and the next morning, more men, including Daphne, gathered to watch the three. Emily and Imenti stood next to Aitong just as they had before. Although she could still only lift one foot off the ground, it seemed as though the two elephants were working together—in a coordinated effort to help Aitong walk again—despite there being little chance of its success.

A few days later, high-pitched trumpets rang out across the orphanage, startling the keepers who rushed toward the commotion. Emily and Imenti squealed excitedly as they dashed from stall to stall. At first, the keepers were confused as to the reason, when their focus shifted to Aitong, standing alone a few feet outside of her stall where they'd left her.

"She put her foot down, lifted it, and put it down again. She took a step—with my own eyes I saw it—she took a step!" a keeper exclaimed, his voice bursting with excitement.

A group of cooks, milk-mixers, and mechanics gathered around, wondering if that was the reason for the elephants' sudden outburst. While they contemplated, Emily and Imenti calmed down, and rejoined Aitong by her side.

Their story unfolded over the next four months, while the two elephants stood by Aitong day after day as she learned to walk again—one step at a time. Finally, she crossed the orphanage from one end to the other, on her own, and before long, the three were able to join the rest of the mini-herd on their daily walks. From the outside, they looked no different from any of the other young elephants. No one could have known the struggles they had overcome. It was a profound example of empathy and of learning to rely on others when moving forward feels impossible.

The way Emily and Imenti leaned into Aitong reminded me of the way recovering alcoholics leaned into me. With every step, supported by patience, courage, and gut-wrenching determination, we both learned how to walk a straight line again.

Though invisible to the naked eye, Aitong still had injuries that the keepers (and the elephants) knew were there. Something was still a bit off in her head. Something was a bit off inside my head, too. I felt a kinship with her, as the injuries of my past were also still present under the layers no one could see. Aitong reacted differently than the other elephants to situations around her. She struggled with perception, got too excited over simple things, and acted in ways that alarmed those closest to her. Emily and Imenti worked hard to keep her in check, much like the people in recovery did with me when either of us felt the urge to veer off in an old, familiar direction.

∞

"What do you see?" Violet asked the same question each time I arrived.

She held the lower leg bone of an elephant and handed it to me. Always eager to uncover a hidden story, I turned it over, inspecting it carefully.

"I'm not sure," I said, puzzled by what she wanted me to find.

"First, we know that this elephant is about twenty years old," she continued.

"How can you tell its age just by looking at a bone?"

"Leonardo DaVinci," she smiled.

In 1490, Leonardo created the Vitruvian Man—or the Human Canon of Proportions—after realizing that simple mathematics applied to a single bone could determine a person's height, and therefore a close estimate of age. The same principle applies to animals, including elephants.

"Texture offers another important clue," Violet said.

The lower part of the bone was smooth, but the top portion, where the knee joint intersected with the upper leg, was rough and dappled. It resembled a layer of hardened bubbles bulging from the surface. My hand moved slowly across it.

"This coarse, irregular, mottled area here," she traced the uneven surface with her finger, "is caused by arthritis. It takes years for it to develop to this point ... which means what?" She looked at me as if I knew.

I felt the scarred bone and wondered what could cause such severe arthritis to develop in an elephant so young.

"That it stood in the same spot for a long time?" I asked, unsure if I was on the right track.

"Exactly. And what else?"

I paused. "The surface it was kept on must have been quite hard," I said.

Violet nodded, as I recalled my days waiting tables, when I had to stand on cement floors for hours. After each shift, my legs ached to the point that I relied on Advil and hot baths to ease my discomfort. At least, I had that luxury; I wasn't forced to spend my entire life on a harsh, unforgiving surface. I shuddered at the thought of the constant pain.

"Very good, yes," she continued. "Just by looking at this bone, we can tell it could only come from an elephant in captivity since we've never seen arthritis like this on any wild elephant at such a young age."

The information from a single bone was astounding, even though the evidence was sad and awful. The elephant would have endured unrelenting pain with that much arthritis built up around its knee joint. Violet explained that the severity of the condition would have been enough to kill it or, at the very least, disable it to the point of not walking normally. That alone would have led to a whole host of other bone and joint issues. It was a common feature she had observed in every elephant leg bone in that museum, a result of being forced to spend its life on unforgiving, cement-like surfaces.

"It is what we call a zoogenic disease," she said.

"Zoogenic?" I had never heard that term before.

"It's a disease *caused* by captivity," she explained. "Zoogenic arthritis is one of the leading causes of death for elephants in circuses and zoos. It's also the primary reason they die at only one quarter of their natural lifespan compared to those in the wild."

"Only a quarter?"

She went on, her tone grim. "On average, an African elephant in a zoo lives to just seventeen years old, and an Asian elephant only nineteen. Even with all of our technology, veterinary science, and ability to feed them healthy food, it's pretty clear when you look at their bones, captivity is what's killing them. Especially when both can and should live well past the age of sixty, just like us."

I knew elephants living in captivity died young, but hearing just how young was not only shocking, but disturbing.

"Jesus," I whispered, absorbing the information.

"Even working elephants who log forests in Asia live significantly longer," Violet shared.

"Like how much longer?"

"Easily more than double the lifespan of an elephant in a zoo," she said.

To hear that while holding a bone so deteriorated by arthritis, belonging to an elephant far too young to have suffered from such a painful condition and one never seen before in wild elephants of the same age, was deeply unsettling. The realization that it was caused solely by us drove that point home in the most awful way.

Until then, I had never considered the separation of diseases between wild and captive elephants. Locked in that quiet room with Violet, surrounded by bones ravaged by equally horrifying 'zoogenic' diseases, I was confronted with that stark truth. Although it made perfect sense, I'd never contemplated that when we alter an elephant's biology so drastically—depriving it of space, food, and family—we set in motion a tragedy so great that not even the likes of Shakespeare could write.

CHAPTER 8

"Why don't you build three?" Jason asked.

"Three what?" I was confused.

"Different presentations on elephants. Since the Rotary gives you only fifteen minutes to speak and you're unsure of what people are interested in, why not create three separate talks to see which one they respond to the most? Then remove what isn't working and keep the rest. Use the Rotary Club as your own personal playground."

As usual, Leslie was right. Jason was the perfect person to ask for advice. Although we had discussed the benefits of preparing multiple presentations on elephants before, receiving an actual invitation made me realize I wasn't sure where or how to begin. The idea of creating several versions and then combining the best parts seemed ingenious. It had the potential to be a compelling way to educate—that is, if I could find the delicate balance between raising awareness and inspiring change.

Once we had selected three random topics about elephants, I created a unique presentation around each one, polishing them during my night shifts between calls. Then I reached out to my friend Phil, from the Rotary Club, and asked him to set a date.

On the day of my talk, I was incredibly nervous, even with only twenty people or so in attendance. Jason was there to evaluate me, to help make sure I was on the right track. At first, I thought everything was going well until a single, drawn-out yawn interrupted my rhythm. Soon, a few more fanned across the room, and my confidence crumbled. Then I accidentally stood in front of the projector, blocking my slides, and fell completely out of sync. By then it didn't matter—I had already lost them. Before it was over, I made a mental tally of five sleepers.

After gathering his things, Jason walked over, grinning. "And there it is," he chuckled. "Your first barometer. If you can keep at least a quarter of the room from falling asleep, you're well on your way. Otherwise, you might consider a career in lullabies."

"God," I groaned, not finding any of it funny.

He jotted down a few notes on a piece of paper regarding the sections he found most compelling and those he didn't.

"You should ask every crowd you speak to the same thing," he said, handing it to me.

"Like a questionnaire?"

"Yes. And make it anonymous, so they'll be honest with you."

"OK, so how do I get more opportunities?"

"Ask Phil for a copy of their directory. Most Rotary Clubs across the state meet once a week and they all need speakers."

That evening, I sat down with the list and emailed every chapter within a twenty-mile radius. In no time, I had scheduled over thirty engagements for the coming months. After each one, I looked for ways to improve based on the anonymous feedback. While working at night, I rehearsed in the break room with my co-workers. Just when I was convinced I'd built the perfect talk, I showed up at another club and ... *more sleepers.*

After I had spoken at all thirty, I extended my reach and traveled beyond the confines of my local area. I also included Kiwanis Clubs, needing all the practice I could get. Before long, I was booked for the following year, sometimes doing several presentations per week. Every extra dollar I scraped together went toward gas.

Since many of the clubs I visited hosted breakfast meetings, I rarely slept between the end of my late shift and those early morning events. Instead, I stayed awake and rehearsed. When I returned home, I was so exhausted I collapsed into bed. Days turned into weeks, then months. Despite the grueling schedule I'd set for myself, the stories of the elephants kept pushing me forward.

All kinds of things went wrong in those talks: equipment failed, there were power outages, and hecklers harassed me. Each time I was knocked down and swore I would never do it again, I got back up and did. I learned not to rely on my PowerPoint slides and instead memorized my presentations, printing them to hand out just in case. I packed extra batteries and projector bulbs, and worked on comebacks for the occasional asshole who thought it was appropriate to interrupt me when he felt he had something more important to say.

On a particular morning, I cursed myself for agreeing to speak at a breakfast club so far away that I had to be on the road by 3:00 a.m. But it was during that talk that an extraordinary thing happened. Midway through, the entire audience of over a hundred people went *dead* quiet. By then, I had meticulously combined all three presentations into one, fine-tuning specific elephant stories. To my utter disbelief, it worked. I quickly snapped out of my zone and noticed, for the very first time, I had everyone's full, undivided attention. It took me a second to grasp what had occurred, and I had to concentrate to avoid getting ahead of myself. Suddenly, the little girl inside me jumped all over that room screaming at the top of her lungs—there wasn't a single sleeper in the house.

As I drove home, basking in the glory, I gave myself the ultimate challenge: nursing homes. If I could keep that crowd awake, then I knew my new and improved elephant talk was a hit. I arrived at the first one days later, but watched in dismay as over half the room went "lights out" within minutes. It seemed the balloon I had ridden so high upon was torpedoed by a missile before it crashed back down to earth.

Dejected, I sat on a curb in the parking lot and called Leslie.

"Well? How did it go?" she asked.

"Awful," I sniffled. "There was a guy in the front row who snored so loud you could hardly hear a word I said." It was true.

Leslie failed miserably to contain her laughter. "You just keep going and trust your instincts. You're gonna nail this."

"Am I? This whole stupid ordeal is fucking exhausting."

"You are—this is only a blip."

"I'm afraid I'll be trapped in these dead-end jobs forever. Speaking at nursing homes hardly feels like a step up."

"But it *is*. If you can hold their attention, you've got it, my friend," she giggled.

Again, I followed her advice and continued my tour, securing bookings at every nursing home I could find. I was determined to keep that damn room awake if it killed me. This time, I ditched my previous talks and started completely over, building a brand-new presentation focused solely on the behavior of wild elephants.

Previously, I'd shared stories about how several of the orphaned elephants returned for help when sick or injured, sometimes years after joining a wild herd. To me, this type of conduct in the animal world was astonishing, but I was dismayed to learn that many of those who filled out the questionnaire weren't as impressed. They explained that the orphaned elephants must have known where to go since they were raised by humans. Yet, I was aware of wild elephants that did the same thing.

I plunged back into my database and soon found exactly what I was looking for. My new presentation was focused on one individual—an elephant whose story aligned perfectly with the anonymous feedback.

∞

The wild bull was a towering presence from the moment the keepers spotted him, surpassing any other they had seen. It wasn't just the impressive size of his tusks that drew their attention, but that he wandered among their orphaned herd in broad daylight.

Poaching was rampant in that region of Tsavo and a large elephant with long, beautiful tusks was the focus of every man who entered the park illegally. The small remaining herds of wild bulls only came out at night, making any individual that appeared during daylight a rare occurrence.

Due to his frequent visits, the keepers named him Rafiki, which means *friend* in Swahili. His past was unknown to them; he just showed up one afternoon, among the orphans.

In the evenings, when they led the group back to the stockades, Rafiki followed, though he always kept a safe distance. He seemed as wary of the men, as they were of him. Instead of entering the front gate with the others, Rafiki stopped just outside, as if saying goodbye to his class. Each morning, he was right where they left him, ready to escort the young elephants into the wild for another bout of learning, mingling, and play.

Early one day, the keepers found Rafiki sleeping on the ground next to the gate, resting his head on a large rock as a pillow. They wondered if he had been there all along, perhaps rising moments before they appeared. Just when they thought they understood his behavior, something new and unexpected would surface, leaving them impressed once again.

Like so many of the larger bulls the men had known, Rafiki seemed to recognize that his large size intimidated the younger orphans. Whenever they visited a waterhole, the massive elephant would lie down along the edge, allowing the smaller ones to climb all over him. The orphans splashed and frolicked, reveling in the adventure of approaching such a giant without fear.

For several months, Rafiki remained with the group, watching over them, until one day, he mysteriously disappeared. At first, the keepers weren't overly concerned, as bull elephants were known to wander. But one week soon became two, then three. Poaching had reached such alarming levels it was difficult not to feel the whisper of worry.

More than a month after Rafiki was last seen, a frantic call came over the radio while the group was deep in the bush with the orphans. A veterinarian was summoned to treat a large, wounded, wild bull roaming close to the stockades. The men exchanged nervous glances, wondering if it could be him. Two of the keepers ran back to the compound to investigate.

As they approached, they saw Rafiki's unmistakable frame and long, white tusks. Although relieved to find him alive, they couldn't shake the uneasy tension at the thought of his injury, hoping it was treatable. Just then, the enormous figure of another wild elephant limped out from behind a tall bush, and they realized he was the injured one, not Rafiki.

The large elephant had a poisoned arrow deeply embedded in his hip, making it difficult for him to walk. The vet arrived a short time later, and while he anesthetized the wounded elephant, Rafiki stepped away, as if he knew they were there to help his friend. Luckily, the poison was old and therefore weak. The wild bull was unbelievably lucky. As soon as the projectile was removed, the elephant rose slowly while Rafiki stayed by his side. He guarded his injured friend until the two disappeared once more into the Kenyan wilderness.

The keepers reported what they had witnessed when they returned to the group. The others were astonished to hear that Rafiki had brought them another elephant who needed help. Or at least, that's how it appeared. And if that was the case, it meant that he understood the difference between the men who wanted to kill and those whose only mission was to save and protect. An elephant that could barely walk would have been an easy target for a poacher, but Rafiki seemed to realize that the keepers posed no threat. If that had been the only incident, it would have been enough. But as time would reveal, it was just the beginning.

Over the next several months, Rafiki escorted numerous bulls back to the stockades—elephants who would have easily died without medical intervention. Whenever an anxious call rang out over the radio that another injured bull showed up needing a vet, the keepers knew Rafiki would be with him. He seemed to treat it no differently than if I took a friend to the emergency room. They were all treated and sent on their way, only for Rafiki to return a few days later, with yet one more lucky individual who had escaped the mark of a persistent poacher.

Then more wild elephants with obvious injuries began appearing by themselves, without an escort. They paced back and forth within yards of the keepers' night dormitories, as if they had been "told" about the elephant hospital and the men who could help, even though none had been raised by humans.

I could only imagine how terrifying it must have been for those elephants. It was man, after all, who shot the arrow, pulled the trigger, or set the snare. Still, they were able to distinguish between the heroes and the hunters. Without the vet's medical intervention, most would have been dead within days, if not hours. Yet each life was saved, given the chance to live another day, wild and free.

At the end of that year, a massive drought engulfed Tsavo and all the natural waterholes dried up, leaving hundreds of thousands of animals to die of thirst.

Except for those fortunate enough to know a friend.

Rafiki began escorting large groups of wild elephants, including females, infants, and bulls with enormous tusks, through the front gate of the compound, to a waterhole the keepers made for the younger ones housed inside. Throughout all the years they had known him, the men had never witnessed Rafiki enter the orphan's nighttime sanctuary. Now, having figured out how to unlatch the gate, reflecting the cleverness of elephants from the past, he did so regularly, leading large groups of thirsty elephants inside.

Awakened by the sounds of Rafiki's rumbles, he kept the group calm, while the men cautiously peered from behind their windows, detecting their uneasiness. But the elephants' need for the life-saving water surpassed their desire for safety. They drank their fill before slipping quietly back into the darkness.

It was a testament to their sophisticated level of communication and illustrated the elephants' trust in Rafiki. For me, it was another example of the empathy shown by a bull elephant who seemed just as compassionate as any female.

In the 1960s and '70s, scientists labeled bull elephants the "loners of society," a misconception they've been trying to shake ever since. In reality, male elephants exhibit significant social awareness and emotional depth, far exceeding what I've witnessed amongst most humans.

After two years of constant presentations, it had finally shifted. Rafiki's behavior had a profound impact on every crowd I introduced him to. Sleeping during my elephant talks became a thing of the past. It was also the first time I noticed people getting emotional—not due to anything dreadful, but from the overwhelming sense of hope and resilience shared between the elephants themselves. They confirmed what I'd always suspected: the public was largely unaware of such mind-blowing elephant behavior. Finally, they began to see elephants as I did.

I was bombarded by speaking requests after that. Suddenly KOTA's mission to "educate" didn't seem so unsexy after all. Within months, I was asked to be the keynote speaker at Portland's annual Global March for Elephants and Rhinos. I also appeared at various women's clubs, symposiums, law schools, universities and was invited to speak as a featured panelist at an International Elephant Conference.

Finally, I was selected as the first female presenter to speak at Columbia Sportswear's corporate headquarters in two years, shifting the dynamic from the traditionally male-dominated space. It also marked my first experience being filmed by a production crew for a presentation that would be shown to all of their employees worldwide.

Once I had captured my audience's full attention, I realized that change was indeed possible. When I showed them the heart of an elephant, they showed me theirs.

CHAPTER 9

A steel gate slammed shut behind me with a clanking-metal *thud* as an officer led me through a series of chambers. It wasn't the first time I had been in a women's prison. During my final year of drinking, I'd faced a two-year sentence for another DUI. Apparently, they don't like it when you get convicted of more than one that close together.

Part of my community service involved picking up trash on the side of the freeway with fellow delinquents, but one day our supervisor drove us in the opposite direction. As we looked at each other in anticipation, he announced that we were going on a field trip. We all perked up.

"That sounds exciting," said a girl with purple hair. A large snake tattoo wrapped around her neck. "Where are we headed?"

Our supervisor chuckled. "Prison." We all perked down.

They made us wear jumpsuits similar to the ones the inmates wore inside, only ours were brightly colored and distinguishable. Later, we learned it was to prevent anyone from escaping by trying to blend in with us, as had happened in the past.

This time we were instructed to pick up litter on the prison grounds outside the fence. The prisoners lining the perimeter whooped, hollered, and cat-called us while a guard explained what our future home was going to be like. Although it should have been terrifying, I felt nothing. The truth is, I simply didn't know how to stop drinking, so what difference did it make? If prison was where my fate took me, I accepted that.

After a long wait to be released from the last chamber, the officer led me through an outdoor area where a group of inmates were gardening in raised flowerbeds, then into another building. We arrived at a room surrounded by windows, reminding me of a human fishbowl, where guards sat at a desk just outside, observing our every move. Soon, a young Hispanic woman joined me at the table. Her bright blue eyebrows made it difficult to concentrate. I remembered the first time I saw them, when she caught me staring.

"I'm sorry," I had said then. "I don't mean to be rude."

"It's okay," Delilah replied, "they're *asombrosa*, right?"

Hmmm ... I thought. Amazing is one word for it.

She explained that during a weeklong binge and blackout she had her eyebrows permanently removed and two bright blue, jagged lightning bolts tattooed in their place as a mark of loyalty to her gang. It wasn't a case where the black ink had accidentally turned blue—these were meant to be as blue as the sky. It reminded me of some of the bad decisions I had made while in a blackout. Was I really above getting my eyebrows tattooed blue?

No, I totally would have done that.

Delilah placed two books on the table and opened one to where we'd left off last time. I was there to teach her how to stay sober, just as I had been taught. For months, I worked with a group of women in recovery, bringing meetings into prison. She was the only inmate who ever asked to meet privately to learn how I overcame my own addiction. Fresh out of a treatment facility,

Delilah had the same drive I did when I first realized that drugs and alcohol were the main contributor to all my problems.

With two young children, she faced a heartbreaking reality. She'd given birth to her youngest behind bars, but the baby was taken away shortly after. Both of her kids were being raised by their father (a reformed gang member) who had stopped bringing them to see her. Evidently, he didn't want them visiting their mother, strung out and addicted. It was her final breaking point, and Delilah was determined to stay sober, no matter how hard it was or how long it took.

We also helped women with the transition once they were released, supporting their recovery by taking them to meetings and connecting them with community resources. But Delilah wasn't getting out anytime soon. Her sentence was long, and though she never revealed the crime she committed (we were instructed never to ask), it was a short list to get the kind of time she had.

"Inches and seconds," a friend used to say in meetings. "I didn't go to prison due to only inches and seconds."

I knew exactly what he meant. When I was still drinking, I drove under the influence all the time, often colliding with parked cars. Miraculously, I just never hit one with people inside. Looking back, I can't help but imagine the shock and inconvenience I caused to those who found their damaged vehicles the next morning. Those blurry memories served as a stark reminder of my past and the life I could easily slip into if I relapsed.

I took meetings into prison because that's where I belonged. The only difference between them and me was that I got to walk through the front door. I came quite close to living a life in captivity—locked in a cage—and it felt fitting that I should work with others who were. If I ever resumed drinking, prison is likely the best place someone like me would end up. Delilah and those blue eyebrows of hers reminded me of that every single day.

On my way home, I thought about elephants in captivity. Were locked-up humans really so different? Both had a difficult time transitioning back into the wild. Humans had to have "resources" in order to support them, especially if they'd served a significant amount of time behind bars or worse—in solitary confinement. If they didn't have help during the transition, one of two things usually happened: they either reoffended or they died by suicide. You couldn't just let them go to fend for themselves any more than you could simply release captive elephants into their natural habitat without guidance. Both have to be taught how to live free again.

I didn't know of any elephants in the United States who—after any period in captivity—were returned to the wild. I wondered why when they did it all the time in Kenya. The baby elephants at the orphanage were raised by humans and hundreds had integrated seamlessly with wild elephant herds. So it *was* possible. I'd heard the excuses, like everyone else—how zoo officials claimed it was impossible, that a species once locked in a cage could never live on their own again. Although, I'm sure they were right about some cases, but not most.

The real reason, I suspected, was the old and familiar story of corruption, driven by the twin forces of money and power. It would be expensive to ship a captive elephant back to its original home, just as it had been costly to capture it in the first place. One scenario filled their pockets, the other emptied them. It was far easier to simply convince the public it could never be done.

I couldn't imagine the cost of hiring people on another continent to hunt down and trap an elephant, keep it confined, and force it to be completely submissive. Then, ship it thousands of miles across the ocean in a small crate, only to train it not to hate humans, perform ridiculous tricks, and be put on display. It seemed like an enormous investment, but I wondered if it was what investors called *a castle in the sky*—an overvalued stock, unjustified by the expense. How profitable could it be if most elephants in captivity died before the age of twenty, forty *years* before their natural lifespan? But I was dead wrong. Elephants, at any age, generated such high profit margins (as babies or breeders) that it mattered little when they died.

An uncomfortable anxiety crept over me as I drove. Instead of going straight home, I took a quick detour to my new gym. The old one was still full of wilted wildflowers. Exercise, meditation, and recovery meetings were all I had left to calm my nerves once alcohol and drugs were no longer an option.

My therapist taught me about "compound trauma," which some-times affects researchers like myself. In the midst of our work, we unexpectedly encounter information that triggers our own past trauma, whether by reliving disturbing events or learning about someone else's. So much of what I studied involved the suffering and death of elephants. My counselor believed I was indeed experiencing the effects of my chosen profession, and she also thought it explained why I continued to have horrific nightmares.

We developed a plan to help me deal with it as best I could. She didn't want me reading or researching about elephants late at night, when support was difficult to find. The last thing I needed was to be alone in that part of my brain without someone to talk to or a meeting to attend. My homework was to spend more time with the friends I adored and to continue my exercise and meditation routines—practices that worked brilliantly.

ELEPHANT MOUNTAIN

I turned up the speed on the treadmill until my legs begged for mercy. As my pace slowed, a sense of calm washed over me, and the nervous tension that had gripped me earlier melted away. I caught sight of my reflection in the window and thought about the runners I'd seen in Kenya—their long legs and smooth physiques, like gazelles running effortlessly across the plains.

The first time I saw them was at a make-shift roadblock on a dirt road outside Voi. I heard a faint pitter-patter and just as I turned to look, four brightly colored, Nike-clad runners materialized out of nowhere, quiet and out of the ordinary. Their beauty against the backdrop of Kenya was mesmerizing.

Then I saw another group while riding on a *matatu*, a bus, in downtown Nairobi. Distracted by a traffic jam and the pulsating music blasting from the speakers, a common feature among drivers who could rival even the best DJs, a quartet suddenly glided by my open window. I leaned out to look, but like a cloud in the wind, they were gone as fast as they'd appeared.

It was no wonder the runners of Kenya dominated the sport. They had been doing so since the beginning of time. For centuries, it was how messages were sent and retrieved between villages, and in some regions, it still continues. Messengers run up to twenty miles a day, delivering important information wherever they go. When one stops to rest, another takes their place, and the cycle goes on.

One day, a group of strange men arrived at a remote village proclaiming, "The telephone, not runners, is the wave of the future." They argued there was no need for messengers when technology could do the trick.

Despite objections from the local leaders, telephone wire was laid across large stretches of the Kenyan countryside. When the time came to collect payment for the phones—most of which were never installed—the village leaders laughed, since they had no more use of a hard-wired phone than a Chanel suit. Then things got ugly.

The corrupt telephone scheme was eventually exposed as the scandal it was. That may have been the end of that story had poachers not seized on a new opportunity that literally fell right into their laps. Hundreds of miles of unused wire—free for the taking—to use as snares, dropped at their feet. It was collected, cut, twisted, shaped, and formed as a noose to catch, kill, and entangle animals of every size imaginable. And the destruction of wildlife across Kenya began on a scale so massive it was practically commercial.

I turned the treadmill off. It was so depressing I didn't want to think about it anymore. I wiped my machine down and headed to the locker room when something just outside the entrance door caught my attention. Hanging on the wall was a fuzzy, black-and-white photograph. It showed a shirtless man with huge muscles holding what looked like a machine gun, standing next to a tiny, living, furry baby elephant. I stepped closer to get a better look. The caption read, "Nautilus, Inc. founder Arthur Jones, with two of his greatest passions: guns and elephants."

The name wasn't familiar, but I was determined to find out more. I walked over to the front desk.

"Excuse me," I said, pointing. "Do you know how long that picture has been there?"

"Forever, if I had to guess." The young man shrugged.

"I've never seen it before. Are you sure someone didn't put it up recently?"

"Nah … it's been there for years."

How had I never noticed it before? I had gone to that gym and worked out daily since I'd joined months earlier. I must have walked right past it countless times. It felt like an extraordinary clue, whispering to me out of nowhere. As I turned and looked around, every workout machine had a picture of a nautilus shell, a logo, blazed across its side. It was not something I had ever paid particular attention to before. Now, they all seemed to glow while the room darkened—illuminated only by a sea of those shells.

This was it.

Without changing out of my gym clothes or even taking a shower, I grabbed my things and ran across the street to the library, eager to reach the nearest computer, convinced that this was the sign I had been searching for.

CHAPTER 10

Arthur Jones was no ordinary businessman. Long before *Forbes* magazine recognized him as one of the world's richest men, his fascination with elephants set him apart. He admired their strength and resilience, often commenting that they reflected his own ability to survive in the harshest conditions. After all, he was a self-made billionaire who built his empire with nothing more than a ninth-grade education.

As the founder of Nautilus, Inc., he invented (and sold) high-intensity training machines to gyms all over the United States and single-handedly fueled the fitness boom of the 1970s and '80s. He bore a striking resemblance to a real-life Rambo, piloted his own fleet of super jets, had a deep appreciation for cursing—*though I couldn't really fault him for that*—and collected all sorts of exotic animals. Already he had accumulated an impressive collection at his compound in Ocala, Florida, called Jumbolair. Soon his heart was set on elephants.

In the 1960s, Arthur flew to South Africa's Kruger National Park to film animals for *Wild Cargo*, a television series he both starred in and produced. The show featured him hunting, capturing, and killing Africa's most iconic wildlife, either for sport or to display in zoos. He had long since established a reputation as both a guest and a host on various programs. His most popular episode focused on him trapping wild gorillas—one of which he kept for himself.

While filming in Kruger, Arthur soon learned that plans for an elephant cull were already underway. Their migration routes to other areas, parks, and countries had been blocked by human settlement. By the time he arrived, the damage they had inflicted inside the park was unmistakable.

Decisions were made to kill off a certain number, therefore relieving the pressure. However, there was one problem—money. Authorities needed more resources to hire helicopters, shooters, trucks, and trailers large enough to haul the carcasses to the processing plants lining Kruger's edges. The meat from previous culls was harvested as a source of protein known as *biltong* (similar to beef jerky), while the bones were ground into powder for fertilizer and the ivory was removed, carved, and sold to the highest bidder.

Then Arthur Jones appeared, and he had exactly what they were looking for—all the money in the world. As a savvy entrepreneur with a keen eye for profitability, he wasn't interested in the small returns from killing elephants. Instead, he bet on the far greater profits he could make by selling the babies to circuses and zoos. So he made them a deal. In exchange for filming the event for another nature program, he offered to pay for the entire operation.

Immediately, they devised a new plan, unlike anything tried on that scale before. Their first mission was to gather two teams of men: one to set out and capture live baby elephants, and the other to go in afterward to cull the herd in order to meet the quota.

The calves, chosen in advance, were scattered across various family groups. I found snippets of the footage, along with several books and articles retracing the events that took place. Despite the heavy nature of that episode, I also knew there was more to the story than tragedy—there was a brilliant light at the end of this tunnel.

On the day of the mass capture in September 1966, men assembled at their designated base camp along the Letaba River nestled in the Malopenyana Valley, deep inside Kruger. The chosen location was hidden from prying tourists who might jeopardize the entire operation if news or pictures got out. Prior incidents revealed the public's distaste for such affairs. The last thing they needed was any "bunny huggers" getting involved, so everyone was warned to stay on the lookout.

Small groups of men were deployed near the wild herds, while helicopters swooped in to separate the families. Their strategy was to create panic, assuming that it would then be easy to split the mothers from their babies. But they underestimated the power of an elephant.

Those mothers fiercely protected their precious offspring, regardless of how close men or machinery got. Very few panicked. Instead, most stood their ground, one after the next, viciously facing their attackers head-on, with their babies tucked protectively beneath their massive legs. The only way they would let anyone get near those calves was over their dead bodies.

The behavior left the men stunned. They were unaware that elephants would sacrifice their own lives for the sake of their young. In order to separate the mothers from their offspring, they needed to anesthetize both, something they hadn't expected or planned for.

After a short delay, veterinarians were dispatched to the helicopters. Once the elephants were subdued, they were the first to reach the babies to check their teeth. If the tiny elephant still had its milk teeth—which meant it was less than one-year-old—then it was given an antidote and returned to its mother. They knew they couldn't keep a baby, fully dependent on milk, alive, so they were thrown back like bycatch on a fishing boat. All the young calves with their first set of teeth were loaded up and whisked away while the vets stayed behind to wake their traumatized mothers.

With each capture, tensions between the men rose. They weren't prepared for the violent confrontations displayed by the elephants who challenged, charged, and threatened them, whether they were high above in helicopters or face-to-face on the ground. Many were so disturbed they refused to continue. At the time, elephants were not considered intelligent beings or even capable of having feelings, but this experiment suggested otherwise.

What began as a capture operation quickly spiraled into an all-out war, with infighting between them growing too severe to proceed, forcing Arthur to cut his losses. They had captured twenty-seven out of the fifty they'd planned on, but it would have to do.

In the days that followed, seven of the baby elephants were released, proving too violent to tame. The men didn't even try to reunite them with their families. Instead, they simply let them go, miles away from where they were taken, and "hoped for the best." Another two died in their cages from unknown reasons. In the end, eighteen were loaded onto trains for a twelve-hour journey to the nearest port in Maputo, Mozambique. There they boarded a U.S.-based Lykes Brothers cargo ship bound for their new homes in American circuses and zoos.

I did a quick search to see if I could find who purchased the calves. As I worked my way down the list, the hair on my arms stood on end. The fate of three of those baby elephants had led them right to Portland and the Oregon Zoo, before being sent to a place that made me catch my breath—*Elephant Mountain*.

I sat back in my chair as fragments of an old memory emerged: a framed picture that hung in the hallway outside of the main research office at the zoo. It was the front page of a local newspaper from 1979, detailing the death of Elephant Mountain's owner—killed by an elephant he kept there.

One year earlier his partner and the love of his life had also been fatally attacked by a different elephant held on that mountain. Their story had all the essence of a romantic fairy tale, but with a dark and tragic twist.

At the time, I intended to learn more about what had happened, but was so buried in other commitments that I never did. Now the opportunity was knocking on my door, like an echo from the past.

The ping of a text startled me. I rummaged through my bag until I found my phone.

"Just checking to see if you're still coming?" Violet asked.

I cursed under my breath having been so engrossed that I completely forgot to meet her at the secret museum. I quickly responded that I was on my way and made a quick note of topics to revisit once I had the luxury of time. Inhaling deeply, I felt a rush of energy coursing through my body—an unwavering certainty. The path forward was finally clear. Without another thought, I turned off the computer, tucked the list into my pocket, and ran to my car.

∞

"What do you see?"

Violet stood next to my favorite elephant skull, wearing gloves and holding a small brush. She waited while I put mine on. Once

I was ready to begin, she asked her usual litany of questions. I looked across his familiar face, crackled by time. The two large holes at the top of the elephant's head, no longer round and symmetrical, led to the olfactory bulbs, which are widely considered one of their most powerful senses—the sense of smell.

Although small bits of bone were missing due to the skull's decay, the bullet hole remained a perfect circle, as if he'd been shot yesterday. I carefully examined each section, taking my time as I moved around the cart, looking for something Violet already knew was there.

Suddenly, a deformity I hadn't noticed before caught my attention. There was a strange, oblong-shaped hole, located just a few inches from the entryway of the bullet. I studied the features of another skull sitting on a shelf behind me to compare, confirming my suspicion: this anomaly was unique.

The bizarre cavity extended all the way to the back of the elephant's head and resembled no other. It was surrounded by a thick layer of rough, uneven bone. Then I noticed a crack running along the edge, barely visible at first as a hairline fracture. It gradually widened as I followed it, expanding into a jagged fissure that ended an inch or so from where it began. The hole started out rather large, about the size of a silver dollar, but narrowed like a funnel, until it was just wide enough for a single finger to pass through—ending at the base of his brain.

"What is *that*?" I asked.

"That," said Violet, "is an infection."

"What do you mean?" I asked, confused.

"An untreated infection slowly eats away at the bone," she said. "This elephant must have had it for some time. So long, in fact, it grew all the way into his brain." Her finger rested on the smallest part of the opening.

"Oh my god," I whispered. As I absorbed this information, another chapter of this young elephant's life was revealed.

"What do you know about this area?" She pointed to the temporal gland between the eye and the ear.

"It's where elephants are disciplined," I said, while Violet nodded.

There are a few primary training points elephant handlers use—areas where the skin is so thin and sensitive, the slightest prick causes an immediate reaction. The region Violet pointed to, where the injury that led to the infection began, is the most common, followed by their ears, mouth, and the most awful, the anus. I wondered how long it had been present to become so severe.

As if she'd read my mind, Violet continued, "If I had to guess that infection would been there for around ten years for it to have grown that deep."

"If this elephant was only thirteen when he was shot, then he was just two or three when the injury occurred," I said softly.

It was the age when most elephants in captivity are separated from their mothers to begin the brutal regime of training. By then, they're mostly weaned, yet still small enough to handle. The older they get, the larger and more dangerous they become.

"And that means ..." I couldn't finish the sentence.

"When he was just a baby," Violet said, finishing it for me, "he would have been hit so hard, most likely with a bullhook during training, that it actually cracked his skull. And since the injury never healed, suggesting no one knew it was there, the bone continued to deteriorate as the infection grew so large it reached all the way into his brain."

The tragic details of his young life filled the room, as we contemplated his sorrowful existence. The evidence was glaringly obvious and plain for all to see once we knew where to look. Apparently, no one except us ever did.

"If this elephant killed his trainer," she continued, "I wouldn't be surprised. This kind of suffering would have easily driven it mad."

"But had they realized it was an infection, couldn't they have treated it?" I asked.

"Yes," Violet said. "That's the worst part. A simple antibiotic could have cured it, had they caught it early enough, and this young elephant wouldn't have had to suffer the way he did."

That stark fact hit me right between the eyes, just like the bullet between his. Before she put the skull away, I asked to spend a few more minutes alone with him. Still so many unanswered questions. His story was heartbreaking and also common—*too common*. It was hard to comprehend such a young elephant dying in such a cruel and senseless manner.

There was no question I was drawn to him. I visited his skull, the bullet wound, and that infection numerous times throughout that year, and each time I felt the pull. A nagging feeling deep inside, like an invisible tap on my shoulder, the lightest breath across my neck, or the way the wind blows gently through the trees on my daily walks—sometimes I swear I can hear the quiet whisper of my name. It never once occurred to me that this young elephant was as eager to share his secrets as I was to uncover them.

CHAPTER 11

"Three babies are coming," Mishak said over the phone to Joseph, the lead keeper in Voi. "*Moja ni ... maalum.*" One is ... special, he continued.

"*Ana shida gani?*" What's wrong with her? he asked.

"She had a bad *jeraha*, to the head. She is the one who used to walk in circles, but the others, Emily and Imenti, taught her how to walk *moja*," Mishak explained.

"*Sawa*, I've heard of them," Joseph replied. They all had. The newest recruits could hardly believe it when they first learned of their story.

When the elephants turned two, the age most left the orphanage, they were loaded onto a large transport truck for the trip several hundred miles away to Voi. There, they would meet their new matriarch, Eleanor, and her trusted nanny, Malaika, who would introduce them to the wild herds that roamed nearby. The goal of all the rescued elephants was the same: to be returned to their natural habitat on their own terms, when they were ready.

Maintaining the connection between bonded elephants during transfers was crucial, and few unions were stronger than that of Emily, Aitong, and Imenti. Daphne learned through the years that separating them inflicted great psychological stress and could be enough to send a traumatized elephant back down the road of depression. A fate few could recover from once, but rarely twice.

"*Ikiwa* Aitong *atafanya upuzi,*" *If* Aitong *acts up,* Mishak warned, "stand aside and let the two elephants handle her."

"*Unakuja nao?*" *Are you coming with them?* Joseph asked.

"Yes," Mishak said. "*Nitakuwepo pia.*" *I'll be there too.* Before hanging up, he instructed Joseph to inform the other keepers.

Afterward, he wondered why Mishak felt compelled to warn him ahead of time, given that he was accompanying them to Voi. Regardless, he followed instructions and relayed the message to the rest of the team.

When the trucks finally pulled through the front gate, it was already late in the afternoon. Despite the nearly nine-hour-long journey, Eleanor and Malaika stood by, eagerly awaiting their arrival, as if they'd received some sort of advance notice. Ndume, along with former orphan Edo, was also there to greet the newcomers, even though neither had been seen in months. How the elephants, including many wild ones, were able to sense when another group was being transferred remained a mystery.

Ndume and Malaika greeted Mishak with squeals, trumpets, and rumbles. They were as excited to see him as they had ever been to see anyone. Mishak felt the same way. After years of nurturing their emotional recovery and watching them thrive in each other's company, he too was overwhelmed by the reunion.

As soon as the elephants stepped off the truck, Eleanor wrapped a protective trunk around Emily while Malaika took a special interest in Imenti, leading Daphne to wonder if her connection to him was because her blood ran through his. Or perhaps they were related, having both been rescued from the same forest region. Whatever the reason, she made it clear he was her chosen one. Aitong, as the smallest, captured the attention of all the rest.

Days after the trio settled in, Joseph received a call over his radio. A spotter plane had observed a small herd of elephants walking directly toward the compound. Since it was rare for them to advance in such a manner, it likely meant a former orphan was among them needing their help. A keeper grabbed his binoculars and jumped on top of a roof. Moments later, he shouted with excitement that two of the five elephants were orphans they had raised. Soon they understood the reason for the visit. Lissa had recently given birth to her first calf. And was accompanied by her closest friend, Mpenzi, who served as her devoted nanny.

"Look, look, look!" several keepers exclaimed, pointing at the tiny newcomer with excitement.

Wild, former orphans were just as eager to introduce their offspring to the men who raised them as they were to the rest of the herd.

As the group came within sight of the stockades, a blood-curling scream startled everyone. Aitong, who had been calmly eating with Emily and Imenti on the far side of the premises just moments earlier, broke away and charged at the incoming elephants. Her companions quickly turned and chased after her. Then Joseph remembered Mishak's warning.

"Get back!" he yelled, as the crowd scattered.

The approaching herd stopped and went on high alert. Each one, including Mpenzi, shielded Lissa and her baby, from Aitong's oncoming charge. Emily moved swiftly to flank one side of her, while Imenti ran to the other, cutting her off. Aitong screamed her displeasure as they blocked her path. Whenever she attempted to maneuver around them, they acted in unison, anticipating her next move and preventing her from getting past until she regained her composure.

After several minutes, Aitong visibly relaxed. Emily laid her trunk across her head, offering comfort as her breaths slowed and the sanctuary fell quiet once again.

As soon as the two elephants decided she had sufficiently calmed down, they shifted from blocking her to standing by her side, as loyal guardians. Then all three moved as one, as they walked toward the wild females slowly and with caution.

Everyone was stunned as they watched the visiting herd lower their guard and extend their trunks in what seemed like a gesture of welcome. Aitong stayed quiet and still, even after the elephants stepped aside, revealing Lissa's tiny, furry baby tucked beneath her legs.

When Aitong reached out, Lissa shifted her stance, allowing her to approach. The potential for a wide array of mishaps was high. But Aitong remained calm and composed as she gently touched the baby with her trunk.

Moments later, the rest of the orphans arrived, eagerly greeting the visitors and Lissa's female calf the keepers named Lara.

"Wow," Joseph said, when it was all over.

"*Niliwambia,*" *I told you,* Mishak laughed, "Let them handle her. *Bado ana kitu ...*" *She still has something ...* he trailed off, tapping a finger to his temple, indicating the lingering impact of Aitong's head injury.

Joseph nodded, now he understood. He was impressed by the elephants' extraordinary ability to control Aitong and had never seen anything like it before. She had no intention of harming the baby, but due to her uncontrollable excitement, she risked injuring it accidentally until Emily and Imenti were able to calm her down. Over time, those who worked at the sanctuary, from milk-mixers to mechanics grew accustomed to Aitong's spontaneous outbursts, and learned to move out of the way whenever she lost her composure. Each time she did, the other elephants handled the situation with ease.

Over the next several days, Lissa, Lara, and Mpenzi stayed inside the compound while their wild friends, wary of the humans, waited for them just outside. Although Aitong was watched closely, there was little need, as she behaved as normal as any other elephant. The unique interaction between the trio stood in stark contrast to what Joseph had expected when he first began working with elephants.

Nestled in the shadow the magnificent Mt. Kilimanjaro and once surrounded by some of the world's largest tuskers, Joseph was raised in the small border town Taveta, three miles from Tanzania. He was one of the few who had ever seen a living elephant before he was hired as a keeper. When he learned there was an opening in Voi, just a two-hour drive from his home, he immediately applied. Daphne didn't tell him the interviews were conducted by the elephants themselves. If they accepted you, you were in. She realized long before that they were better judges of character than most people, and quite capable of conducting their own assessment.

Luckily, Joseph passed their inspection and began his studies under the one man known as a true elephant whisperer. Mishak taught him everything he knew about their mysterious nature.

Joseph learned all females stayed together for life, separated by just two things: man or death. Transfixed by their stories—where they came from, what they had endured, and the profound trauma so many had overcome—he always looked forward to Mishak's extended stays in Voi.

Eleanor's story was also the first to captivate him. After leading the orphans as the head matriarch for thirty-three years, she finally transitioned into the wild. Malaika stepped into the role as the new matriarch, where she took charge of the orphans for the next several years until she went into labor with her first calf. After nearly two agonizing weeks, both she and her baby tragically died. Mishak was devastated, knowing there wasn't anything he or anyone could have done to save her.

A blanket of sorrow descended upon the compound. Emily and Aitong dedicated themselves to the mini-herd, offering solace and support wherever they could. Then they stepped into their dual roles as matriarchs, following in Maliaka's footsteps and those of Eleanor before her.

Each day, the two elephants took turns sharing the role, revealing another odd quirk to their friendship. It was unusual to have more than one elephant stepping in as the matriarch, but they shared the responsibility as if it had always been done that way.

On their daily walks, Imenti preferred to stay at the back, taking the last position in the long line of elephants, rather than joining his companions at the front. Joseph wondered if he was serving as their protector. Every morning, as they headed out, the large elephant waited until every orphan fell into place, then he followed from behind. No other bull he'd known had ever done that. Then Joseph remembered something else Mishak shared with him one day.

"Everything they do is on purpose," he said. *"Ni uamuzi."* *It's a decision.*

The startling truth in that statement struck him. Just when he thought he had heard it all when it came to their behavior, they surprised him again. It seemed there was so much more to learn, yet already he was astounded.

"They care about you like *familia*," Mishak's words replayed in his mind.

At the time, he'd struggled to comprehend the depth of their bond. That the elephants might see the men as more than mere caretakers, but as their actual family. What he couldn't have known was that the opportunity to test that theory was about to present itself sooner than he expected.

∞

It was a warm summer morning in mid-December, as the group began their day like any other. Emily took the lead at the front, with Aitong next in line, as they guided the orphans into the Kenyan wilderness. Holding his usual place at the rear was Imenti, followed by Joseph, Mishak, and the others. At six years old, the three elephants towered above the rest.

After walking for a few miles, Emily came to a sudden halt. She flared her ears and lifted her trunk, while Aitong stood next to her, alert and ready.

"*Ni nini?*" *What is it?* Joseph asked, balancing on his toes for a clearer view.

"*Sijiu,*" *I don't know,* Mishak whispered. "*Karibu zaidi.*" *Get closer.* He waved to the stragglers to catch up.

Suddenly, Imenti whipped around and darted behind the keepers. Lowering his head, he drove them toward the elephants. At the same time, the matriarchs trumpeted, pushing the startled elephants back the way they had come. With Imenti holding the rear, blocking any escape, the scattered line quickly transformed into a tight circle. Mishak and Joseph were tucked into the middle, baffled, unable to grasp what was unfolding.

Aitong stayed at the front with Emily, facing a danger they

could not see, while Imenti held his position. Without warning, Aitong peeled off and stood halfway between the two larger elephants. The temporal glands gushed liquid down the sides of her face—a vivid testament to her intense emotional state. At the same moment, Imenti pivoted and faced the same direction. The large elephants had aligned to form a massive defensive wall. Then they froze.

The faint sound of pounding hooves could be heard in the distance before a herd of antelope leapt from the dense scrub brush, narrowly missing them, followed by the unmistakable roar of a lion.

The screams of the three large elephants rivaled the lion's bellow. Blocked by their towering frames, the keepers couldn't see beyond them. But as they shifted, the men caught sight of what they feared most: a large pride of growling, ferocious carnivores.

One by one, more slithered from the dense brush. They peeled off in slow motion and surrounded their circle. Mishak held his breath, knowing that a pride smaller than this could easily overpower them had it not been for the towering presence of Emily, Aitong, and Imenti. The chances of a lion bringing down an elephant of their size were slim. However, if the lions broke the perimeter, which was clearly their intent, one of the younger elephants or a full-grown man would make for a substantial feast.

Aitong viciously charged, daring them to take one step closer. As the lions shifted, the trio mirrored their movements, threatening any audacious enough to strike.

Two individuals attempted to breach the formation, but Emily and Imenti held the edges while Aitong continued her charge, forcing any lion that came too close to retreat. The keepers clung to the younger elephants amid the chaos, trembling with fear.

The lions desperately searched for weak points to pick off their prey. Aitong ran from one side to the other, issuing urgent calls. Panic was what the pride was betting on. If they could panic just one, the circle would break, and it would be easy to isolate any of the vulnerable individuals—elephant or human.

Emily bellowed long and deep, communicating with the terrified youngsters. To everyone's surprise, the elephants did not panic, did not break out of their circle, and did exactly as they were told.

Despite their persistent attempts, the lions' efforts remained futile. After a grueling hour, they finally surrendered in a chorus of parting screams. But one brave individual refused to budge, expressing its anguish with a roar so intense that it left the entire group breathless. Eventually, it too slinked away, vanishing into the heavy brush with the rest, leaving nothing but the sound of their pounding hearts.

Emily waited for several minutes before she stretched out her trunk to one of the young elephants, offering comfort. Imenti turned abruptly and took his usual place. The matriarchs also pivoted as they gently coaxed the orphans down the path in the direction they came, this time with Imenti in the lead. Aitong tucked herself into the middle, remaining on high alert and maintaining vigilance against further threats. Emily, at the rear, paused every few seconds to survey the surroundings, detecting lingering signs of danger.

Soon, Imenti stopped and relaxed, as if giving them all a silent signal the threat had passed. Joseph sank to the ground, joined by several keepers in the shared weight of what they'd just survived. He glanced up at Mishak, who leaned against one of the smaller orphans; his expression mirrored the profound relief that washed over each of them. There was no need to say anything. The elephants had saved their lives and protected the men as they would the youngest and most vulnerable individuals in the herd.

In the wild, the largest adults shove the smallest and most defenseless into a tight bunch while they guard the edges. But the orphans—like Imenti, rescued too young to have had a similar experience—practiced the same behavior. They surrounded and protected the men as they would their own families, just as Mishak said they would.

Their actions on that day spoke to the roles they would come to define. Emily had established herself as a strong matriarch, Aitong as a fierce warrior, and Imenti earned the title of 'The Brave,' one which he would carry from that point forward.

I looked out the window, taking a moment to reflect. There was a reason I had returned to the stories of those three remarkable elephants—why my hand had stopped on the one notebook that held them on that night I was overwhelmed by terror. I needed to remember what it was like to feel fear, yet be brave anyway.

For the sake of the elephants.

For the sake of me.

CHAPTER 12

The night sky stretched above as I looked up from my tilted lawn chair, a kaleidoscope of familiar stars and constellations. I was struck by how different it appeared from Kenya. The unfamiliar landscape of the Southern Hemisphere was filled with unrecognizable symbols, like the Southern Cross, which my guide, Ibrahim, pointed out on an evening similar to this. I wondered what the keepers and the elephants were doing at that very moment. A slight breeze picked up, chilling the air. I hugged my arms tightly, trying to ward off the cold as a bank of clouds rolled in, obscuring my view—the calm before a storm.

I gathered my things and went inside to make some tea. Several months earlier, I had moved to a beautiful town called West Linn, located ten miles outside Portland. My studio was a mother-in-law unit attached to a large home, making it virtually invisible from the street. The house sat close to the banks of the Willamette River, next to a wooded trail I walked daily. Surrounded by nature and wildlife, I felt myself finally relax. Since leaving my exposed apartment in the city, the ever-present feeling of being secretly watched disappeared.

I had a rare gift: four consecutive days off. At last, I had a substantial stretch to pull on a thread and see where it would lead.

Despite my therapist's warning against researching after dark, I found myself unable to resist. When a subject captivated me as much as Elephant Mountain did, sleep became impossible. I could hardly wait to dive into the depths of this mysterious and tragic love story. Once my printer was loaded with paper, I made myself comfortable, opened my laptop, and prepared for the long night ahead.

∞

Deep in the heart of Blue Earth County, a hundred miles south of St. Paul, Minnesota, Howard Morgan Berry, Sr. was born and raised in the rural town of Mapleton. There, he met his wife Estella who worked as a nurse in the local hospital. The small railroad community was quaint and charming. Surrounded by golden fields of wheat and corn, it resembled the serene clarity of a Grant Wood painting. After graduating from law school, Howard established himself as the town's only real estate attorney. Since the government offered dirt cheap land loans toward the end of the first World War, business was booming.

Howard Morgan Berry Jr. was born on July 30, 1911, on Estella's twenty-fourth birthday, as their only son, followed by a handful of sisters. Gifted with a natural talent for music, Morgan could play practically any instrument he touched. By the time he was a teenager, he had mastered the bass (similar to a cello). Soon he'd caught the attention of the world's most prestigious musical institution, securing a spot at the famous Juilliard School in New York.

His first paid job came at the height of the silent film era, when live bands performed in front of the stage, bringing the stories to life. It was a time before *talkies* revolutionized cinema, and the dazzling 1930s ushered Hollywood into its golden age.

While settling into his new routine, Morgan caught the attention of the legendary band leader, Red Sievers, who recognized raw talent when he saw it. Within days, Morgan was picked up for a tour with the Red Siever's Big Band Orchestra performing in ballrooms across the Upper Midwestern states.

After months of relentless shows, the excitement of playing every night in a new city took a toll. Feeling homesick, Morgan asked for some time off to see his wife, Louise, and their infant son, Howard III. It was a decision that would forever change the course of his life and one that seemed orchestrated by the very hand of fate herself.

On October 16, 1941, days after arriving home, he received a devastating phone call. During the early hours of the morning, the band's tour bus collided with a cattle truck in thick fog. The crash was so severe that it sheared off the entire left side—including the very seat assigned to Morgan, killing the musician who took his place.

Tragically, Red Sievers, along with six other musicians were also killed, while several more were critically injured. Had Morgan been on that bus, his name would have been listed among the dead.

He was left shaken, unsure of what to do next, when a colleague presented him with an unexpected opportunity: a position in a large jazz ensemble on a cruise ship. As the world turned its gaze to foreign destinations to escape the grim headlines of World War II, the cruise industry flourished. It wasn't just another chance to play music; it was a lifeline. With his second baby on the way and financial pressures building, Morgan packed his bags. He embarked on a journey to places he'd only ever read about in books: The Orient, the Kingdom of Siam (modern Thailand), Vietnam, and Formosa (modern Taiwan).

At a port stop, one of his band mates insisted he join him for a "surprise" since he had followed the call of the Siamese Dancing Dragons before. A strange noise caught Morgan's attention as his friend led him to a well-known street market within walking distance of the docked ship.

"What was that?" he asked, but the young man simply laughed and waved for him to follow.

As they rounded a corner into the bustling area, Morgan realized he had indeed heard the roar of a tiger, locked in a cage so small it could barely turn around. Hardly believing his eyes, he took in the scene: row after row of caged, exotic animals—all for sale to anyone with cash. Though Morgan wasn't paid much as a musician, it was more than enough to buy a leopard or two. He stowed his purchases in the bowels of the cruise liner near the ship's employee kitchen and quickly became the most popular man on board.

When he returned home, he sold the leopards so fast that he could hardly believe how this new business venture had fallen into his lap. Men were so desperate to show off rare and unusual animals that he charged whatever he wanted. The sky was the limit.

Within a few years, Morgan had saved enough money to quit the band. Long gone were the days of music—selling animals was his thing. By then, he'd moved his family to Seattle, where he had made a new friend, the Woodland Park Zoo's director, Ed Johnson.

But his first expedition as a bona fide importer didn't quite go as planned. He purchased 30,000 goldfish, a few tropical birds, and several monkeys when disaster struck on his way home. Unbeknownst to him, the ship he had rented was carrying a load of nitrate. If it came into direct contact with water, it could explode and had to be unloaded before they could continue, a process that took seven days. During that time, no fresh water was allowed onboard necessary to keep his precious cargo alive, and all the goldfish died. He was devastated as he watched his entire life savings poured overboard.

Once he returned to Seattle, he met with Ed at a local diner.

"I guess it's all over now," Morgan said, dejected.

"What do you mean?" asked Ed.

"Well, what am I supposed to do with four kids at home, a mortgage to pay, and a small collection of animals to feed? I'm out. I'm broke."

"That's what I wanted to meet with you about," Ed said, patting him reassuringly on the shoulder. "I talked with the zoo board, and we agreed to take everything you've got, and we'll pay you top dollar. But here's the thing see, I got them to make *you* our number one animal importer."

"What?" Morgan replied, unsure if he had heard that correctly. "Really?"

"Yes, really. You have a contract with us, and I'll bet with any other zoo you want to work with, too. Now stop wallowing in your soup, go back out there, and get us some more exotics!" Ed said, grinning.

He sweetened the deal further by offering space to house the rest of Morgan's animals, including those he planned to sell elsewhere, all at the zoo's expense.

"They can stay in the empty bear grottos," Ed added with a shrug. "Besides, it'll give our guys something to do."

Morgan struggled to grasp the full extent of the offer. His previous trip, which had disguised itself as a total failure just moments earlier, had been a much bigger success than he ever could have imagined. He raced home, shared the good news with Louise, and re-mortgaged the house.

Over the next two years, Morgan's business exploded. Every zoo in the country was desperate for the rarest creatures he could find. And due to the public's overwhelming desire for more, people everywhere started their own private zoos and collections as thousands popped up all across the United States. Exotic species of all kinds were kept in backyards and farmers' barns, while caged rare animals lined popular highways as "roadside attractions." Everyone, it seemed, wanted in on the game.

In March 1952, Morgan visited a familiar haunt in Bangkok when he learned about a baby elephant being offered in a jungle village outside town. A few hours later, he fell in love. Hiding behind the leg of the man who owned her was the tiniest elephant he had ever seen. The one-month-old baby was covered in furry skin with small pink eyes, and in that instant Morgan knew, he would do absolutely anything to have her.

He'd discovered that most logging camps, which depended on mature elephants for labor, simply gave the babies away. A working female distracted by a needy calf couldn't put forth the effort required to log another forest. Since the baby elephants wouldn't become "working elephants" for several years, it was more practical to get rid of them rather than slow production.

It was the perfect set-up: the logging camps gave their calves away to men like Morgan who lined the streets, eager to take as many as possible. It is how an absolutely staggering number of Asian elephants made their way into American circuses and zoos.

Morgan's home in the Fremont District of Seattle was surrounded by large trees and offered the perfect cover for his animals to roam free, away from curious onlookers. Although it was hard to hide the occasional roar of a tiger, a monkey scream, or the squeal of a baby elephant, the neighbors eventually grew accustomed.

Belle, as the young calf was named, became the queen of the Berry home and could roam wherever she pleased. At first, she slept on a bed of hay in Morgan's basement with his two sons, Howard and Kenneth. They were tasked with her nightly feedings and for waking every few hours to stoke the furnace fire, which kept the animals warm on the coldest Seattle nights.

Morgan bought a pink Cadillac convertible and enjoyed driving around town with his family and Belle in the backseat. Everywhere they went, people stopped and stared. Once, the boys walked her to school for a show-and-tell, but that caused such a massive traffic jam they were asked politely not to do so again. At least, not without alerting the police department ahead of time.

At the end of that year, Belle had grown too large to fit comfortably in the basement or in the back seat of a car. Ed stepped up once more, thrilled to put her on display at the zoo, and soon she was transferred to his care. There she would have the company of two circus elephants, Billie and Wide Awake, who were temporarily on leave from their performance rotations.

In order to keep Belle occupied, Ed and Morgan trained her to give elephant rides. For a small fee, members of the viewing public could climb onto her back for a short walk around zoo grounds. Their insightful business venture exceeded even their greatest expectations. The Woodland Park Zoo began attracting record numbers of visitors and generating more money than it had ever seen, while Morgan received a substantial cut of the profits.

Having Belle out of the house allowed him the time he needed to get her a mate. A few days after Belle's fifth birthday, Morgan learned about another five-year-old elephant who seemed to be exactly what he was looking for. He'd sought guidance from experienced mahouts in East Asia—those who'd worked with elephants over generations. They had instructed him on how to select the best breeding candidate for Belle. Their advice was to acquire a tall bull with a well-proportioned back, ample girth, and sturdy white tusks. However, Morgan's quest to find this "perfect" match had taken him much longer than expected.

Thonglaw Punyanitra, Morgan's business partner in Thailand, was both an attorney and a cunning entrepreneur. He dabbled in whatever made him a profit: gun trafficking, money laundering, or exporting animals. And he could easily handle all the necessary paperwork to ship exotic creatures out of his country.

"Whaddaya want?" Thonglaw would ask his customers. "Bird, monkey, snake?"

No matter what the person desired, he'd always reply, "Done." And it was. The chosen object usually appeared within a day or two.

During one of Morgan's visits to Bangkok, Thonglaw was alerted to a situation that benefited them both. A Greek man, previously living in Cambodia, had been kicked out of the country (for reasons no one cared to know), a few days earlier. Now he was just down the street with nothing more than the clothes on his back, his young daughter, and a five-year-old healthy, easy-to-please elephant he was willing to sell to anyone who would take him. Thonglaw arranged a meeting later that same afternoon.

The young bull was the first to meet all of Morgan's requirements, and within minutes, a negotiation was underway. In the end, an exchange was made that included two bicycles, twenty dollars, and a few odd things Thonglaw threw in for good measure.

"See? Whatever you want, I can get it for you." He slapped Morgan on the back, leading him and the young elephant away.

Overwhelmed with excitement, Morgan couldn't believe his luck. Soon he would have a breeding pair. The mere possibility of two of his elephants having a baby made him giddy, as it hadn't happened since 1918. Prince Utah was the last calf born in captivity in the U.S., but he died just prior to his first birthday from a congenital heart defect.

"You don't understand," Morgan beamed, "I have plans for this guy." He patted the elephant's shoulder, who stood nearly as tall as the men. "I'm going to make him more famous than Jumbo!"

The great circus wizard Phinneas T. Barnum had put his African elephant Jumbo on display in 1882 at Madison Square Garden in New York, after purchasing him from the London Zoo. Jumbo remained there for eight months, where he generated an astounding $2 million in revenue—equivalent to around $60 million today.

"Oh really?" Morgan's business partner said, stopping in the middle of the street. "If he's going to be that famous, why don't you name him after me?"

"All right then. Thonglaw it is." Morgan agreed.

Once they were back in Seattle, Belle and Thonglaw adjusted to each other quickly. Before long, they were both giving rides to the paying public, and the pair became one of the city's most popular attractions.

Two years later, Morgan returned from Bangkok with his third baby elephant, an adorable pigeon-toed female named Pet. From the moment she arrived, Belle embraced Pet as her own. As she grew, her feet turned further inward, giving her a unique gait that only added to her charm. The bond between Belle and Pet deepened, and they became inseparable. Often seen sleeping side-by-side, with their trunks intertwined, it was a testament to their unbreakable connection.

The Woodland Park Zoo's governing board had shifted by then, and was no longer keen on Morgan's previous agreement with Ed Johnson who had moved on. They didn't like that he stowed his purchases at the city's expense or that he bought and sold his growing collection of exotics on zoo grounds.

As tensions grew, Morgan called his friend, Jack Marks, the director of the Oregon Zoo, who was still mourning the loss of the zoo's second elephant, Buddy. Weak and severely malnourished, the four-year-old arrived with legs so bowed that he could hardly stand. It was likely that he suffered from Metabolic Bone Disease, or Glass Bone Disease, a common killer of young elephants back then, and Buddy died before he even had a chance to truly settle in. A short time later, another Portlander donated a baby Asian elephant he'd received as a gift—a female named Tuy Hoa (Tee-Wah)—and the city's grief was replaced with elation.

Jack was thrilled to hear about the trouble Morgan was having in Seattle, and recognized an opportunity. He offered Morgan's elephants a permanent home, as it would also create the first official herd in any U.S. zoo. They were already familiar with each other, since Morgan transported them to Portland each year due to the milder winters. In the spring, he brought them back to Seattle to resume their busy performance and ride schedules.

A few weeks later, Morgan's three elephants were loaded into trucks, headed for their new home at the Oregon Zoo. However, there was more to the story—something Morgan suspected but kept to himself.

In July 1960, he had witnessed Belle and Thonglaw mate in Seattle, and wondered if Belle might be pregnant. Little was known then about the length of an elephant's gestation period, and he wanted his herd moved in and settled long before any sign of a potential birth. If there was a baby on the way, he imagined the media frenzy such news would attract.

Within weeks of their arrival, Dr. Matthew Maberry, the head veterinarian at the zoo known as 'Doc,' confirmed on October 27, 1961, that Belle was definitely expecting. When the announcement finally came, the Woodland Park Zoo in Seattle kicked themselves for their colossal mistake.

The birth of Packy, on April 14, 1962, hit the national news like an atomic bomb. The donations, notoriety, press, and ticket sales surged to levels unlike anything ever seen at any zoo across America. Television crews and reporters from all over the world converged on the city to have their very first look at a baby elephant, filling the local hotels. Hundreds of thousands of people (including scores of celebrities) flocked into Portland to catch a glimpse of the new arrival.

Radio stations held naming contests even replacing their daily bulletins with daily *Belle*-tins. A lucky winner, Wayne French, came up with a playful twist on *pachy*-derm and the name was an instant hit. News reports featured nightly Packy segments and nearly every store in Oregon sold Packy merchandise—from stuffed animals to ashtrays—all of it selling out within days. Portland's economy received a boost that other cities could only dream of.

It is often said that the revenue from Packy's debut even surpassed that of the World's Fair, held in Seattle that same year. Zoo attendance records exceeded one million visitors, no small feat given that the entire population of Portland was only around two million. There was no denying that his birth sparked an unprecedented wave of public fascination and profit: an event that remains unmatched in the city's history.

Employees at the zoo, from animal keepers to maintenance staff, were treated like local celebrities, but none more so than Morgan. His name appeared in hundreds of newspapers around the world. *Life* magazine, the most widely circulated publication at the time, even ran a staggering eleven-page spread dedicated to the occasion.

Offers to buy Portland's elephants began pouring in from as far away as Europe. Zoos and private owners were willing to pay any price to bring that same level of chaos to their cities. But the zoo didn't own the elephants, Morgan did, and he had the right to sell them to anyone, without warning, and remove the very thing that had put Portland on the map.

Immediately, a negotiation was underway. Morgan promised Jack first dibs, as his friend, and set the price at $30,000 for the sale of Belle and Packy. He also asked for a commitment not to separate them and allow him to visit whenever he wanted. Jack agreed to everything, but there was a catch: Morgan needed the payment in full within two weeks.

The zoo immediately launched a "Save the Elephants" campaign, leading to the largest fundraising crusade in Oregon history. There were telethons, bowling alleys sponsored "Bowl for Belle" money-makers, and public donation drop boxes lined the city. Local news stations dedicated hours of free advertising to the cause. Car dealerships donated portions of vehicle sales, and hundreds of schools held "penny drives," collecting what turned out to be thousands of dollars in pennies. A fight promoter even promised to donate half of his earnings from a heavyweight boxing match at the city's grand auditorium. Within a week, the zoo had far exceeded its goal.

Due to the public outcry to keep the elephants in Portland, Morgan donated Thonglaw and Pet as well, but with the condition that they keep his herd together. As a result, the Oregon Zoo became the first in the nation to actually "own" all of its elephants.

After three years of making the four-hour commute between Seattle and Portland, Morgan was exhausted. He spoke with Louise, and they agreed it was time to move. They searched for somewhere with more privacy, away from prying eyes, yet spacious enough to accommodate their ever-expanding menagerie. Proximity to the Oregon Zoo was a priority, along with an airport, to make travel as convenient as possible for prospective buyers. Their realtor offered to show them an old, out-of-commission, 80-acre cattle dairy thirty miles north of Portland that sounded promising. Even so, they were reluctant to get their hopes up, as everything else they'd looked at was disappointing in one way or another.

After a short drive off the I-5 freeway, they followed a dirt road that wound through a dense forest toward the peak of a small mountain just outside Woodland, Washington. Near the top, they came across the largest barn either of them had ever seen. As part of the existing property, their agent gave them a tour of the vast structure.

Built to accommodate a massive herd of cattle, it seemed to go on forever. It featured hundreds of stalls, spacious equipment storage rooms, and a hay loft with the capacity to hold thousands of bales. It even had a colossal indoor arena ideal for training the largest animals. There was an abundance of space for Morgan's collection, with plenty of room to spare. Then their agent took them to the very top of the mountain.

"This is the view you could have if you built a house right here," he said, standing in the middle of a wide slab of granite.

The Berrys stepped beside him, speechless as they took in the impressive landscape. From where they stood, they could see the entire valley dotted by forests and small towns. Directly below them were two islands, Martin and Burke, submerged between the immense Columbia and Lewis Rivers before both bodies of water converged into one. And just beyond that was the very beach where the great Lewis and Clark expedition camped in 1805, in full view of the Chinook people whose presence shaped the river's history.

"It's brilliant," Morgan said. He envisioned the house, full of windows facing the breathtaking view.

"And there's a creek that runs right through the property," the real estate agent said, as if things couldn't get any more perfect. Louise squeezed Morgan's hand, and they signed the papers later that day.

News of their arrival and plan to turn the cattle dairy into a private wonderland made the front page of all the local newspapers, and the Berry family was welcomed with open arms. By the end of 1965, animal traders from across the United States congregated like children in a candy store. Morgan took their orders and sold anything they wanted: wolves, camels, birds, snakes, hippos and, if they could afford it—elephants. Soon, he became one of the world's largest dealers of caged, wild animals. Though his new home was originally named the "Elephant Farm" after its most lucrative, star attractions, the press began calling it *Elephant Mountain* and it stuck.

Morgan's business partner, Thonglaw, helped him acquire hundreds of elephants over the next several years and most stayed on the mountain before they were sold. When I learned that, my heart lurched. One man, all by himself. *Hundreds of baby elephants.* Yet he was far from the only importer doing so. Exotic animal traders soon shifted their focus primarily to elephants, due to their significant profit margins, as thousands were driven, flown, and floated away from every East Asian country that had them. All were destined for a lifetime in a zoo or trained for a circus.

In 1976, just fourteen years after Packy's birth, the once booming population of wild Asian Elephants collapsed. The scientific community finally caught on and they were officially listed as Appendix I on the CITES* list: the highest, most urgent listing a species gets before it disappears forever. To this day, no one wants to talk about the role the United States played in the downfall of Asian elephants—that is still being blamed on "the poachers." But the numbers are hard to ignore.

Raman Sukumar, one of the greatest Asian elephant scientists in the world today, estimated in his book *The Living Elephants* that around 100,000 were taken from the wild in just Myanmar (formerly Burma) and Thailand alone. Those that survived ended up in zoos and circuses across the United States and Europe. However, a high number died before their first birthday due to the trauma of being separated from their families or the brutal training tactics used against them.

As the inventory of Asian elephants dried up, men like Arthur Jones flew to Africa on multiple occasions, returning with jumbo jets filled with African elephant babies, to replenish the stock. I watched his last mission in 1984, when he flew to Zimbabwe and

---

* CITES (Convention on International Trade in Endangered Species) is an international treaty that helps protect species by regulating their trade across borders.

captured sixty-two on just that trip alone. It was filmed and aired later that same year for the television show, *20/20*, featuring Hugh Downs and Barbara Walters.

If men like Morgan and Arthur could take so many elephants in such a short amount of time, then it wasn't hard to imagine any species collapsing entirely. Poaching also took a toll, but combined with the removal of live elephants for captivity—there wasn't a population on the planet that could withstand losses like that. Especially not one which takes nearly two years to reproduce.

From the moment Morgan opened Elephant Mountain, orders piled up as he fed America's insatiable desire. It didn't matter if it was for a zoo, a circus, or just some random guy who wanted his own personal gorilla. The trafficking of all things wild, it seemed, had the same effect on people as heroin. But like a drug dealer supplying an addict—it was never enough.

I lay back on my couch and took a deep breath. The details of what I'd learned floated around my living room as I wondered just how awful this story could get. A storm raged outside as torrents of rain pounded against my windows. I closed my eyes and imagined myself climbing into a rubber raft in the shallows surrounded by calm water. Then I put on my life jacket, secured my belongings, and braced myself before grabbing an oar to push myself toward the unknown, toward the mouth of the river, and deeper into darkness. The likelihood of rough water ahead was clear—dangerous rapids. This journey had only just begun and already things felt choppy.

CHAPTER 13

I screamed for help, but no one could hear. The underwater light appeared right in front of my face as I sank. The water line was just out of my reach and for a single, terrifying moment, I wished I knew how to swim. Elephants were born with this gift, but I had yet to learn that skill. Now, I'd made a deadly mistake.

Above me, I saw the fuzzy images of the parents in the stands. I must have drifted into the middle of the pool, so I yelled, "Mom! Help!!" as tiny bubbles of screams swirled above my head. I had never been in the deep end before, though I had imagined the dark mystery of it many times. Seeing it up close, it was scarier than I expected.

A grate at the bottom pulled me downward. I tried to get away, but its pull was stronger than I was. A faint, muffled sound caught my attention, and I turned in search of it. My lungs burned as panic tightened its grip. The rumbling grew louder, as I desperately scanned my surroundings, until a strange shape emerged out of the gloom at the far end of the pool—a large, gray outline of something swimming toward me. At first I was scared, until a long, soothing rumble began to calm me down. Slowly, the blob came into focus, and I saw her.

Eleanor.

She reached out her trunk, and I reached back. Her amber-colored eye stared into mine, and I felt my body transition to peace and warmth. The two of us floated together, deep underwater, and while I drowned, she held onto me. Her rumble grew steadily louder. Though I knew the end was near, I was no longer afraid.

After a few moments, she released me and drifted farther away. Confused, I reached out for her wanting to follow, but couldn't. The sharp burning in my chest returned, progressively getting worse. Panic clawed its way up my throat as I called out to her. I heard one last rumble before it was replaced by a distant roar that grew louder by the second.

"Come on." The words rose like a soft echo from a deep canyon. "Breathe!"

I didn't care. I wanted only to stay with her. Eleanor slipped further away as I pleaded. For a moment she stopped and looked at me. *Please don't go,* I begged.

"Debbie, breathe!" The faint voice increased in intensity.

Eleanor disappeared into the darkness as I twisted in circles, searching for her. The pain was so intense, it felt as though I would break. But she was gone. The noise rose in a terrifying crescendo until it slammed into my chest like a freight train and panicked screams surrounded me from all directions.

"DEBBIE—"

I vaulted off the couch, gasping for breath. My eyes, wide with panic, frantically scanned the room as familiar items pulled me back to the present. I collapsed into the cushions, still soaking wet from that dreadful flashback.

The raging storm from the night before had turned into a soft, peaceful rain. The light sound of it against my windows was soothing. I wrapped myself tighter in a blanket until I calmed down. It was a classic night terror, only this one was taken from my vault of traumatic "real-life" events. My chest ached, just as it did each time I relived it.

My living room looked like it had been hit by a bomb. There were papers everywhere, covering every inch. The light on my printer was blinking, waiting to be fed. My light was blinking, too—I was starving. I glanced at the clock and realized I'd slept later than intended, never having made it to my bed. After my breathing stabilized, I dragged myself to the kitchen for some much-needed coffee. As it brewed, my thoughts replayed the details of that awful memory.

I hadn't wanted to go to my swim class that day. It was freezing, and I hated getting into a cold pool in the middle of winter, but my parents insisted that, at eight years old, it was time. My instructor wasn't feeling well, so instead of being in with the rest of us, he sat in the shallow end with his feet dangling over the side while we got to do whatever we pleased.

A young friend and I broke away while we engaged in a dangerous game. We let go of the wall in deeper water to see if we could roll onto our backs and float, something we hadn't fully mastered. Before we sank, we grabbed the pool's edge, or if we missed, we grabbed each other, pulling ourselves to safety. The risk was exhilarating. After a few minutes, she got bored and rejoined the group, while I stayed and played by myself.

When my fingers slipped, there was no one to pull me back. At first, I was determined to kick myself to the surface, but my knee hit the wall pushing me further into the depths. No matter how hard I struggled, hope faded.

My mother was in the stands, distracted by another parent. Moments earlier, she'd leaned over the metal railing to check on me and saw that I was with a friend, directly below her, but out of view. Meanwhile, my little sister, Carrie, sat quietly next to her, preoccupied with her favorite coloring book. A few minutes later, my mom noticed the girl I'd been playing with had rejoined the rest of the class, yet I was not with her. She stood and checked the spot where she had just seen me, but I wasn't there either. Her eyes anxiously scanned the pool until she caught sight of a blurry blob in the deep end. Without thinking, or saying a single word, she flew over the guard rail and dove in.

The loud splash startled everyone. They stood to see what had happened when a voice shouted, "There's a kid down there!"

Immediately, another parent jumped in while others positioned themselves at the edge to grab me as soon as my mother dragged my lifeless body to the surface. They yanked me out of the pool, pounding on my back and chest. Everyone was shouting in panic, but I heard nothing. I was with Eleanor and wanted only to stay with her. Paramedics raced to the scene, and I was beaten, pounded on, and screamed at until all the water held in my lungs came gushing out. It was sheer luck that I'd survived that day and only due to the quick thinking of my mother.

On the way home, I curled up on the front seat and watched her in disbelief. Each time she touched the pedals, her shoes made a squishing sound. She hadn't even taken them off before she jumped in, and I found that funny. If the sharp pain in my chest wasn't so unbearable, I would have laughed. I never imagined an adult jumping into a cold pool with all their clothes on and wondered if the drivers next to us noticed we were both soaking wet.

I looked at my six-year-old sister, Carrie, in the back seat—always quiet and calm. Her long dark hair cascaded down her shoulders, framing her perfect, baby-doll bangs. She was already fixated on me, peacefully sucking on a lollipop given to her by someone at the pool. Her large brown eyes blinked as she reached out her hand offering another one for me. I smiled as I took it, and she grinned, leaving me curious about what had happened to her favorite coloring book.

A few months later, after being cleared by my pediatrician, my parents threw me back into a pool. My fear was no excuse, they said. I never had to return to the place I nearly drowned, but resumed classes in a neighboring town until I, too, learned how to swim like an elephant.

My phone startled me—it was Leslie.

"Hey," I said, grateful for the interruption.

"Are we still on for dinner tonight?" she asked.

"Oh ... yea—"

She laughed. "You forgot, didn't you?"

"OK, yes, I did," I admitted with a smile. "But I will be there. Besides, it'll give me something to look forward to after I get through this mess."

"Good, I can't wait to hear all about it. We need a proper catch-up ... and I have some news to share with you." Leslie sounded strangely serious.

"What is it? Is it bad?"

"No, it's not a big deal. We can talk about it tonight. I just miss you, that's all."

After we hung up, my mood lightened. Although I knew the history of Elephant Mountain ended in tragedy, I wasn't quite prepared for the direction we were headed. I looked across my living room floor, still covered in paper. With somewhere to be, I felt a sudden urge to get to the end. I quickly finished my breakfast, made more coffee and dove, once again, into the deep end of the story.

ELEPHANT MOUNTAIN

∞

Within months of Packy's arrival, four more baby elephants were born at the Oregon Zoo, and Portland found itself in a perpetual whirlwind. It was the only zoo in the northern hemisphere with one newborn elephant, let alone five. Eventually, Thonglaw sired a total of fifteen—setting a record unmatched by any other bull at that time. His success earned him the status of a breeding icon, just as Morgan promised his namesake he would be.

A few years after the excitement surrounding Packy settled, Morgan came up with an even grander idea—something nobody had ever tried. In 1966, an untrained baby elephant was worth $2500 in the United States; a trained one, however, could easily fetch twice that amount. Morgan believed his newest venture would catapult his reputation to even greater heights. He planned to assemble a troupe of performing elephants called The Tuskers of Thailand, composed entirely of *bulls*. That distinction alone would set them apart, since no one dared put five males in the ring together at the same time.

Back then, all elephants were referred to as "bulls," though few were. The term applied to both sexes. But Morgan wanted to be the first to have a group of *actual* bull elephants sharing the stage. He knew how dangerous it was, and he anticipated the large crowds it would draw as a result. It would also secure his legacy as one of the world's greatest elephant trainers—that is, if he could pull it off.

Young males were no different from females when it came to training until they enter a state known as *musth* (pronounced must). During this time, their testosterone levels surge, leading to a noticeable increase in aggressive and sexual behavior.

When in musth, bulls often stop listening to commands, grow highly agitated, and can turn violent without warning. And when it happens to a full-grown, towering, ten-thousand-pound animal, few things are more dangerous. It's one of the reasons that being an elephant keeper is ranked among the world's deadliest jobs.

While, in some ways, musth is similar with rutting behavior seen in species like deer, it also has distinct differences. Rutting occurs only once a year during mating season, but unlike most animals, elephants have no official "mating season." Elephant bulls can mate whenever they chose, musth or not, which made the timing of its onset that much more confusing.

For some, the condition lasted only a few days, whereas for others, it continued for months. The only reliable indicator most elephant trainers used back then was a liquid (called temporin) secreted from the temporal glands on the sides of an elephant's face. Once they spotted the telltale sign of wet streaks running down their cheeks, they automatically presumed the elephant was in musth.

What no one realized then was that temporin, as the primary indicator, was unique *only* to the Asian elephant species. African elephants secrete temporin whenever they experience social excitement of any kind, such as family separations or reunions, and when they're under stress. And it happens in both sexes, not just the males as it does with Asians.[*] The way the phenomenon manifests differently between the Asian and African species highlights a distinct divergence on the phylogenetic tree, offering insight into where the two split.

No one knew how to make musth stop or what brought it on. Even worse, the absence of effective methods to manage an

---

[*] Female Asian elephants also produce temporin, but in such small quantities that it is rarely detected.

elephant experiencing it only added to the confusion. Of course, mahouts in East Asia were familiar with it, and Morgan consulted with them often. They implemented several well-documented strategies, some more successful than others. These included isolating the individual for weeks and sometimes months at a time, to keeping them chained in one place and starving them until it passed, since bull elephants in poor health seemed to exit the condition faster than healthy ones.

They also tried beating them senseless, yet if they survived this brutal treatment, which many did not, most went insane and had to be killed anyway. The inability to control musth led to experiments conducted on male elephants, so horrific they made my blood run cold.

Upon seeking advice from his contacts across Asia, Morgan was convinced that, although he might not be able to stop it from affecting his tiny Tuskers, he was confident he could manage them in spite of it.

Thonglaw had entered the state years earlier and isolating him at the zoo had worked, or at least kept him alive. What no one realized, however, was that Morgan had a trick up his sleeve. He had developed an entirely new approach, one that he believed was even more effective than all the previous strategies others had tried.

"What are you working on?" Doc asked. He found Morgan hunched over a workbench in the barn, fiddling with something.

Doc, the vet from the Oregon Zoo, and his wife were visiting Elephant Mountain as they often did. After dinner, while the women stayed inside, the men walked down the hill to check on the elephants.

"This is a new idea I've come up with," Morgan said excitedly. Laid out in front of him were pieces of an old, disused neon sign he'd taken apart.

"I take these," he continued, holding two of the unattached transformers, "and attach them to this." He wrapped the exposed cords around a long broom handle and taped them in place. "Then all I gotta do is plug it in and poke." He jabbed the stick into the air.

Doc was confused until Morgan offered to show him in person. Thonglaw had just been placed in isolation after one of his keepers noticed the telltale sign of temporin running down his face. He agreed to meet Morgan in the elephant barn the following evening, after the zoo closed, though he didn't know what to expect.

When he entered the building after work the next day, he was surprised to see it full of men he had never seen before—keepers, he assumed, from other departments. It was late, well past time for everyone to have gone home. Among the sea of unfamiliar faces, he spotted one he recognized: a regular elephant keeper who'd apparently agreed to stay behind, off the clock. The two nodded.

Morgan was deep in conversation with someone on the far side of the room when he noticed Doc enter. He looked up, waved, and said, "Glad you could make it," before returning to his discussion.

Then a different stranger began hosing Thonglaw down with water through the bars of his stall.

"Are we giving the elephants baths at night now too?" Doc asked, half-joking.

The man chuckled and gave a slight shrug. Once the elephant was soaked, Morgan leaned in and placed an apple into Thonglaw's mouth, rubbing his massive head. The gentle interaction between the two surprised the keeper who worked with him daily. He had grown accustomed to the elephant's highly unpredictable nature.

"Are we ready?" Morgan asked, as he reached for the handmade contraption.

Everyone nodded, while Doc watched in anticipation. A signal was given to plug in the wire at the end of the long stick. The live transformers hissed and spit, as Morgan gripped it tightly, then stretched between the bars and laid it against Thonglaw's wet body. Instead of pulling it back giving him a quick zap of electricity—like a cattle prod—he held it against the elephant's hip for several minutes, without letting up.

That's when Doc realized they used the water as a conductor, delivering the most powerful shock. Thonglaw screamed and tried to escape, but there was nowhere to go; his stall was barely wide enough for him to turn around. When it was over, the large elephant leaned against a wall, appearing listless and drained. Before everyone left, they agreed to meet in the barn a few days later to do it all over again.

If Doc disapproved of those late-night sessions, he kept it to himself. He raised no concerns about the practice and instead, voiced only admiration for Morgan's ability to do what no other man could in his memoir *Packy and Me*. He was convinced Morgan had developed a technique that genuinely worked.

Over time, as the electrocutions continued, Thonglaw experienced multiple injuries. Once, Morgan shocked him for too long, accidentally paralyzing his trunk for over a week. The keepers, who had not been allowed anywhere near him for their own safety, had no choice. The elephant, unable to care for himself, had to be fed and watered by hand.

During his recovery, he accepted the help offered. It was only after he regained the use of his trunk, that Thonglaw once again attempted to attack anyone who got close. Had electrocution effectively shifted him out of musth, there would have been no more temporin drizzling down the sides of his face, but there it remained.

Eventually, Thonglaw no longer fought the painful intrusions. He simply leaned his massive body against the farthest edge of the tiny stall and waited for the convulsions to begin. The weakness he exhibited each time it ended was misinterpreted by Morgan as surrender, who was convinced that electricity was the secret to yank bull elephants out of the mysterious condition.

There were several other people, however, who were not comfortable with Morgan's approach, reflected in the books and testimonials that emerged over the following decades. Still, no one spoke up at the time. None of the men in powerful positions, those with impressive degrees, or any of the veterinarians who'd witnessed it over the years ever questioned Morgan or his methods, and I wondered why.

Then I stumbled across an important and telling clue: Morgan's business card. Underneath his name was his title—Zoologist.

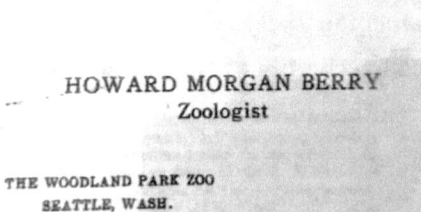

And there it was. Had Morgan been an actual zoologist, it would have meant he had spent years in school learning about the behavior and anatomy of animals. Yet he had no formal education outside of Juilliard. I could almost hear his voice in my ears.

"I capture animals for zoos, so I'm like ... a zoologist."

Someone who captures animals for zoos is not the same as a person with an *actual* degree grounded in scientific study. I understood the paradox, but wasn't sure he did. And without that education, without understanding what he was actually doing, Morgan inadvertently caused lasting, irreparable harm. That false, made-up credential, I assumed, was most likely the reason no one ever questioned him.

Back then, most elephant trainers believed that the intense behavioral changes experienced by bull elephants in musth were similar to psychiatric disorders in people. In the 1930s, electroconvulsive therapy was first introduced as a therapeutic approach for individuals suffering from mental illness.

When electric shocks were given to dogs, scientists noticed it had a "tranquilizing effect," and by the '40s and '50s, they were routinely shocking humans in psychiatric wards across the country. News of this innovative treatment was everywhere and likely where Morgan came up with the idea.

In 1967, two psychologists, Martin Seligman and Steven Maier, revealed an unexpected observation when it came to experimenting with electricity on mammals: a concept they termed "learned helplessness." They discovered that once an animal reaches a state of complete helplessness, especially due to something as painful as an electric shock combined with the inability to escape, their mental health declined stunningly fast. The "tranquilizing effect" was nothing more than the animal's retreat into severe depression, or worse—total psychosis. And it wasn't specific to just rats and dogs used in their experiments; it applied to every living mammal, including elephants and humans.

When Thonglaw first arrived from Seattle, he was a happy, gentle giant. Throughout the years, the keepers who cared for him enjoyed a good working relationship. It was mostly during bouts of musth that he became too dangerous to get anywhere near. Once it ended, he always reverted to the gentler elephant he once was.

Until he was electrocuted.

Shortly after Thonglaw was shocked for the first time, he tried to attack anyone who dared get close. And not long after his initial session, he descended into what people who worked with him described as total and complete madness.

No one was allowed to interact with Thonglaw again, except for tossing him food through the bars of his stall. Morgan was the only person who could handle him, work on his overgrown toenails, or let him out to be with the other elephants. Forced to come to the zoo daily, he arrived each morning to bathe the massive elephant and to shovel the large amounts of waste piled up inside his tiny stall. From that point forward, Thonglaw spent the rest of his short life dependent upon his sole caretaker for almost every aspect of his care.

Unfortunately, word got out about Morgan's method of electrocuting elephants, and its reach extended across the globe. Doc's glowing endorsement of the practice likely didn't hurt.

During the 1960s and '70s, most zoos and circuses decided it was simply easier to kill elephants once they entered musth and start over with younger ones not yet affected by the condition. Even if the killing of young bulls hadn't been so well-documented across history, it was easy enough to find. A quick look through databases of death records revealed just how few lived past the age of twenty. Besides, the killings were hardly a secret. A multitude of keepers, trainers, zoo directors, and veterinarians wrote books with details so gruesome they could make even the most resilient stomachs churn.

Despite the obstacles, Morgan remained undeterred, forging ahead with his performing troupe as he placed another order with his business partner in Bangkok. Soon, five baby Tuskers would begin their new life on the mountain. No one could have foreseen the profound impact those little elephants would have, or the extent to which they would drastically reshape the course of our lives—both Morgan's and mine.

CHAPTER 14

In 1968, Morgan welcomed his first young elephant into the performing troupe. Born at the Oregon Zoo to Pet and Thonglaw, Morgan collected Rajah shortly after his second birthday. But he wasn't alone for long. Within the year, four more calves arrived from Bangkok and The Tuskers of Thailand were complete. While the five settled in, it marked the beginning of a new chapter on the mountain.

At first, Morgan kept the elephants in the basement of his home, where it was easier to manage their nightly feedings and maintain warmth. During the day, he allowed them to roam upstairs in his living room, surrounded by windows offering stunning views. He enjoyed taking the miniature group on long walks, exploring the forests on his property. As the five grew, Morgan took note of their unique and distinct personalities.

Rajah was well-behaved and, since he'd lived on Elephant Mountain longer than the rest, he dominated the others by throwing his weight around. Morgan didn't like the name he was given at the zoo and renamed him Teak (after the wood his relatives still logged in the Asian forests). He was the fattest of the five, noticeably smart, and quick to take direction. He reminded Morgan of Thonglaw in his eagerness to please.

Thai was shy at first to anyone new and unfamiliar. But once he felt comfortable, he transformed into an adorable, mischievous, and playful little elephant. He and Teak sparred whenever they had the chance. However, once Thai got into the performance ring he became overwhelmed easily. Sometimes, when one of the keepers got impatient or yelled too loudly, he was paralyzed with fear, unable to move until the situation calmed down. Occasionally, Thai would panic and run away, but Morgan always coaxed him back.

Tunga (or, as some called Tonga) was the tallest in the group. He was two years older than the rest, at age five, quite gentle and did whatever he could to please, just like Teak. He was kind and patient, earning the nickname "Tidy Tunga" for his unique bathroom habits—he preferred to poop in the same spot, unlike the others who were less particular.

Buddha was the smallest of the group. He had a mild temperament and stood out as the fastest learner among them. By the age of three, he'd already conquered the hardest trick of all: a one-foot-stand balancing on a ball. And he had done so in the span of only a few short weeks, a feat which took the others months to master. He was easy to identify by a single, small tusk. The other eventually grew, but always remained noticeably shorter.

Ranchipur was named after *The Rains of Ranchipur*, a film starring Lana Turner and Richard Burton. Since his name was already a familiar one, thanks to its recent success in the cinema, Morgan knew audiences would adore him. Ranchi, as he was called, had an adventurous streak. He learned how to slip out of his chains early on and escape into the forests nearby. When a keeper came looking, he followed without incident, as if playing a thrilling game of hide-and-seek.

Morgan soon realized he needed seasoned professionals who knew how to effectively train elephants to perform the tricks he envisioned. For this, he recruited the best he could find: Smokey Jones and Eloise Berchtold.

Robert 'Smokey' Jones was only fourteen when he ran away from home. He jumped onto an empty car on the nearest freight train, looking for a one-way escape—lucky for him, the train's last stop was right next to a lot rented by a traveling circus. Cold, tired, and hungry, they took him in and gave him a job on the crew. After days spent riding the rails, his body was coated in thick, black soot, earning him his famous nickname.

Smokey started out caring for horses and mules in several circuses, but his passion and skill eventually led him to elephants. Over time, he steadily rose through the ranks, gaining more responsibility and experience with each new role. Until one day, he was offered an opportunity that few in his field could possibly dream of. At just twenty-five, he was put in charge of all fifty elephants at the largest circus in the world: *The Greatest Show on Earth*—Ringling Bros., becoming the youngest man to ever hold such a prestigious position.

Several years later, when Ringling closed most of its traveling shows due to falling ticket sales, Smokey was out of a job. When he and his wife Beverly, also an elephant trainer, heard that Morgan was looking for experienced handlers, they jumped at the chance and headed up the mountain.

Eloise Berchtold was, by all accounts, one of the most famous female circus trainers in the world, let alone the United States. Her story made nearly as many headlines as Morgan's. Not only did she have the beauty of a pin-up girl, but she was among the few to have actually trained a male African elephant. Although it was unheard of at the time, Eloise had successfully performed with him for years. Circuses typically avoided African elephants due to their larger size and more aggressive nature, preferring their calmer, more amiable cousins. As a result, far fewer were imported, making them a rare sight in the industry.

Morgan was thrilled when Eloise accepted his offer. He wasn't aware that she had arrived with a heart deeply broken, having just lost the love of her life: an African elephant named Koa. She would do anything to understand what happened, how the sad end of their relationship could have been avoided, and how to prevent such a thing from ever happening again. Morgan didn't realize this at the time. Like everyone, he was drawn to Eloise's beauty and talent, blind to the grief she carried.

It was the beginning of a spectacular union and a most tragic love story. Eloise reminded me of Pandora in Greek mythology. All she wanted was the answer to one simple question: how to keep bull elephants alive in spite of musth. There had to be a better way than just killing them. More than anything, she longed to understand how Morgan did it. But like the Greek tragedy, once she opened the lid of that box, a flood of calamity and misfortune was unleashed, never to be contained again.

Eloise Carolynn Berchtold was born on December 30, 1935. As the youngest of three, she had a natural passion for animals from the start. By the age of eleven, her parents, Clifford and Esther, enrolled her in the Cincinnati Zoo's volunteer program, just miles from her childhood home.

One day a local hunter donated a bear cub he had rescued after killing its mother. After keeping it for several days, zoo officials determined it was too wild and aggressive to handle. Instead of putting it down, Eloise begged them to let her have it, so they did.

She added the cub to her growing assortment, and "Teddy" quickly surpassed all expectations. Within a year, he topped the scales at over two hundred pounds. Eloise trained him to perform a wide variety of circus tricks, then brought other animals into their act. Soon, they hit the road, performing all across the country, and at fifteen her fate was sealed.

By the time she turned twenty, Eloise had dyed her red hair blonde and was dazzling audiences with her impressive routines. In 1955, she caught the eye of John Cuneo, Jr., one of the world's most eligible bachelors. As heir to his father's Chicago printing empire, his wealth rivaled that of only William Randolph Hearst, listed among the wealthiest people in the country.

However, John had no interest in printing. Like many young men of his generation, he had been bitten by the circus bug. He grew up on his family's grand estate in Vernon Hills, Illinois, previously owned and built by Edward M. Smith, Thomas Edison's personal secretary. After Edward lost the home and went bankrupt during the Great Depression, John Sr. bought it on the cheap. He refurbished the 31,000-square-foot Italian Renaissance mansion, added servant's quarters, and raised a most elegant breed of horse—the Hackney. Then he established a massive dairy, later known as the Hawthorn Mellody Farm. Visitors were charged admission for anyone who wanted to see what it was like to milk a cow.

But it was John Jr.'s petting zoo that turned the tides. Animals of a different sort attracted far more spectators than a measly cow. Soon, the Cuneos added a real-life ghost town—a remnant of the old Wild West—complete with a country store, several odd museums, and a steam train. They transformed the thriving dairy into an even more popular tourist attraction. Building on his petting zoo's success, John launched the Hawthorn Corporation, leasing lions, white tigers, bears, and elephants to circuses and fairs nationwide.

It was his bear act that originally brought Eloise to Vernon Hills. John needed a trainer for a new traveling circus he planned to launch, and she had everything he was looking for. At twenty-five, he had an eye for the ladies and a trust fund large enough to run a small country.

Eloise was stunned as her car wound down the road toward their palace. The pink "Italian Villa of the Prairie" looked more like a castle than a home. In the foyer, she stood for several minutes staring up at a towering medieval knight standing guard at the bottom of a massive staircase.

"He's not real, you know," John chuckled, tapping the knight's shoulder and jolting her from her trance.

Then he gave her a tour of all thirty-two rooms. She walked slowly, taking it all in. There was art and opulence everywhere she looked. Eloise was transfixed by the Italian frescos painted on the ceilings. Marble pillars lined extravagant hallways filled with fine art and paintings by some of the world's most famous artists, living and dead (though mostly dead).

There were gardens of flowers, gardens of sculptures, and meticulously manicured lawns that seemed to never end. John led her by pools, ponds, and a ballroom adorned with ornate decorations. The size and scale was so opulent that she could almost imagine the Queen twirling gracefully in the center, her billowing gown shimmering with fine jewels.

Eloise began performing with John's bear act but soon graduated to big cats when he bought her a baby leopard as a gift. The two were married shortly after they met on February 28, 1956, in a quiet ceremony at the St. Louis Church in Chicago with just their families in attendance.

After mastering all of John's other animal routines, Eloise aimed for an even grander prize: elephants. Her new husband's recent acquisition, a baby African elephant named Koa, captured her attention from the moment she laid eyes on him. She had never heard of any African elephants in captivity or trained in a circus and wanted to be the first person in the United States to claim that honor.

Every day, Eloise worked with two-year-old Koa at John's private zoo. Before long, they were making appearances at local fairs and venues. Then she began incorporating him into her existing animal acts, those involving big cats and bears. Eloise knew the variety of animals appearing together would drive the crowds wild, and she was not wrong.

Although it was publicized that Eloise was the first person to train an African elephant for a circus, she wasn't. It had been done before, just not by someone who had an uncanny resemblance to Marilyn Monroe. Before her marriage to John ended, less than a year later, she left with Koa and never looked back.

Years later, John found himself at the center of controversy. He became the first person in U.S. history to have an elephant forcefully removed from his care by the government due to severe abuse. Despite this, he paid their fines and resumed his business without delay, showing no intention of shutting down.

In 1994, scandal struck again involving another African elephant he owned, an eighteen-year-old female named Tyke. In the middle of a performance during a circus, she killed her handler, before running into the streets of Honolulu, Hawaii. Cornered and with no escape, she was shot eighty-seven times in front of horrified spectators and rolling cameras.

Then, in 1997, came the most famous incident of all when Hawthorn's trainers attempted to ship an elephant named Nicholas to Puerto Rico for a circus performance fully aware that he had tuberculosis. Not only was it an egregious violation of the Animal Welfare Act, but a serious public health risk.

Officials intervened and further investigation revealed that fourteen out of the eighteen elephants on his farm also carried the deadly disease. And worse, it was the first-known strain of tuberculosis that could spread from elephants to humans. Then they discovered that two elephants had recently died of the disease, yet the authorities were never notified. The Centers for Disease Control and the USDA classified Hawthorn as "high risk." John was fined again, and his exhibitor's license was revoked.

This time, not even the best legal defense could save him. John's business venture was eventually forced to close, and Hawthorn Corporation would go down as one of the worst private zoos in history.

As Eloise and Koa crisscrossed the country, few performances gained more notoriety and press. Her spectacular routines made her as famous as any movie star. She was at the peak of her career until the day Koa almost killed her. Perhaps he wasn't feeling well, or she missed the cues, but during a performance Eloise stumbled and fell at his feet. The elephant dropped to his knees and drove his tusks deep into the ground, trapping her between them. As he raised his head, preparing to strike a second time, another trainer intervened and yanked her beneath a protective wall.

A few weeks later, during a normal training session, Koa knocked Eloise down with such force that, had no one dragged her to safety again, he most certainly would have killed her. In that moment, noticing temporin running down Koa's face, she feared the worst and determined he was in musth. Eloise was mistaken, though she couldn't have known it at the time.

The true nature of musth wouldn't be thoroughly explored until years later, during Dr. Joyce Poole's landmark ten-year study on wild African bulls in Amboseli National Park, Kenya. Her work, published in 1987, revealed that male elephants weren't entering full-blown musth until an average age of twenty-nine, with the earliest case recorded at twenty-four. However, captive African males were observed exhibiting musth symptoms as early as eleven, prompting speculation that the harsh conditions of captivity severely influenced the phenomenon.

Both male and female African elephants produce temporin whenever they feel excitement about anything. If a helicopter chases a herd, the stress triggers a heightened emotional state, causing every elephant to secrete temporin. And when one herd is reunited with another close-knit group after any period, pure excitement stimulates it once more.

Though temporin is also observed in African bulls during musth, it serves as only one of many factors when combined with several unique behaviors to diagnose the condition—unlike Asian males, where just the sight of it serves as the primary indicator. In African bulls, simply seeing the appearance of temporin is no more a sign of musth than a single cloud is a forecast for a storm.

Koa, like so many captive African elephants before him, was misdiagnosed as being in musth when the temporin running down his face was due to nothing more than a biological response to stress or excitement. At just six years old, he wouldn't have entered the condition for some time. Unfortunately for him, he didn't live long enough to find out.

After isolating Koa for over a year, Eloise turned him over to the Toledo Zoo. Following another extended period in isolation, he was diagnosed as being in a state of "chronic musth" as the wet streaks of temporin never stopped. He was transferred again to Eloise's alma mater, the Cincinnati Zoo, as they continued to wait for the condition to pass. But it never did. Eventually he was shot, like so many before him, after being labeled as a "rogue" just days after of his eleventh birthday.

The pain of that loss weighed heavily on Eloise as she stepped out of her vehicle and walked toward the massive barn on Elephant Mountain. When she arrived, Morgan was already there, waiting to greet her. From the moment she set down her bags, Eloise felt a spark of intrigue. He welcomed her warmly, dressed in a crew neck sweater and nice slacks—far more polished than she'd expected. She had imagined a more rugged type, not someone who could easily be mistaken for a college professor. Morgan's hair was cut short, his face clean-shaven except for a crisp goatee, and he wore sleek, black brow-line glasses. Even his scent was unexpectedly pleasant.

By then, Morgan had been married and divorced twice, leaving him single again—though not for long. Soon after Eloise settled in, the two became partners, both in business and romantically. Then they got straight to work training The Tuskers of Thailand.

Several months later, they were interrupted by a phone call. Morgan left Smokey and Eloise with the Tuskers while he ran to answer it.

"You'll never guess what that was about," he said excitedly when he returned. They stopped and stared at him, their faces a mixture of confusion and curiosity.

"A guy named Arthur Jones is looking to sell three of his elephants." Morgan continued, noticing their puzzled looks. "African elephants!"

Eloise's calm, cool demeanor changed instantly. She squealed and jumped into his arms, surprising Smokey and everyone else. They had never seen her act so giddy or out of character—she was usually in full control of her emotions.

"All right, all right now," Morgan laughed, unwrapping her from around his neck. "We still have a lot of work to do if we're going to have eight elephants roaming around this place."

One week later, two African females, Durga and Owalla, along with a young male named Tshombe, joined their miniature herd. Morgan presented them as a gift to Eloise. He knew she had always harbored a profound desire to also be the first person to train a group of performing African elephants, and this was her opportunity.

While they diligently worked with the five Asian elephants on the mountain, they displayed the three newest babies at the Oregon Zoo to generate much-needed revenue. Once the Tuskers were performance-ready, they brought the young trio back to start training for their own act.

In the spring of 1969, Morgan and Eloise set out for their first series of performances. They captivated circus audiences far and wide, showcasing the two rarest groups of performing elephants anywhere in the world: The Tuskers of Thailand and The African Trio.

They were a massive hit, just as Morgan dreamed. With Eloise by his side in the ring, their status soared to superstardom, and profits surged to levels neither had experienced before. But trouble was coming. This time, it wouldn't merely threaten their success—it was about to transform their greatest triumph into their darkest nightmare, bringing their glamorous lives to a sudden and catastrophic end.

CHAPTER 15

*E*loise was killed by one of the Tuskers in the middle of a circus performance in Canada. There were 615 spectators in the audience—*eyewitnesses*—along with 109 circus personnel and 100 or so additional crew members hired by the individual acts. Over eight hundred people saw the tragic accident firsthand, yet after an exhaustive search, I was unable to find a single account from anyone who was actually there. Instead, there were numerous conflicting versions about what happened on that day, with some articles appearing to describe an entirely different event. My first significant challenge was piecing together the circumstances leading to her death—a tangled web that left me both curious and confused.

Some newspapers reported the elephant had accidentally stepped on Eloise, crushing her. Others alleged that someone in the audience startled it, causing the Tusker to bump into Eloise so hard that it killed her. Additional articles claimed that when the elephant realized Eloise was injured, it ran to her side, and stood guard over her body as a way to protect her.

But given my knowledge about elephants, particularly those in musth, I knew nothing could be further from the truth. None of it made any sense.

Despite the sheer number of eyewitnesses, it was nearly impossible to determine which versions were accurate. Each article, filled with detail, varied so widely from one to the next that it was difficult to follow. This was the tragic death of an iconic person who, in my opinion, deserved better. But something about it also seemed intentional.

The story peddled to the American public felt more like a watered-down version of *Dumbo*, where elephants were portrayed as gentle giants longing for our friendship. It appeared deliberately obscured to fit someone else's narrative. The question was: why and by whom?

One of the more frustrating aspects of this story was separating facts from fiction. But to learn the truth was to learn about underlying motives, marketing spin, and the old familiar saying: "The show must *always* go on."

I began by organizing each article into a large spreadsheet, sorting them by how close they were to an eyewitness account. Yet, in my sizable stack of commentaries from across the U.S., there wasn't a single first-hand perspective from anyone present during the tragedy. It seemed unlikely that no one had come forward to share their story after witnessing such a tragic event.

There were a few second-hand testimonies, and I organized these into the second column of my spreadsheet, while third- and fourth-hand statements were placed in the third and fourth columns. I noticed that the last columns contained the most articles, far removed from anyone present during Eloise's death, and filled with of all kinds of conflicting information.

Once I had each article organized, I made lists of repeating items. Strange anomalies emerged from those last columns including embellishments that seemed out of place. I disregarded them entirely, as these slight but noticeable elements were likely nothing more than additions by a newspaperman, trying to make a name for himself. I was looking for the Holy Grail: an eyewitness account from someone who was actually there that day.

I eventually found two, buried deep within a circus database, raising even more questions as to why they were so difficult to find. Next, I contacted several libraries across Quebec, where Eloise was killed, and that's when I stumbled upon an absolute treasure trove. There were multiple databases containing dozens of descriptions from people who were there, rich with striking detail from French newspapers, books, reports, and magazines. It was clear that those who were present during the horrific event had a story to share, and they did—just as I'd suspected. And surprisingly, most of their versions matched up, in stark contrast to the sheer number of articles from American newspapers with odd and varying details.

The revelations from the Canadian databases were shocking and left me feeling angry and sad. I reflected on the complexity of my admiration for Eloise—how a love for elephants can coexist with respect for someone who caused them pain. But what I learned shed light on just how remarkable she was, her work ethic, and the loneliness of standing on a pedestal where no other woman before her had stood.

∞

When Eloise created her final act, Peace in the Jungle, she not only included her repertoire of lions, tigers, bears, and jaguars, but she also added seven stark-white German Shepherds. She combined the predator and the prey—sixteen animals performing together in the same ring. It was yet another historic milestone, never attempted by anyone before. There was little doubt her latest ensemble would leave audiences spellbound.

By that time, Morgan and Eloise had shared the stage for over a decade with The Tuskers of Thailand and The African Trio. The elephants, now impressively sized teenagers, helped make them one of the most famous circus couples in history.

The large training ring in the main barn on Elephant Mountain was the ideal place to prepare Peace in the Jungle for its upcoming debut. The show was scheduled for a two-week run in Quebec, Canada. Eloise was booked to perform her solo act, followed by a joint performance with Morgan and The Tuskers at the Gatini Circus. The tour, which traveled through the eastern townships, was set for the spring of 1978, and due to their busy schedule, Eloise had just a few months to train all the animals during the winter break. She dedicated every waking minute to perfecting her newest act.

Morgan continued his business of buying and selling exotic wildlife, including elephants, while Eloise rehearsed in the indoor arena each morning before dawn. In the afternoons, Morgan liked to watch her work from his office on the second floor, which featured a spacious viewing gallery lined with a large bank of windows overlooking the ring. Full of circus memorabilia, it also served as a place to entertain their most honored guests, who sat at tables sprinkled across the vast room while they took in the remarkable scene below.

Eloise employed several young men, trained to keep the bears occupied by dipping their spoons in honey until it was their turn to enter the ring. If they gave them too much, the bears missed their mark—too little, and they wanted more. But some were more polite than others. Sometimes not even the crack of Eloise's whip could distract a hungry bear, which is why being the "honey guy" was almost as dangerous as working with the elephants.

The Gatini Circus ranked as the fourth-largest touring circus in the world, yet Eloise had her sights set on number one: Ringling Bros.—the biggest of them all. Her two-week engagement was her opportunity to gain the attention of the leading players in the industry, who would also be there looking for new entertainers to cast in their upcoming shows.

Gee Gee Engesser, who scouted acts to fill the Gatini tents, had once worked as an animal trainer herself. She was instantly captivated the moment she first saw a teenage Eloise performing her daring bear routines and had followed her career closely. When she heard about Peace in the Jungle, she knew it was the perfect choice. Gee Gee's intention was not only to include Eloise's newest act in the circus, but to give her the highest honor any performer could receive: the privilege of being the "show opener."

"I can't go with you this time," Morgan said, as he approached Eloise in the arena. She had just finished loading the tigers into their cages, ensuring each door was latched and secure.

"What do you mean?" She turned to face him.

"It's Buddha. He's gotten too unpredictable. It just isn't safe to perform with him in the ring anymore."

Eloise knew it was true; even she hated working with him. Just days earlier, Buddha had lunged at another recent hire. Fortunately, the young man had made a narrow escape, but quit on the spot, like so many others who had come too close to the dangerous elephant. Eloise remembered the first time she had encountered the wrath of Buddha—an experience that left a lasting impression.

∞

Moments after The Tuskers of Thailand finished their act at the Miller-Johnson Circus in Flagstaff, Arizona, a disturbance occurred.

As the elephants exited the performance ring, Morgan couldn't hear the commotion above the deafening crowd. He was always the last to leave the arena, but caught sight of a panic-stricken circus hand frantically waving at him through the exit curtain. Morgan shoved past Ranchi and ran into the smaller tent, just as Buddha got down on his knees and aimed his one tusk at the unconscious torso of someone lying beneath him.

"Buddha! NO!" Morgan shouted, whacking him with his bullhook.

The elephant retreated, but to Morgan's horror, he realized it was the limp body of Eloise tucked underneath. He quickly backed Buddha away, then secured him in chains. When Morgan rushed to Eloise's side, members of the staff had already dragged her to safety and placed her on a cot to assess the full extent of her injuries. Luckily, she regained consciousness a short time later, revealing nothing more than a bump on the head.

"What happened?" Eloise asked, struggling to sit up.

"It was Buddha," Jim McGowan, also known as The Elephant Man, said. He was a seasoned animal wrangler at the Miller-Johnson Circus and renowned for his skill in handling the toughest elephants. "He came at you from behind and hit you so hard you flew about twenty feet. You're lucky. He was just about to finish you off by the time we got there."

Once Morgan was assured Eloise would be fine, he returned to his Tuskers and quickly realized one was missing. The crew members he'd instructed to collect the rest of his herd had not been able to gather Thai, who stood terrified at the back of a small tent. The angrier the strange men became, the more the shy elephant retreated, paralyzed by fear. As soon as Morgan appeared, Thai broke out of his trance, eager to obey—leaving everyone astonished.

In 1969, following news of the Flagstaff incident, the Miller-Johnson Circus changed its name to Circus Vargas, partly to avoid the negative publicity. However, it wasn't long before similar stories emerged from other performance rings and venues, revealing disturbing reports of keepers, wranglers, and trainers who had been lunged at, grabbed, or hit by Buddha. Over the years, no one could approach him without the risk of being attacked, except for Morgan.

He was unsure what had caused Buddha's drastic change in behavior and attributed the aggression to the elephant's unique temperament. If he didn't want to do something, he lashed out. It was perplexing given that none of the other elephants in his care behaved that way. Morgan couldn't explain Buddha's shift, especially since he hadn't yet shown the telltale sign of musth.

∞

Eloise was finally forced to admit that no one other than Morgan could control him in the ring, despite their long history of performing together as a team. The elephants had grown so large that having a volatile bull in the arena was a risk they could no longer take. With that, the five Tuskers were reduced to four.

"Now that we've lost another man we have to hire somebody else, and you know how hard that is." Morgan said, as he fiddled with a nail on the wall.

Eloise sorted through a pile of props at her feet, organizing them for the next training session. She already knew where the conversation was going.

"I'm sorry, Eloise, but I have to stay. With Buddha. No one can control him like I can."

"Fine Morgan. I'll go by myself."

"We'll get you some help ... for the Tuskers and for your act ... it's a good one, Eloise." But when he turned to face her, she was gone, having disappeared down the long, dark hallway leading to the room that held the big cats.

On the morning of her scheduled departure to Canada, Morgan and a small crew stacked twenty-two cages filled with Eloise's Peace in the Jungle act onto a heated semi-truck attached to a forty-eight-foot trailer. Then Morgan loaded the four Tuskers into a separate truck filled with food and supplies. A young couple had also joined as Eloise's assistants, although neither had much experience working with wild animals. Morgan was confident that she would get more help once they arrived at their first destination.

Without saying a word, Eloise waved out the window with a muddy, gloved hand as she pulled away from the barn's entrance, driving the longest of the two trucks by herself. Morgan couldn't make out her face through the dense fog that clung to the forest-covered mountain, and she disappeared like a ghost. He patted the truck holding his remaining elephants and waved to their driver, Ken Stevens, a seasoned long-haul trucker, who slipped into the haze and vanished behind Eloise.

The two made few stops as they drove across the United States from Washington to Maine, likely due to the unpredictable spring weather. When they entered Canada and arrived in the town of Coaticook, Quebec, it was Sunday evening, April 30, 1978—the night before their first show. An unexpected storm had already dumped several inches of snow, prompting a chaotic rush to unload the animals into one of the heated circus tents.

Eloise barked instructions to the men who came to assist, but Ken, who had promised to help with the elephants upon their arrival, was nowhere to be found. The young couple struggled to be useful, leaving the heavy lifting to Eloise and the circus men, those who could handle the hard labor required to work around dangerous animals.

When Eloise asked where Ken was, a member of the crew told her he said, "I don't know a damn thing about elephants—I'm only getting paid to move them from one place to the next. If anyone asks I'll be at my hotel." And then he left.

Later, Ken revealed that at a stop along the way, an elephant had lunged at him, while another tried to grab him with its trunk. Convinced they were too dangerous, he stayed noticeably absent until it was time to transport them to their next circus destination.

Manuel Ruffin, Jr. appeared from behind an open flap in the heated tent. He was one of the few Black men ever hired to work in the industry, and the first to earn the prestigious title of head tentmaster at any circus.

"Where's your crew, Eloise?" Junior asked. The two had been friends for years.

"I am the crew, Junior," she said, without missing a beat. "Don't worry, I've trained these animals, including the elephants, since they were small enough to curl into your lap."

It was unusual for acts as large as hers to travel unaccompanied by a team of staff to assist with setup and breakdown. The young couple took on menial tasks, but were not equipped to handle the tougher work. From Junior's perspective, Eloise seemed to have it all under control, regardless of whether she had help. Instead of staying in a nearby hotel with the other circus performers and crew, she slept in the semi's camper. Junior assumed she wanted to stay close to her animals, which made him respect her even more.

After settling in, Eloise joined her friends Giovanni Iuliani, the circus's artistic director, and Pierre Jean, the ringmaster, in

Giovanni's trailer. The three had worked together for years on various circuses and had a tradition of sharing hot chocolate the night before their first performance. As Eloise sipped her drink, gently swirling the contents of her mug, she took a deep breath before revealing a secret that left both men stunned: she was broke.

Giovanni looked at Pierre Jean, then asked, "How much?"

"Over $100,000 dollars," she said, her voice barely a whisper.

Eloise explained she had even turned down a $10,000 winter performance, because it would have disrupted her preparations for Peace in the Jungle, on which she'd bet everything. Every dime she earned from her performance salary was essential, including the amount she saved by not renting a room at a local hotel.

The next evening, when Eloise took the stage as the show-opener, it appeared her gamble had paid off. Just as Gee Gee had predicted, Peace in the Jungle brought down the house. As Junior watched from behind the curtain, he found it difficult to believe she was the same woman he'd seen wearing blue coveralls with her blonde hair wrapped in a bright red handkerchief one day earlier. She had transformed herself into a heavily made-up, glittering superstar who commanded the ring.

After her opening act, Eloise hurried backstage to change her outfit. While Junior's wranglers loaded her animals into their cages, she prepared The Tuskers of Thailand for their Canadian debut. But instead of bringing all four elephants into the ring, she brought only three. Eloise had heard Tunga viciously kicking the inside of his trailer shortly after their arrival the night before. Once he was unloaded, she saw the dreaded temporin running down his face—he was in musth. Eloise immediately walked Tunga back into the transport truck, chained his legs to the floor, and didn't let him out again.

Instead, she introduced the crowd to Teak, Thai, and Ranchipur, and all three elephants performed to perfection, never missing a single cue. The audience was awestruck as they watched Eloise seamlessly execute two spellbinding acts. First, in her black bodysuit as she directed five species of dangerous animals through a flawless routine inside a dome-shaped cage. Then, in a glittering white leotard for The Tuskers of Thailand, commanding the only group of performing bull elephants anywhere in the world. It was more than Gee Gee or the circus owners could have hoped for.

At dawn the following morning, with the trucks loaded and tents broken down, they moved to their second destination, a few miles away in Magog. As Eloise removed three of the Tuskers from their trailer and Ken disappeared back to his hotel, one of the men Junior assigned to help her gasped.

"Do you see that, Eloise?" he pointed to the long stream of temporin running down Ranchi's face.

"Yes, I see it," she said, tossing him a stake to secure a chain around the elephant's leg.

The circus hand let it drop, the metal clanging against the ground as he slowly backed away until he reached the entrance of the tent and stopped.

"Are you just going to stand there?" Eloise shouted, but it was clear he was.

She stomped over, picked up the stake off the dirt floor and drove it in with a mallet, convinced that if anything needed to get done, she would have to do it herself. Once she got the elephants out of the trailer, except for Tunga, more men gathered. No one could believe their eyes. Streaks of temporin ran down the sides of each elephant's head. All the Tuskers were in musth at the same time.

Crawling between their massive legs as she staked them to the ground, Eloise noticed a group of circus hands staring in stunned silence. One elephant in musth was enough to make news, but four? That was unheard of. Yet Eloise appeared unfazed, reminding everyone that no one knew her animals better than she did.

During the matinee performance, she once again entered the ring with three elephants. Backstage, circus personnel held their breath as they gathered, peering through every crack in the tent. Word quickly spread that the most dangerous show on earth was about to begin.

In the middle of her act, Ranchipur refused to acknowledge Eloise's commands. She tried twice before giving up and turning her attention to Teak and Thai. Then Thai stopped listening to her, too. Although the audience was blissfully unaware of what was happening, Junior watched nervously from the sidelines. But Teak performed each trick as expected, so Eloise focused on him, ignoring the other two.

The crowd cheered, and she adapted her act on the spot, improvising in response to their energy. Without warning, Teak suddenly turned and rammed his massive head into Thai's belly, nearly knocking him over. Thai quickly regained his balance, screamed in fury, and charged at Teak. The thunderous clash of their locked tusks reverberated throughout the large room while they engaged in a fierce sparring match.

The audience erupted, convinced it was all part of the act, while Junior shouted at his men to get into the arena and help. Eloise bravely jumped between the elephant duel, separating them, while a wrangler led Ranchipur out the back unnoticed. Having gained control of Teak and Thai, Eloise swiftly took a bow, and walked out the direction she came, with her elephants following like two dogs on a leash. No one had any idea how close to danger they all were.

After it was over, she called Morgan and explained what had happened.

"This is too dangerous," he said. "You can't work with three elephants in musth, Eloise, it's too much."

"Just tell me what I can do, Morgan. I'm not giving up after coming all this way."

The two devised a new plan. The next day, when the circus moved to the parking lot of the Rock Forest Shopping Plaza* in a suburb of Sherbrooke, Eloise was confident it would succeed.

Instead of using three Tuskers in the ring, they decided it would be best to work with only one: Teak. He was quick, smart, and without the others provoking him, Morgan and Eloise believed he would be the easiest to manage on his own. And they were right. Teak performed in two shows each day, executing every trick just as he had been trained. He stood on a ball, did a one-foot stand on a metal tub, and performed his baton-twirling routine flawlessly.

Due to the large crowds and increased ticket sales from both Sherbrooke, the capital of the Eastern Townships, and the town of Rock Forest, the circus decided to extend their stay.

Late Wednesday evening, two nights before Eloise's last show, Junior was awakened by a noise coming from the main tent. When he went outside to investigate, he found her, all alone, meticulously operating a pulley system to rearrange the cages, each holding an animal weighing 200 pounds or more.

She washed the inside of each animal's crate, while carefully transferring her collection of big cats and bears, to ensure their

---

* The Rock Forest Shopping Plaza was formerly known as the Woolco Shopping Center.

safety and comfort. The temperature was below freezing, and Junior wondered if she ever slept at all.

Although Eloise managed most of the hard work by herself, he understood the back-breaking effort it required. He recognized how much more difficult it was for one person. Junior could scarcely imagine another man daring to take on such a daunting physical feat by himself, cementing her reputation as a true legend in his eyes.

On Thursday, Eloise's fourth day with Gatini, she performed with Teak again during both the matinee and evening shows, and everything proceeded smoothly. But after the last performance, she was confronted by the circus manager.

Leo Duplessis, a towering figure and retired boxer, had recently been promoted as the general manager. It was a quite a leap from his previous position managing carnies at local fairs to becoming the manager of the fourth-largest circus in the world. Although, most likely, it was due to his partial buy-in, making him a part-owner, that landed him the role. Eager to prove himself, he got into a heated shouting match with Eloise, overhead by many.

"My audience is paying to see the Tuskers, Eloise—plural—not the lone Tusker of Thailand," he yelled, waving a flyer in her face.

"I understand that, but—"

"This is false advertising! Either you put them all back in the ring or take your show with your one elephant somewhere else. This is a violation of your contract and not what we agreed to." Leo threw the paper on the ground and stormed off.

When Eloise contacted Morgan again, he was having dinner with a close friend, Charlie Wilson, who overheard the couple's last conversation. She told Morgan what had happened.

"You need to leave," Morgan urged. "If I was there with you,

I could handle at least one of the elephants. But you … all alone? It's just too much."

"They could withhold payment, Morgan. He said I'm violating my contract. I've worked too hard to risk coming this far for them not to pay me." Her voice shook with anger.

Morgan wasn't aware of the full extent of Eloise's financial troubles. Because they weren't married, they kept their money separate. He didn't realize that without that paycheck, she was broke. Eloise had no way to cover the expenses of getting her animals home. Stranded in a foreign country, she couldn't even access what little she had left in her U.S. bank account. As a performer, she would only receive payment upon completing an agreed number of shows, therefore fulfilling her contract.

Morgan turned away from Charlie and whispered into the phone, "We'll figure it out, Eloise. This is just a tough break. Come back to the farm, and we can sort everything then. I'll call the driver Ken to load up the elephants first thing in the morning."

When they hung up, he thought he had convinced her. Morgan knew that Eloise's dream was to headline at Ringling Bros. and that, at forty-two, she felt her time was running out. Though she believed she had outgrown the youthful pin-up image of her past, Morgan was certain that Eloise was still considered one of the world's greatest circus performers. Once the Tuskers came out of musth, he was confident that her star would rise to the top again.

The following morning, Morgan contacted Ken at his hotel and told him it was time to bring the elephants home, then waited for confirmation once they were on the road. When his phone rang hours later, it was not the call he expected.

"Morgan—Morgan! You need to get here! They—something happened—chaos, one of 'em ran away."

"What's going on? Who is this?" Morgan demanded.

"It's just that Eloise—I'm one of the guys—"

"Never mind that. What's going on? What happened?" Morgan's voice sliced through the chaotic shouting in the background.

"He got her. She's hurt real bad. You just need to get here. An elephant is in the ring and he attacked—he's attacking—"

"Is there a vet?" Morgan interrupted, desperately piecing the situation together.

"I don't know, I-I think so—"

"Just do whatever needs to be done and tell everyone I'm on my way."

Morgan slammed the phone and immediately called his friends: Oregon Zoo veterinarian Doc Mayberry, the new director, Warren Illif, and his close friend Jack Barker, a local fish & wildlife officer who lived nearby. Warren quickly organized a private jet to fly Morgan from Portland to the Dorval International Airport, as Doc and Jack rushed up the mountain. Knowing that he would need money, they gave him all the cash they had on hand, stuffing wads of bills into his hastily packed suitcase. Morgan promised to pay them back as soon as he returned.

He made a final call to his son Kenneth in Seattle, then raced to Rock Forest, where he learned the devastating details of what had happened to his beloved Eloise.

CHAPTER 16

A sudden snowstorm dropped several inches the evening before the tragedy. Junior had set up space heaters across the big tent to prevent it from collapsing under the snow's heavy weight. At the time, he hadn't realized that the tank holding the performing seals had also sprung a leak.

The following morning, Friday, May 5, 1978, as Junior entered the main tent, he immediately noticed a large bulge in the carpet lining the performance ring. Due to the snowmelt from the heaters and the leaking seal tank, it was soaked. Junior and his crew quickly set to work, drying and stretching it before the first circus show that evening. With a warm break in the weather approaching, substantial crowds were expected for a busy weekend full of shows.

The head of the Zamperla Bareback Riders, Napoléon—known affectionately as Papa—was concerned. His family performed acrobatic tricks, balancing on decorated horses as they galloped around the ring.

"It's too dangerous," he warned. "One of our horses could trip on that bulge, causing a stampede. Or worse, a family member could fall to their death."

Junior's team stretched the carpet to its limit before Eloise opened the evening's six-thirty matinee. But during her first act, she tripped over a large wrinkle. Though she hardly missed a step and finished her routine, it was all Papa Zamperla needed to pull his family off the schedule.

"You're up next!" Leo shouted.

Eloise jumped as he flung open the curtain to her dressing area. His stern gaze met hers, a reminder of the command he had given her the night before. Normally, she would have had more time to prepare, but the sudden change left her scrambling. Clowns were sent out to distract the crowd, and the concessions gave away free snacks while the show was frantically adjusted backstage. Junior barked orders at his men to help secure all of Eloise's animals, while she stripped off her black leotard, replacing it with a bright, sparkling white one. Then she ran to the tent holding her elephants, where she unhooked Teak and Thai, leaving Ranchipur behind. Eloise knew Leo would be furious that she wasn't performing with all three elephants, but at least two were better than one.

Junior opened a tent panel for her as she entered the arena, head held high, as if all the confusion and disorder from moments earlier was an expected part of the show.

"Good luck, Miss Eloise," Junior whispered as she passed by.

If she noticed, he couldn't tell. Eloise walked swiftly, exuding confidence, followed by the two elephants. As she placed them into their starting positions, a quiet hush fell across the crowd. Her routine began as it always did, while Junior watched from a small opening. Eloise arranged the tubs for Teak and Thai to climb, and they executed each trick with precision while the audience laughed and squealed with excitement.

She positioned Thai at the back of the ring for the next part of the performance, near where Junior was watching, allowing her to concentrate on a baton-twirling act with Teak. Eloise tossed the first baton, which he caught and twirled with ease. She repeated the process with a second, and everything went according to plan. The problem arose with the third and final baton. She threw it to Teak, who dropped it as intended, but when Eloise told him to pick it up and toss it back to her, he refused. She gave him another command, and he ignored her again. Teak curled his trunk over his head, still holding the other two batons. Junior had seen the routine enough times to know that something was different.

Eloise scolded the elephant for his insubordination by delivering a witty comment to the crowd. Although Junior couldn't hear her exact words, the audience's uproarious laughter made it clear. She then walked over and picked up the baton, still lying at Teak's feet. But when Eloise took a step backward, her foot caught on the carpet bulge again and she fell—landing in a sitting position.

In a fraction of a second, Teak dropped to his knees, pinning her between his massive tusks. Junior was startled by the elephant's loud trumpet, followed by a grinding sound as the ivory pierced the carpeting and scraped against the asphalt beneath.

"Get him off me!" Eloise screamed.

Several men rushed into the ring, desperate to distract Teak without risking their own lives. But before anyone could intervene, the elephant lunged again—this time, his left tusk drove straight through her torso. For a heartbeat, Junior and the performers froze, watching the scene unravel in slow-motion. Eloise clung to the tusk as Teak rose, lifting her impaled body high above his head, her white leotard blooming red as she tried to shout commands. Her muffled voice was drowned out by the circus band's upbeat tune as the crowd's laughter dissolved into a stunned, uneasy silence.

The band played on, uncertain and trembling, as Teak's fury escalated. With a sudden, violent motion, Teak hurled Eloise to the ground. Then he dropped to his knees, crushing her beneath the weight of his massive skull.

The music came to an abrupt halt, instruments poised midair, as the reality playing out before them sank in. Thai, who was at the back of the arena, panicked and rushed toward the performer's entrance, only to find the ringmaster, Pierre Jean, blocking his planned escape. Eyes wide with terror as the elephant charged straight at him, Pierre bolted, yanking the microphone cord right out of the box. At the last moment Thai veered off, tearing through a side panel of the tent, and disappeared into the night.

Then the crowd erupted into total, sheer pandemonium.

Terrified people were suddenly everywhere—screaming, crying, and running for their lives. The crew backstage struggled to control the frightened animals as a wave of panicked circus-goers surged toward them, splintering in every direction.

Teak loomed over Eloise's body while the tent cleared, his eyes scanning the fleeing crowd. Amid the chaos, a few brave souls remained, determined to protect their fallen friend. Papa Zamperla didn't hesitate. Armed with a crowbar, he jumped into the ring and tried to draw the elephant's attention from his relentless attack on Eloise.

The musical director and organist, Rick Rosio, grabbed a second microphone—an unexpected stroke of luck, since just the day before he had requested there be two in case one failed. He tossed it to the artistic director, Giovanni, who took charge guiding the panicked crowd while Rick and several crew members continued distracting Teak. Spectators in the lower bleachers, within reach of the rampaging elephant, scrambled to escape, while those seated higher up waited anxiously for instructions.

Once everyone was evacuated to safety, Rick grabbed the microphone and began shouting commands at Teak—the same ones he'd heard Eloise use in their many rehearsals.

"Foot up, Teak! Foot UP!"

To their surprise, it worked. While Rick kept the elephant occupied, Papa picked up a piece of plywood from the floor and used it to hide behind, to get closer to Eloise. He carefully rolled her body toward him, inches at a time.

Outside, a bank of payphones became a hub of frantic activity. Emergency calls were made to paramedics and police, who rushed to the site.

Sergeant Richard Tremblay was among the first officers to arrive. He cautiously entered the main tent and saw a small group of people facing the large elephant, undeterred as they tried to divert its attention. He recognized Dr. Tétreault, the head veterinarian from the Granby Zoo, with his colleague, Dr. Girard. The two men were in the process of loading their tranquilizer guns, their expressions tense.

The first dart struck Teak's shoulder, but he quickly plucked it out and coiled his trunk. In a split second, everyone dove for cover as Teak hurled the projectile back at the veterinarians, barely missing them. Packed with M-99, it held enough lethal power to kill a man with the slightest prick, adding a chilling edge to the already desperate scene.

Sergeant Tremblay realized the situation called for more drastic measures as he slipped out of the tent and radioed dispatch. He requested that anyone with the most powerful weapons available—including big game or moose hunters—come to the circus grounds at once.

Additional police and emergency personnel arrived as news of the incident spread. Spectators and onlookers flooded the area, causing a massive traffic jam which delayed the paramedics. Patrol units from surrounding areas were called in to handle the growing crowd and escalating crisis.

Amid the frenzy and confusion, no one noticed a small, eleven-year-old boy, who was peering through a gap in the tent, quietly watching the scene unfold. Paul Langlais was captivated by the circus and had visited every day since they had set up in Rock Forest, a short distance from his home. He helped wherever he could, and in return, the crew allowed him to watch the show.

Just outside, he listened to a group of police officers urgently discussing the need for big game hunters. Determined, he approached them.

"Excuse me," the young boy said, but the men, engrossed in conversation, ignored him.

Paul raised his voice and tugged on a deputy's coat. "Excuse me!"

The deputy looked down, annoyance evident on his face. "What is it, kid? You shouldn't be here."

"But I can help," he insisted.

The group exchanged skeptical looks, and an officer scoffed. "Help? How's that?"

"My father is a big game hunter."

"Yeah? Who's your father?" another deputy asked.

"Claude Langlais," Paul answered. The men stopped, their attention snapping to the young boy.

Officer Langlais was a well-known and highly respected figure, as a firearms instructor at the Sûreté du Québec, a provincial force in Sherbrooke with broader jurisdiction than the local police in Rock Forest. He had trained most of the young officers.

"Do you know where he is right now?"

"No," Paul said. "But today is his day off."

An officer tracked down Claude, urgently requesting his help. Fortunately, he was close to a precinct in a nearby town, where he borrowed a patrol car and raced to the scene. At the circus grounds, officers escorted his son to safety.

A short time later, fellow Sûreté du Québec officer Louis Côté—equipped with a much larger weapon than what the police force were issued—reached the staging area along with Claude Langlais. Sergeant Tremblay, the highest-ranking official, decided that Louis and Claude, both armed with the most suitable weapons, would accompany him inside the tent. Unfortunately, the anesthetic administered by the vets had failed to take effect, and Teak was still fully alert. Meanwhile, law enforcement from various branches and local authorities mobilized to secure the scene, find the missing elephant, and ensure the safety of everyone left on the circus grounds.

The three officers tiptoed into the tent, with Louis moving along one side and Claude covering the other. Sergeant Tremblay positioned himself in the center, using hand signals to guide their approach toward a small group of men who were still scrambling to divert the elephant's attention.

Suddenly, Teak picked up a sledgehammer and lifted it over his head, prompting everyone to duck for cover once again, aware of the danger it posed if he chose to hit the mark. The officers raised their guns and held their positions, watching closely to see what he would do next. Instead of throwing it, Teak used it to scratch his back. As the tension eased, Louis and Claude inched closer along the edges of the tent, while the sergeant advanced up the middle.

After over two hours of following Rick's commands, Teak finally began ignoring them. Whenever Rick or Papa Zamperla got too close, he charged, forcing the men to flee. Other circus crew members scrambled to distract the huge animal by picking up leftover snacks from the ground and tossing them toward him. A partial bale of hay kept Teak occupied until he took notice of the three officers approaching. He dropped the sledgehammer, and everyone froze. Without warning, the elephant lowered his head and charged directly at Louis.

In a panic, Louis fired several shots, but his 7mm-08 Remington was ineffective against such a large creature. Claude fired his weapon from the opposite side as Teak suddenly pivoted and lunged at him, allowing Louis time to run for cover. The elephant closed in, forcing Claude to duck under a large bleacher. With the elephant momentarily preoccupied, Sergeant Tremblay seized the opportunity, grabbed Eloise's body, and sprinted outside.

Louis fired more shots as Teak turned and charged at him again, giving Claude a moment to carefully aim his .300 Magnum Winchester rifle. He discharged two more rounds, dropping Teak to the ground. Before the elephant could get back up, Claude quickly approached, delivering the final shot to his head. It took fifteen bullets to end Teak's short life; he was just twelve years old.

An ambulance waiting outside rushed Eloise to Hôtel-Dieu meaning 'Hospital of God,' but it was too late, she was already dead. Her body was taken to the coroner's office, where officials awaited a full investigation into her death.

Morgan arrived in Canada at 11:30 a.m. the following day. At Dorval International Airport, a police helicopter stood by to take him to Rock Forest. During the flight, an officer briefed him on the events of the previous night.

"Under instructions from command, you have six hours to collect the runaway elephant and gather the rest of Ms. Berchtold's animals," he explained. "Otherwise, we'll have them all killed."

Morgan's heart raced as he asked, "And Ms. Berchtold? How is she?"

As the helicopter blades whirred overhead, the cabin fell silent. The officer, unaware that Morgan hadn't yet been informed, looked at him with deep sorrow.

"I'm sorry," he said. It confirmed what Morgan already feared: Eloise was gone.

They continued the rest of the trip in silence as Morgan grappled with the enormity of the situation. Half an hour later, they landed in the Rock Forest parking lot, where two of Eloise's closest friends anxiously awaited his arrival. They knew that Morgan would have learned of Eloise's death during the helicopter ride and offered their support.

Wade Burck, a renowned tiger trainer traveling with his famous group of white tigers, and Giovanni had witnessed the horrific incident and were deeply shaken. The two joined in the search for the missing elephant, as they struggled with the loss of their friend.

Morgan learned that officers had located Thai in a nearby thicket. He was grazing peacefully on the exposed vegetation, now visible under the melting snow.

Relieved, Morgan leapt from the police vehicle.

"Thai! It's me ... come here."

The shy elephant instantly recognized Morgan's voice and ran straight to him. After being surrounded by law enforcement for hours, the reunion was a touching conclusion to what could have been another tragic episode. Soon, Thai was secured in a transport truck, bringing a very long night to a close.

Upon their arrival back at the circus grounds, Morgan was surprised to find the large tent buzzing with activity. Preparations were already in full swing for the afternoon performance. The urgency to move on from the incident was unsettling. It highlighted the painful contrast between Morgan's personal loss and the circus's relentless pursuit of entertainment: *the show must go on*, regardless of the cost.

Morgan stepped out of the patrol car, as an officer approached.

"Mr. Berry?" he asked.

"Yes."

The officer offered his condolences. "I'm Sergeant Tremblay, and I'm in charge of the investigation into Ms. Berchtold's death."

"I understand," Morgan said.

While Wade and Giovanni unloaded Thai, Morgan spoke with the sergeant inside a private circus trailer. After the interview, he was permitted a final goodbye to Teak. The elephant's body had already been loaded onto a large tow truck. After the investigation, his remains would be sent to a local rendering plant for processing. In the meantime, they would be stored at a nearby warehouse.

Morgan slowly circled the elephant when he noticed one of his tusks was missing. "What happened?" he asked.

Before the sergeant could respond, Leo Duplessis, the general manager, approached from behind.

"I took it," Leo said. "As a souvenir."

Morgan turned and saw him holding the bloody tusk that killed Eloise in his outstretched hand. The thought of it being treated as nothing more than a "souvenir" made his stomach churn. Overcome with despair, Morgan looked away and whispered a swift and final goodbye to Teak before the elephant's body was removed.

"Do you want us to take you to her?" Sergeant Tremblay asked.

Morgan learned that a representative from the circus—whom he didn't realize was Leo Duplessis at the time—had already met with the coroner the night before and positively identified Eloise's body, as required by law.

"No, no." Morgan shook his head. "I don't think I can take much more."

The sergeant passed a folded sheet of paper into his hand—a preliminary report from the coroner. Morgan scanned the brief summary, his eyes catching on the phrase: "polytraumatic injuries," and multiple fatal wounds. The clinical language did nothing to soften the reality of what Eloise had suffered. The extent of her injuries left cremation as the only option. After making the difficult call to Eloise's mother, Esther (her father had died four years earlier), they decided to divide her ashes between them.

By that afternoon, Morgan and the truck driver, Ken, had loaded her remaining animals, including the Tuskers, onto the two trucks for their journey back to Elephant Mountain. After they said their goodbyes, he reflected on the young couple he'd hired to assist Eloise as they drove away. Giovanni had informed him that the Canadian immigration authorities had deported them days earlier because they were unaware that a visa was required to enter the country.

A wave of helplessness washed over Morgan as he realized just how alone Eloise must have felt. He wished he could have known the true extent of her isolation. For the next five days, with the road stretching before him, he buried his grief and focused on the task at hand. Meanwhile, a carefully curated story emerged in the media, pleading the circus's case to the unsuspecting public.

The circus's four owners gave numerous interviews to the Canadian press, desperately trying to save both their business and their reputations. Leo Duplessis posed for a local newspaper, still holding the bloody tusk as if it were some grotesque badge of honor. Another owner, Robert Daoust, gave several infuriating statements to The Daily and Voice of the East newspapers.

"She was a proud woman and refused to follow our advice," he said. "We didn't ask her to suspend her act because she had worked with wild animals her whole life and knew what she was doing."

Yet following their "advice,"—or a not-so-thinly-veiled threat—was partly what led to her death. Eloise had performed with Teak alone in four performances with no problem before Leo's deadly ultimatum. Of course, there was no mention of how he pressured her to put multiple elephants in musth into the ring at the same time. Nor was there any whisper that the payment Eloise so desperately needed to get home could be withheld if she didn't.

Besides, it wasn't as if a circus owner would advise any animal trainer to "suspend their act" when it was the very thing that lined his pockets. Especially considering that The Tuskers of Thailand was the highest-grossing performance in the history of the Gatini Circus until then. It was a nauseating display of hypocrisy. Less than four days after she was killed, they rewrote the narrative, using her as a scapegoat to cover their own ignorance and missteps.

Michel Gatien, another owner, publicly vowed that elephants would never appear in their shows again. Behind the scenes, however, negotiations were already underway to do just that. At nineteen, Carol Buckley and her elephant, Tarra—trained by

Smokey Jones to roller skate—took Eloise's place shortly after her death.

Years later, Carol went on to establish two of the three recognized elephant sanctuaries in the United States, dedicated to healing elephants from the extraordinary trauma of captivity. Today, she lives at the Elephant Refuge North America (ERNA) in Attapulgus, Georgia. Tarra, now fifty-two, and other formerly captive elephants, roam freely across 850 acres, living a life no longer burdened by chains.

After Morgan returned to the mountain, he learned that Canadian authorities had ruled Eloise's death as 'accidental.' News of the tragedy had already spread throughout the global press, and overnight, his once-thriving business collapsed. It marked the turning point of an era and should have put to rest any remaining notion that dealing with bull elephants in musth was safe. But as I would soon learn, it was just the beginning of a story far more complex and unbelievable than I ever could have imagined.

CHAPTER 17

"Holy shit!" Leslie slammed her glass of water down on the table. She stared at me, her eyes wide with disbelief. "That story is awful. I had no idea elephants could be so ... *brutal*."

"I know, right?" I shook my head, still shocked.

"What happened to her husband after Eloise was killed?" she asked.

"They weren't married, but Morgan returned to the mountain and met his own violent end a year later, almost to the day she died."

"How?"

"Another elephant killed him, but I don't have all the details yet."

"You're kidding!" Leslie's fork clattered onto her plate. "Wow. You *have* to tell me what happened when you find out—I'm dying to know." She paused, looked down at her dinner salad, and asked, "Are you taking care of yourself?"

"Yeah ... as much as I can, I guess." I fiddled with my knife, avoiding her gaze.

Leslie took a deep breath. "I can't hear about animal abuse without feeling sick. This must be really difficult for you to witness and live with. It sounds like a pretty dark place."

"It is, but—" I paused before continuing. "I just feel like if I can make it to the end of this story, then I'll be able to move on," I said, trying to convince her as much as myself.

"What do you hope to gain from learning about it?"

"I don't know ... there are countless details here that just don't make any god damn sense."

I folded my arms and leaned back in my chair.

"There were so many articles written in the U.S. about what happened to Eloise, about her death, yet they were all different. There were all kinds of quotes defending how Teak was just protecting her, that he didn't mean to kill her, or that he was actually trying to save her."

I shook my head and took a deep breath.

"Perhaps those were the stories the reporters thought everyone could hear because the public couldn't face the reality of what really happened. Or maybe it was a calculated choice—a well-constructed press campaign to sugar-coat the horror. I mean, when you think about it, how many people would buy a ticket to a circus to see elephants, to ride one, or get close enough to touch them if they were aware of the truth you know? Then there's Teak ...

Several articles said that he was *gently* put down while in his sleep, instead of being riddled with bullets. I've seen the photographs, splashed across newspapers all over Quebec and it's obvious he was shot multiple times. The police reports even showed the final count of every bullet pulled from his body, so let the record show he did not die peacefully. Is everyone just terrified of the truth?

I get that back then, they didn't know that much about musth but an elephant in musth kills people all the time. They always have. It's why so many have been killed in captivity. Yet, even today, nobody seems to be aware of that. And it's not like female elephants don't kill their keepers, too.

Nobody seems to recognize how similar their brains are to ours, and how trauma changes them the same way severe trauma changes us. We push these herbivores, animals that are normally terrified of blood, and that have no natural enemies except for humans—we force them into such unnatural circumstances by constantly separating them from any elephant they've bonded with by trading them with another zoo. We take their babies when there is nothing more important to them or we beat them senseless to do what …? A circus trick? My God, we've left them no choice but to fight back.

But it stuck, you know? The false assumption about elephants' behavior—it stuck. And people bought it. They kept coming back to circuses, coming back to zoos, elephants keep attacking and killing their trainers, and these … these reporters helped, changed, and even supported the entire fake story of elephant behavior. Every article I came across, where an elephant killed its trainer, stated that the elephant was simply trying to *protect him* or accidentally *stepped on him*—crap like that. I just feel, somehow, that the mystery of how it all began starts here, right here with Morgan on that mountain. There's something … something keeps pushing me in that direction, so … I'm going."

The music, which had been playing over the restaurant speakers moments earlier, had stopped, allowing my voice to carry farther than intended. The people who sat at tables on either side of us were staring at me, listening intently to my rant.

Leslie looked at them and giggled before she cleared her throat, and leaned in.

"All I'm saying is that I'm concerned about you. This information you're learning is awful."

I nodded. I knew she was right. Then she said something that caught me completely off guard.

"Don't forget about Michelle."

My heart skipped a beat. The story of what happened to Michelle, my favorite researcher, haunted me as deeply as the stories of the elephants. Michelle McNamara stalked serial killers the way I stalked elephants. Through the course of her research, she had to relive the traumatic experiences of others, and she understood horror. It played with her mind the way learning about the horror elephants faced played with mine.

She created one of the first original blogs, *True Crime Diary*, dedicated to tracking serial killers—years before hundreds of podcasts followed her brilliant lead. Leslie and I read it faithfully. I was intrigued by Michelle's ability to process unimaginable trauma while uncovering the dark secrets of the human predators she chased. Yet no one realized the full extent of her struggle, how all-consuming it became. Or how deeply it affected every aspect of her life ... until months after she mysteriously died.

The day her autopsy report was released is a day I will not soon forget. At first, Leslie and I speculated it was foul play. Perhaps one of the serial killers she hunted had caught her, or maybe it was a simple explanation like an aneurysm. She died in her sleep, after all. Michelle was only forty-six, only a few years older than I, so young it just didn't make sense. At least, not until the truth was finally revealed.

Michelle, it turned out, died of an accidental drug overdose. Apparently, she had not been coping as well as everyone thought.

She was plagued by night-terrors too. Sleep eluded her, nightmares kept her awake, and she was consumed by solving the great mystery of the Golden State Killer: one of California's most notorious and elusive serial killers.

She had started using Adderall (an upper) to wake up, recharge, and concentrate. I learned that when I smashed and snorted the pills like a line of cocaine, I felt the effects within seconds. Then she used Xanax or Percocet (downers) to come down off her "research high" to be able to sleep. I'd done that, too. When she couldn't get prescriptions, she'd turned to street drugs, which is likely why fentanyl was also discovered in her system, a deadly ingredient a doctor would never prescribe. She was chasing a different kind of evil—*addiction*—one that made the Golden State Killer look like an amateur.

Although they also found a hidden heart condition, the combination of the two sealed her fate. Michelle's death shook me quite hard. Her story could have so easily been mine. We both played with dark monsters. We were united by horror. By learning details about an elephant's death, whether captive or wild, I also discovered terror, distress, alarm, and panic—a shared connection between the stories she followed and mine.

I had to find a way to make sense of it all. If I didn't, I was afraid it would consume me, too. Leslie had shared her concern with me before, as had most of my friends. Once I found a hot trail, it was difficult to let go.

Leslie looked down at her food. Something was obviously on her mind.

"Shoot, I'm sorry I rambled on about that," I said. "Let's focus on what's going on with you. You have something big you wanted to share."

Instead of looking happy, she seemed alarmed. I had known Leslie for over a decade, but in that moment, I realized I'd never seen her look the way she did then.

"Oh God, what is it?" I put down my fork.

To my relief, she looked up and smiled. The music had started up again and the diners at the tables closest to ours had stopped paying us any attention.

"I have breast cancer," she said as I froze. "And it's … it's bad."

Whenever someone shares devastating news with me like that, I always try to be extra careful to focus on my reaction and let them have the full space without feeling they also have to take care of me. But that hit me unlike anything before. Leslie was my best friend, my unwavering support, and my anchor.

When I looked up after she said the worst thing I'd ever heard, and her eyes filled with tears, it felt as though all the blood drained from my body.

"It's okay," she sniffled. "It's all going to be okay because I have a great doctor and we have a clear idea of treatment—"

Everything blurred after that. It was as if the world stopped rotating on the word "cancer," and time stood completely still.

Throughout the rest of our dinner, I heard more bad words like "Stage 4," "metastasized," and "triple negative." She had one of the hardest, most aggressive cancers to treat, and as she talked, the world stopped again and again. I like to think that I held myself together for her, that when she looked at my face, my agony remained hidden, but I cannot say for sure.

What I was certain of as we left our familiar booth at Seasons and Regions was that our days were numbered, and I would never step foot inside that restaurant again. Somehow, I knew with absolute certainty that this was a battle she would not win. And if she were gone, if Leslie didn't survive—something almost impossible for me to even imagine—the question was: how on earth would I?

∞

I sat on a bench along the quiet, beautiful Willamette River. The early morning dawn was just beginning to break, the water hidden beneath a layer of mist. I stared into the murky abyss, lost in thought, as the faint echoes of invisible geese gliding close to its surface coaxed me back to the present. One brilliant ray of sunshine penetrated the fog, then two. I looked up at the sky where beams of light burst through a cloud as if opening a secret entrance to heaven.

My thoughts drifted to Leslie, wondering what our future held. The image of her just hours ago lingered. She tried her best to seem confident and full of determination, but the unease in her eyes told a different story. Death was not something I was afraid of; it was pain and suffering. And I would do anything to prevent her from enduring either. She agreed to let me take her to the hospital for the first of several surgeries before we met the two-headed dragon: chemo and radiation. I wasn't looking forward to any of it, but I would not let her walk alone, no matter what.

"We're in it together or not at all," she always said, her words fading into the mist.

Now it was my turn. Whatever was coming, whatever waited on the other side of that door, would also have to face me. The weight of this new reality settled heavily. There were no tears, only quiet acceptance and the hint of a looming breakdown.

The wind picked up suddenly; I leaned back and looked up at the trees swaying above. That's when I heard it—the whisper of my name. I jumped up, searching for the source, but I was the only one there. Then I heard it again. An eerie chill swept over me like a shadow as the wind blew even harder. Either I was losing it, I thought, or something was trying to get my attention. Whichever it was, I had a sudden urge to head home.

When I walked through my front door, I looked around my living room for some sign, some clue—but nothing. I went to my bookshelf, closed my eyes, and ran my hand across the bulging notebooks filled with thousands of pages of elephant stories. Nothing jumped out to me there either. *What was it?*

Nearly every inch of my floor was still covered in paper. It was a chaotic sea of research, newspaper clippings, books, and scientific journals. As I scanned the mess, my eyes were drawn to the only news article lying face up, standing out amidst the disarray. I walked across the room, the sound of paper crinkling beneath my feet, and picked it up. It was the front page of the Woodland newspaper announcing the death of Morgan Berry—the same article displayed in the Oregon Zoo hallway that I'd printed the night before.

I lowered myself to the floor, pressing my back against the couch. Years had passed since I last read it, but now that I understood the events that unfolded in the year before his death it felt like I was reading it for the first time. What lay ahead would test me in ways I could never have imagined, the full weight yet to be revealed. They say when the student is ready, the teacher will appear—and the elephants were about to deliver their most powerful lesson of all.

CHAPTER 18

The phone's piercing ring shattered the tranquil melody of crickets, and the forest surrounding Morgan's house, fell silent. From the outside, it appeared occupied; lights glowed warmly from within, spilling onto the front porch and casting shadows on the overgrown lawn. The door hung open, as if Morgan had simply stepped out into the warm summer night, intending to return at any moment. But the idyllic scene was nothing more than an illusion, and that phone would never be answered again.

Charlie Wilson lived ten minutes away in the town of Woodland, Washington, and though it was unusual for Morgan not to pick up after one or two rings, he kept trying. His concern grew with each attempt. At 9:30 p.m., after a half hour of unanswered calls, he reached out to their mutual friend and Morgan's neighbor, Joe Wodaege, and asked him to check the house while he headed to the barns. Both men had worked on Elephant Mountain before as part-time keepers, and were somewhat familiar with the elephants living there. After Eloise died, Morgan insisted he wanted to be left alone and slid into a deep depression, which made his friends increasingly uncomfortable.

In the months after her death, he sold most of his exotic animals, keeping only nine elephants and a pair of wolves. Then he fired all the keepers, wanting—he explained—to remain a recluse.

In addition to the four surviving Tuskers and The African Trio, Morgan had also acquired two more Asian elephants: Me-Thai (formerly known as Abbie), a gentle female who had spent years rotating between circuses and zoos, and Winkie. Morgan rescued her after she yanked a young girl through the bars of her stall and trampled her to death at a Wisconsin zoo.

Morgan's closest friends, concerned about him managing so many elephants on his own, made him a deal. Each night, one of them would call at 9:00 p.m. to ensure everything was fine. If he didn't answer, they were to assume it wasn't.

After a quick search of the house, Joe and his wife Mary found no sign of him. Morgan typically walked along a dark forested path that led from the front door of his home, down a long hill, to the entrance of the main barn, so they waited outside, hoping for his return.

Soon Charlie's car approached, its headlights highlighting the couple standing in the driveway.

"Anything?" Joe asked.

"No, I counted only seven elephants between the two barns," Charlie replied, after he parked and got out. "But no sign of Morgan anywhere."

Joe pointed his flashlight into the darkness. "There's one right there, which makes eight."

The men walked closer, locking eyes with the elephant. Nearly hidden along a narrow access road, the massive creature stood tethered between two trees. Its legs were secured with chains, attached to hefty, homemade weights resting on the ground. Eloise had welded them herself, allowing Morgan to move the elephants around the property without escaping.

"There should be nine," Charlie said, shining his flashlight into the surrounding forest. "The three Africans are in the barn, so the missing elephant is definitely one of the Asians."

"Morgan's probably gone off looking for him." Joe replied, checking his watch.

Their conversation was abruptly interrupted by the jarring sound of chains being pulled tight as the elephant lunged toward them, its trunk extending perilously close to Joe. He reared back just in time, narrowly avoiding its reach. The shocking speed of the elephant's movement left the men startled.

"It's a good thing you noticed him over there," Charlie exclaimed, as they scrambled up a short embankment. "That guy is in musth, did you see the sides of his face?"

"I do now," Joe said, nervously rubbing his chin.

The three went back inside the house, where they decided it was safer to wait than outside with a runaway elephant on the loose. After another hour passed, Charlie called Kenneth, Morgan's son, who lived over a hundred miles away in Seattle and worked as a primate keeper at the Woodland Park Zoo. Kenneth assured them he would get there as fast as he could.

Little did they realize that within hours, the mystery of Morgan's disappearance would spiral into a global sensation. The details of that summer night, Tuesday, June 26, 1979, would dominate local headlines for months and attract international attention. *Life*, the most popular magazine in the U.S., dedicated an eight-page spread to the events surrounding that evening and it would spark a fierce debate. Even I remember seeing it in our newspaper, though I was only seven at the time.

As midnight approached, in the neighboring town of Kelso, located twenty miles north of Elephant Mountain, Sheriff Dan

Sheridan, and Deputy Brad Bright were finishing their coffee at a local diner before heading out to begin their usual overnight shift. Drawn by the bizarre chatter on his radio, off-duty officer Tom Hudson slipped into the empty restaurant where he knew they'd be. A self-proclaimed night owl who lived around the corner, Tom couldn't resist the intrigue of the initial reports hinting at something unusual unfolding on the other side of Cowlitz County.

Several concerned drivers reported random sightings of an elephant. Unfamiliar with Morgan or the animals he kept on the mountain, the three were stunned as they listened. They were in the middle of discussing the strange situation when dispatch radioed, instructing them to join the search. A group of fellow law enforcement officers had already assembled at the scene after Kenneth called requesting their assistance. They were directed to Morgan's big barn: ground zero for all responders.

"Want to come with us?" Brad asked Tom as he tossed a bill on the table and grabbed his jacket.

"Are you kidding? I wouldn't miss it!"

Tom jumped into the passenger seat of Brad's patrol car while the two vehicles flipped on their lights and headed to the scene. In a county surrounded by old-growth forests, fueled by the logging industry where nothing strange or unusual ever happened, this was already an unprecedented event. Soon, they arrived at the staging area where a cluster of uniforms stood in tight conversation.

"What kind of place is this?" Dan asked, as he stepped from his car.

"Exotic animal importer," the officer replied. "Keeps a herd of elephants up here and one of them is also missing."

"Do you think he's just gone searching for it?" Dan wondered.

"Yeah, probably. But there's no sign of him so far. We keep

getting reports on the missing elephant, though. Seems kind of dangerous walking around at night in a dark forest looking for the guy with a wild elephant on the loose."

Just then, dispatch interrupted. Another shocked neighbor had reported seeing an elephant further down the road. Dan and Brad were instructed to investigate.

"Let's go!" Dan gestured with a swirling motion of his hand.

As the two patrol vehicles gradually worked their way in the direction of the sighting, they turned on the spotlights attached to the sides of their car. Dan directed his beam into the forest on one side while Tom and Brad swept theirs across the other.

"I never could have guessed this would be in my job description," Brad spoke softly, carefully scanning each shadow.

"You can say that again," Tom chuckled. "It's not like they can teach you how to catch an elephant in the police academy."

The vehicles cautiously approached the area where the elephant was last seen. As they rounded a corner, Dan abruptly slammed his brakes, with Brad nearly rear-ending him. Piled high on the road in front of him, illuminated by the glow of his headlights, was a towering heap of dung, the kind that could only be made by a very large animal. The Sheriff opened the door with one leg still inside the car and stood up just as a massive elephant emerged from the dense forest, moving directly into their path several yards ahead.

"What the ..." Brad whispered, as Tom leaned further out the open window for a better look.

The elephant paused in the middle of the road, turned toward them, and held its ground as the stunned men stared. They had never seen an elephant before—not this close, anyway—and had no idea how large they could get. The officers were captivated by its impressive size. After a tense stand-off, Dan looked back at his deputies and shrugged.

"What should we do?" whispered Tom.

"Not a clue," replied Brad.

The elephant continued staring at them. Dan flicked on his police lights, hoping that would scare the animal into returning home, but it remained still. Then he waved his arms and yelled, but that didn't work, either. After a few moments he turned to face his deputies.

"Turn on your siren," Dan whispered loudly. Brad hesitated for a moment before he hit the switch.

The sudden loud noise startled the large animal. It flapped its ears, whipped around in a circle, and took a defensive stance. For a brief second, it looked into the forest, as if contemplating its next move. Just when they thought it might run away, the elephant let out a thunderous rumble, lowered its head, and charged straight at them.

Dan scrambled into his vehicle, his panicked voice screaming at his fellow officers.

"Go! Back up! GO! GO! GO!"

They slammed their patrol cars in reverse. Dan's front door swung open, as there was no chance to close it during the hasty retreat. The elephant thundered toward them with astonishing speed, quickly closing the distance. Dan turned to see it was nearly on top of him. He covered his face and closed one eye, bracing himself for the impact, when it veered off at the last second disappearing once again into the dark forest.

The officers finally came to a stop as they took several minutes to regain their composure. They maneuvered their vehicles into a driveway a safe distance away.

"Well, that wasn't exactly what I expected," Dan said, shaking his head, as the three stood beside their patrol cars.

Then the men broke into spontaneous laughter while they replayed the event: how they'd barely escaped with their lives—not from a bullet, as was the nightmare of every police officer—but from a runaway elephant. The absurdity of it made them laugh even harder, releasing nervous tension. Once their humor died down, Dan sighed deeply.

"I suppose we need to call for some backup," he said.

As word of the "situation" spread, law enforcement from other precincts gathered at the big barn. After all, it wasn't every day one got to witness the take down of the world's largest mammal. A short time later, two more deputies from a neighboring county arrived, selected for their experience hunting big game in Africa and each owning rifles powerful enough to kill an elephant.

"It's probably in musth," one of them said, "and we can't take any chances." He grabbed a long rifle out of his trunk.

In the pre-dawn hours, Dan placed another call to the head elephant keeper at the Oregon Zoo.

"Are you Roger Hanneous?" he asked.

"This is him," he mumbled, having just arrived at his office for an early start to the day.

"We need some assistance up here with a runaway elephant." Dan explained what had happened.

Although they were not close friends, Roger knew Morgan and was shocked by the unfolding developments. After hanging up with the sheriff, Roger contacted the zoo vet, Dr. Michael Schmidt, who'd taken over after Doc Maberry retired. Then he placed another call to enlist the help of Doug Groves, a fellow elephant keeper at the zoo.

Doug had traveled with the Tuskers for years to their circus performances and knew Morgan and Eloise well. He, along with Kenneth, was the most familiar with the elephants. Within the hour, Roger, Doug, Dr. Schmidt, and his veterinary assistant, Anne Moody, headed up the mountain.

A beautiful sunrise painted the sky, signaling yet another hot summer day while a police escort led the group through the area. Large crowds of spectators, reporters, and photographers already lined the main road, evidence of how swiftly word had spread. Despite warnings to stay indoors, clusters of local residents chatted excitedly standing in driveways while holding their first cups of morning coffee.

Several officers had located the elephant in heavy brush by the time they arrived. Positioned further down the road next to a flatbed truck for transporting the lost elephant home, Roger, Doug, and Anne wrapped long chains around their torsos to secure the animal's legs, while the tranquilizer was prepared. The big-game hunting deputies loaded their massive guns, ready for a "worst-case scenario," and they set out for the elephant's last known location.

As they approached, a loud trumpet rang out. They waited until Dr. Schmidt could determine its exact position to dart it with a sedative. The hunters flanked the edges, prepared to intervene if things took a dark turn.

The elephant lifted his head out of a thicket and Doug recognized him instantly.

"Thai! Hey, it's me ... your old friend Doug, remember?"

Thai trumpeted and chirped as he stepped out from the dense underbrush, appearing excited to see someone familiar. Just as he broke through the cover of vegetation, a dart hit his shoulder, but he didn't even seem to notice. Instead, Thai seemed relieved to be in the presence of a keeper he once knew.

"It's okay bud, it's okay," Doug comforted him.

Everyone stood back, the hunters lowered their guns, and a few members of the crowd clapped and cheered. While Doug escorted Thai toward the waiting truck on the main road, the elephant suddenly collapsed on the hard asphalt. The tranquilizer had taken effect.

"He's too hot," Doug yelled. "Can we get any water on him?"

A neighbor ran to their house arriving a short time later with a water truck as they drenched Thai's body to cool him down until the effects of the sedative wore off. Then, due to the stress of it all, combined with the rising heat, several people also laid down in the middle of the road, seeking shade next to their parked vehicles, to catch a quick nap before Thai woke up.

Joel Sternfeld, one of the many photographers on the scene, caught that moment in a timeless picture called "Exhausted Renegade Elephant." At first glance, the photo looked more like a mass shooting rather than what it actually was: a group of people and an elephant peacefully napping together in the middle of a rural country road.

Thai woke shortly after to the sounds of his favorite female companion, Me-Thai, who another keeper had brought down to coax Thai home. Due to a minor injury he suffered to a leg, likely the result of his sudden collapse, he offered no objections when Doug and Roger loaded him onto the flatbed truck to be driven home. By the time he was reunited with the rest of his herd, Kenneth had arrived from Seattle.

Most of the officers were stationed at the large barn, while a few remained up the hill at Morgan's house. With increasing concern,

Kenneth wondered where his father could possibly be now that they'd found Thai. He walked over to Joe, just outside striking distance from the angry elephant still tied to the tree, when something caught his eye.

"What is that?" he asked, pointing to an object on the ground that had the elephant's attention.

"I don't know," Joe shrugged. "I think it's a blanket, or maybe an old deer hide. He's been playing with it for a while."

The elephant picked it up a few times, twirled it in his trunk, and tossed it to the side. Kenneth walked away, returning moments later holding a pitchfork.

"Can you go over there and distract him so I can grab it?" he asked.

Joe stood on the opposite side, waved his arms, and diverted the elephant's attention just long enough for Kenneth to fork the object. He placed it on the ground to examine it when he realized it wasn't a blanket or a deer hide, but a pile of uniquely folded clothing. With Joe standing over his shoulder, he carefully opened a shirt, section by section. Inside the right sleeve was what appeared to be a long string. Then he laid out a pair of pants, which had another string tucked inside one of the legs. While Kenneth continued inspecting it, Joe leaned in.

Suddenly Kenneth lurched, nearly knocking Joe over as he staggered.

"What is it?" Joe asked, alarmed.

Kenneth's reply was barely a whisper, his face a horrifying shade of gray as he rubbed it with trembling hands.

"It's ... *him*," he choked out.

"What do you mean? How can that be?" Joe asked, frantically studying the pile closer. A moment later, he saw what made

Kenneth lurch—the blurry outline of Morgan's face. The strings were skin, and all that was left of his arms and legs.

The grim discovery caught the attention of several officers standing nearby. Before long, more converged on the scene. While waiting for the coroner to arrive, they dug through the tall, matted grass, uncovering more items of clothing, including pieces of the back brace Morgan wore along with a single shoe.

Everyone looked at the menacing killer elephant, wondering how such an unbelievable tragedy could have happened. Somehow, he had gotten a hold of Morgan and obliterated him. Every bone, every organ—crushed beyond recognition. All that remained was the haunting impression of the man he once was.

By the following morning, news of Morgan's death not only made its way down the mountain but also graced the front pages of most newspapers across the Pacific Northwest, accompanied by the name of his killer—Tunga. The fact it was the gentle giant *Tidy Tunga* who killed Morgan was shocking and sad. Of all the elephants, he was the one I'd least expected.

Later that same day, Tunga was executed with two bullets to the head, like so many young male elephants before him. The mystery of how Thai escaped from his chains that night remains unsolved. It's possible he was with Tunga when Morgan was killed and simply ran away, as he so often did when afraid, but we will never know. Within months of Morgan's death, all the elephants were sold and shipped to their new homes, ending the long reign of Elephant Mountain once and for all.

I closed my computer and sat in stunned silence. It was not at all what I expected. Morgan's story was even more awful and spectacular than whatever I'd imagined. His grand experiment, controlling elephants in musth, ended in complete, abject failure. It not only cost him his own life but that of everything he loved.

As I began clearing the papers off my living room floor, the name Tunga flew into my mind, and I stopped. It flipped around for a moment before it disappeared. I continued tidying until it happened again. *Tunga.* I sat back on my knees racking my brain, feeling as though I had heard that name before, like it was familiar somehow before I'd known anything about Morgan or the elephants he kept on the mountain. *Tunga*—I distinctly recalled an elephant named Tunga at the Oregon Zoo, one of the bulls used in their breeding program.

But how could that be? Surely, I was mistaken. Tunga had only ever lived on Elephant Mountain before he was killed at age fifteen. There was something about this story that didn't make sense. I got up and paced across my living room, retracing every detail of what I'd just learned.

All of a sudden, a clue dropped out of nowhere. While working on the research project, we stumbled upon a document with the names of all the elephants that had ever been kept at the Oregon Zoo. If Tunga had lived there, his name would be on that list. I rushed to my closet and pulled out a stack of boxes hidden deep in the back. I sifted through papers and files until I uncovered the hard drive I was looking for. My stomach churned as I plugged it in, waiting for the computer to detect the file.

A few minutes later, it appeared. My finger shook as it scrolled through a lengthy list of names, stopping at one—*Tunga.* I covered my mouth with my hand. My heart beat so fast I had to take a deep breath to calm down. *What the fuck was going on?* I quickly opened another database that listed the transfer date for each elephant, including where they came from. Perhaps there were two elephants named Tunga. Or maybe Tunga and Tonga were indeed separate individuals.

But there was only one, and he was sold to the Oregon Zoo on October 25, 1979 for $15,000, four months after Morgan's death. The zoo's director, Warren Iliff, called the purchase "a steal" and bought Tunga as a breeder, just as I'd remembered. He lived in Portland for over a decade before being transferred to the notorious Hawthorn Corporation, owned by Eloise's ex-husband, John Cuneo.

Five years later, Tunga became one of the first elephants infected with the strain of tuberculosis that could be transmitted to humans, ultimately leading to his own death in 1996. Nicholas, the elephant they attempted to ship to Puerto Rico despite knowing he too had the disease, turned out to be Tunga's offspring.

I was struck by the irony of this story, how it completed a full circle and looped back to the very beginning like a serpent swallowing its tail. I dug through all the papers strewn across my living room until I found the articles that included old photographs of Tunga on the day Morgan was killed. There were only three: one showed him tied up between the trees, another revealed two men standing in front of him, guns drawn, and the third depicted him lying on the ground moments after he was shot. Each caption identified the elephant as Tunga.

So who was that, if not Tunga?

My mind raced as I tried to connect the dots. I needed to track what happened to the other elephants in order to reveal the killer's true identity. Ranchipur and Me-Thai were sold to the Manizales Zoo in Colombia, near where Morgan's first wife, Louise, and their grown children lived. Later, they were transported again to their final destinations. Me-Thai joined Thai at the Houston Zoo (and, at this moment, were both still alive) while Ranchipur was purchased by the Wild Animal Park in San Diego, then moved once more to his permanent home at the San Diego Zoo until his death in 2016.

Winkie was first sold to the Oregon Zoo and then to the Wildlife Safari in Roseburg four hours south of Portland, where she died not long after in 1982. The African Trio ended up with a former elephant keeper, leaving only Tunga and Buddha. A final search revealed no evidence whatsoever of Buddha ever having left Elephant Mountain.

I thought back to the frantic events of that day. The reporters wouldn't have been able to identify which elephant was tied to that tree, nor the neighbors, police, or volunteers. The only people who could have positively identified it were the keeper, Doug Groves, or Kenneth. But once Doug returned Thai to the barn, law enforcement had already cordoned off the area upon discovering Morgan's remains, leaving only Kenneth.

The horrifying scene had left him so traumatized that, by that point, it was doubtful anyone would have even bothered to ask. The reporters were unlikely to place much significance on the elephant's real name. Their primary mission was to get the sensational story out as fast as possible: Morgan Berry, the great elephant trainer who swore he could manage bull elephants in musth, was just killed by one.

No, the identity of Morgan's killer mattered little to anyone except me.

I sat back for a moment, as the pieces fell into place. It wasn't the gentle giant "Tidy Tunga" who killed Morgan. Instead, it was the elephant long labeled a "rogue" and known as one of the most dangerous in the country—*Buddha*. I reread each article, those which misidentified Tunga, replacing his name with Buddha's.

Details I hadn't paid particular attention to earlier slowly emerged. I grabbed my computer and searched the name Buddha as Morgan's killer, curious to see what it would reveal. To my surprise, it was flooded with articles from across the U.S., correctly naming Buddha and providing even more clues about his life. Ironically, only the local newspapers got it wrong, confusing the two elephants and adding to the chaos of an already tragic story.

As I jotted down each new detail about Buddha on my notepad, I noticed something I couldn't have seen had it not been written. Shortly after he arrived on the mountain, Buddha's temperament changed drastically. He went from a kind, playful elephant to totally vicious seemingly overnight, confusing many of the people he once had a good working relationship with.

After the Arizona incident, when Buddha nearly killed Eloise, a trainer commented on a circus blog post that Buddha wasn't right in the head. He pointed to a suspicious indentation that he claimed grew more pronounced over the years. A different news article featured an interview with Morgan where he also mentioned the unusual dent and agreed that it was the most likely cause of the elephant's sudden change in demeanor, though he didn't know why.

The hair on my arms stood, and a chill worked its way up my body. I held an article, a eulogy of sorts, someone had written for Buddha. The former keeper ended his reflection with relief that even though Buddha was young, just thirteen when he was shot, he could finally rest in peace next to the stream on Morgan's property where he was buried—a serene end to a violent life.

Suddenly I stopped. Everything blurred as I pushed myself to my feet. The articles in my hands fluttered to the ground like leaves caught in a breeze. Details flashed before me. *Bullet right between the eyes.* Buddha. *Deep dent in his skull.* Buddha. *Buried along a river bank.* Buddha. *Killed his trainer.* Buddha. *Thirteen years old ...*

"It's BUDDHA!" I screamed.

The skull I had been so obsessed with in the secret museum belonged to none other than the very elephant who killed Morgan Berry. I felt Buddha's spirit fly across my living room.

"It's Buddha," I sobbed, dropping to my knees.

He was my quiet whisperer in the woods all this time. My chest tightened as my cries grew louder, making it harder to catch my breath. I cried for Buddha, I cried for Leslie, not knowing which tore at my soul more.

The breakdown no longer waited on the sidelines, but descended upon me like a tidal wave. Defeated and overwhelmed, I gave in. With no will or fight to stop it, the floodgates burst open as a surge of emotions slammed into me.

CHAPTER 19

"His name is Buddha," I said to Violet, lightly touching his skull.

She looked at me with wide eyes, disbelieving at first. I unzipped my overstuffed backpack and spread a large stack of news articles and photographs across a long table—pieces of a complicated puzzle. Each detail revealed a fractured life, and soon we were surrounded by his old memories.

There were several pictures that showed Buddha performing with The Tuskers of Thailand. He balanced on balls, twirled in skirts, and did a perfect one-foot stand, just like they said. Even as a young elephant, we could see that the left side of his face appeared different—his skull had already been cracked by then. As the years progressed, the dent became significantly more pronounced.

In his final photograph, taken moments before Buddha was killed, he was chained and angry-looking. His trunk coiled over his head like a rattlesnake preparing to strike, and his eyes looked strange, almost demonic. The infection would have already entered his brain.

Once we had reviewed each part of Buddha's life and met each character in his story, Violet placed a gloved hand on his skull. We exchanged a look, as she suddenly realized why I insisted on meeting her at the secret museum with such urgency, and why my face was still red and swollen.

"Oh Buddha," she said softly, as a single tear slid down her cheek. "It's *you*."

An eerie peace filled that room, as if he were there with us, reliving every moment of his short life.

"How could they not have known?" Violet whispered.

"About what?"

"The infection," her gloved finger touched the area.

But there was no answer. How *could* they not have known? How could it have been such a mystery when there was an unmistakable dent on the side of his head? How much force had it taken for someone to hit him hard enough to crack his skull when he was just a baby? It was tragic to realize that Buddha's suffering could have been prevented with something as simple as an antibiotic, at least until the infection spiraled out of control.

We held hands and gave him a final farewell, then gathered our things and walked outside. As we prepared to part ways, Violet turned to me.

"How you figured all this out, how it unfolded—it's really remarkable. I just wanted to tell you that."

I hugged her and left, still confused why the ghost of Buddha had tracked me down, why he wanted me to learn his story, and what it meant moving forward. I could have lived a long and happy life without ever knowing the awfulness of his.

Instead of going home, I sat in my car, parked on a city street, and stared through the sunroof into the wide branches of an old oak tree. The gnarled bark, weathered by seasons past, bore witness to its history. Several limbs were covered in a beautiful shade of green moss. Some were large and outspoken, rustling loudly as fleeting streaks of light danced across my face. Smaller ones lingered in the background, whispering to each other with the nudge of a gentle breeze.

The city seemed unusually quiet, then I remembered it was a Sunday afternoon. The gorgeous spring-like day signaled a clear shift from the cold, rainy winter. The sun's warmth felt comforting. I rolled my window down, allowing it to penetrate my pale skin.

My mind drifted to a news clipping I'd stumbled across that provided more details about the people who had uncovered Buddha's remains. In 1984, an archaeology professor from Lewis and Clark College, a few miles from where I lived, reached out to Morgan's son, Kenneth, to see if his class could conduct an archaeological dig. The students were taken to the bank by the stream, to the very spot where Buddha was buried by the man who put him there. Just as I thought, it wasn't some accidental find.

They planned to showcase his bones at the Oregon Zoo, but there were no elephant skeletons when I worked there. Perhaps, in the three decades since, he had already been dismantled or was on display somewhere else. How his skull ended up at the secret museum would remain an unsolved mystery.

The details surrounding Morgan's death were also troubling and inconsistent. Many of the news articles suggested he died of a "heart attack," after collapsing at Buddha's feet, where he was then squashed like a bug. The reason, they said, that the angry elephant lashed out at anyone who approached? Well, he was simply protecting what remained of the friend he loved. Buddha must have accidentally crushed him when he lay down to sleep next to his master. Others implied he was only trying to help once he realized Morgan was injured. After all, he would *never* deliberately hurt the man who raised him. It was all just one big misunderstanding—an accident. A very, very unfortunate event.

The articles detailing what happened to Morgan mirrored those written about Eloise, watered down and sugar-coated to such an extent that most of the facts never did find their way home. The more I read the more unsettled I became, unable to shake my growing desire to uncover the truth.

When the Cowlitz County Coroner, D.F. Winebrenner, was asked by a reporter for *The Oregonian* whether Morgan *could* have died of a heart attack instead of being trampled to death, I couldn't help but smirk at his answer.

"He might possibly have survived a heart attack," he said, "but he certainly wouldn't have survived these injuries."

Morgan's cause of death was listed as "multiple traumatic injuries by elephant trampling," in the coroner's report. Pathologist, Dr. William J. Elton explained there wasn't enough tissue left to examine under a single slide. There was no brain, kidneys, liver, pancreas, lungs, or heart.

Without biological matter to analyze, the cause of death could only be determined by the most obvious evidence. Morgan's body was pulverized, and they found nothing more than small fragments of skin and bone.

I was mystified by the sheer amount of force it required to shatter a grown man's femur into rubble in a field of soft grass. In less than twenty-four hours, Morgan was reduced to dust by an elephant suffering not just from musth, but from an infection in his brain that would have made him crazy enough to do worse.

What Dr. Winebrenner didn't include was nearly as intriguing as what he did. There was no mention of a "secondary cause of death." Coroners have access to a deceased patient's medical records, and though he noted Morgan was taking a statin (a medication used to lower bad cholesterol), the health issue was not specified. While it's possible that a heart condition may have been the reason for the prescription, if the coroner believed it could have contributed to Morgan's death—even as a remote possibility—then it would have been listed. But that box was left blank in his report. The deeper I dug, the more elusive the facts became.

The Sheriff's spokesman, Gary Waddell, also played a substantial role in spreading the false narrative. He rattled off a bevy of inaccuracies about elephant behavior, which I doubted he came up with on his own. He even stated to a local newspaper, *The Daily News*, that "elephants sometimes will try to pick up a trainer who has fallen," offering that as some sort of explanation. However, his claim did nothing to clarify how Morgan's body ended up in the condition it did.

Mr. Waddell was also quick to mention the heart attack theory. The Sheriff's department had access to his death records, including photographs from the scene along with the coroner's and autopsy files. Yet his peculiar statements found their way into several articles and eventually books, reinforcing the misleading portrayal of events. Who, I wondered, was pulling the strings of so many puppets? Considering that each report detailed, in chilling and grotesque clarity, what was observed, leaving little doubt as to what happened.

I unexpectedly discovered the truth when I read a book called *The Astonishing Elephant* by Shana Alexander, who took a deep dive into the story. She became famous not only for her best-selling books, but also for an iconic *Saturday Night Live* skit.

Shana, a liberal columnist, was credited in part with the early success of the news show *60 Minutes,* due to her political acumen. She was beautiful, witty, and featured in a weekly segment called *Point/Counterpoint,* where she sparred against a conservative writer named James "Jack" Kilpatrick. The two engaged in such lively debates on hot-button issues of the late 70s, that audiences tuned in just to watch the fireworks.

From the first episode, she caught Jack off guard, surprising him with her knowledge of subjects outside the kitchen. Soon, comedians Dan Akroyd and Jane Curtain took notice when they portrayed the real-life characters of Shana and Jack in a skit on *Saturday Night Live*. The parody, featuring Dan's famous retort: "Jane, you ignorant slut," turned it into one of the show's most memorable moments. It was a classic example of how some men resort to demeaning tactics when unable to outsmart their female colleagues.

While visiting Portland to write an article on the birth of Packy, Shana and Morgan became friends. As the first woman to join the staff of *Life* magazine as a writer, she helped introduce them both to the world. For years they stayed in touch through letters, and their friendship deepened. When she learned of Morgan's death, she hopped on a flight to find out exactly what had happened.

It was the title of Shana's article in *Life* called "For the Love of Elephants: An Inquiry into the Violent Death of an Old Friend," that first caught my attention. It suggested she wasn't going with the whole "Morgan died peacefully of a heart attack" scenario.

After discovering the truth from her own research and interviews, she confronted Doc Mayberry, whom she had also grown close to over the years. She wanted to know why the story of Morgan's death was being inaccurately portrayed in the press. The explanation he gave was that if the public were aware of the true danger of keeping elephants captive, they would "insist" on them all being killed. He admitted what Shana and I had already suspected: the details were deliberately altered.

Though Doc wasn't entirely wrong. Modern American history is haunted by spectacles of elephant executions. These final, tragic moments were often captured on film and in photographs, the images splashed across newspapers. Captive elephants who'd killed humans were purposely poisoned, hung, shot, and electrocuted in public squares nationwide. Still, Shana was the only person I could find who ever confronted those men, which made me admire her even more.

Until I discovered another individual who shared our concerns: George W. "Slim" Lewis. With over thirty years of experience training elephants for the circus, he wrote a letter to *The Oregonian* three weeks after Morgan's death. In it, he questioned why so many reporters—the newsmen being fed by the zoomen—went to such great lengths to create the impression that Morgan had died from a heart attack.

He clarified that in his experience (as the author of the best-selling book *I Loved Rogues**), when an elephant repeatedly stomped on a person's body, it was to ensure the individual was dead. And when it lashes out and seems to threaten anyone who comes near, it wasn't a loving gesture toward the man it just killed, but a warning to everyone else that it was capable and willing to do so again. After all, Slim had learned this firsthand, having survived similar attacks. One incident, in particular, elevated his status to a legend.

While working outside at the Brookfield Zoo in Chicago, with a bull elephant named Ziggy, Slim was thrust into a deadly showdown. Ziggy knocked him to the ground, got down on his knees,

---

* George W. "Slim" Lewis's book was originally published in 1955 under the title "Elephant Tramp" and later republished in 1979 with a new title "I Loved Rogues: The Life of an Elephant Tramp."

and repeatedly tried to crush him. Each time the large elephant lunged, Slim twisted onto his side and positioned his skinny frame right between the bull's tusks, narrowly avoiding getting stabbed. He remained trapped inside a cage of ivory until Ziggy lifted his head to try again. With the agility of a professional athlete, Slim rolled across the yard with the massive elephant persistently chasing and pinning him, until he finally managed a perilous escape.

Not only did the attack earn Slim his famous nickname, but a lucky spectator captured the entire event on film, and photographs of the deadly charge were featured in the *Chicago Tribune*. Newspapers nationwide picked up the remarkable story.

Slim did not make it out unscathed, however. He spent several weeks in intensive care recovering from a long list of broken bones, crushed organs, and other severe internal injuries. After spending most of that year in the hospital, everyone agreed it was a miracle he had survived.

Although he didn't have a formal education, Slim's knowledge of elephants went far beyond what I would have expected. It was clear that he wasn't your typical elephant man. He understood their behavior, biology, and mental abilities long before the scientific community did, and it was impressive.

Even in 1955, when *I Loved Rogues* was first published, he recognized striking parallels between elephant brains and ours. While many scientists emphasized the similarities of apes and humans, Slim was steadfast in his belief that elephants were more like us than any other animal species. I never imagined the pride and admiration I could feel for yet another circus trainer—but there it was.

Chilling stories of men being chased down and crushed to death by elephants graced the pages of *I Loved Rogues*, mirroring the tragic fate of both Morgan and Eloise. Given space outside of a cramped stall, it seemed they regularly knocked their trainers to the ground, dropped to their knees, and used their massive heads to shatter fragile bones. As I researched photographs and footage of various elephant attacks, I realized just how similar they were. This method of elephants crushing humans was far more common than I previously understood. It's no wonder Slim was incensed by the portrayal of Morgan's death; it was a gross misrepresentation of reality.

For Dr. Marlowe Hildebrandt, known as Ditty, the truth was straightforward and transparent. What happened to Morgan was not a mystery to her. She was a physician who had her own practice in Portland until shifting her focus to animals. After working as Doc's assistant at the zoo, she met Morgan and moved to Elephant Mountain, where she helped care for the animals left behind while he and Eloise were on the road.

In his book *Elephants Don't Snore,* author Leverett Richards recounted how Ditty directly contradicted her former colleagues.

"I think Morgan had a death wish," Ditty said, "I think all of those bulls were in musth. And he knew the odds. I don't buy the heart attack theory." She had spent as much time around Morgan's elephants as anyone.

A gentle breeze brought the giant oak to life as everything started to make sense. Now that all the articles were fresh in my mind, it was obvious that the reporters rarely ventured beyond the comfort of official statements. They relied heavily on professionals' testimony, doing little independent research of their own. Back then, the local press was nothing more than a mouthpiece for the zoo. If the sheriff's spokesman offered questionable details or influential zoo officials deliberately shaped the narrative, no one apparently ever thought to question it.

In hindsight, the deception was hardly surprising once I understood what was at stake. Exposing the truth would have jeopardized the zoo's lucrative enterprise, one built on the backs of baby elephants.

Hundreds of crows suddenly flew overhead, landing in the tree above me. Their noise was deafening, and I wondered if it was a feud, a long-awaited reunion, or a solemn gathering due to the death of a close friend. For a moment, I wished I knew a crow who could translate.

Patterns are a researcher's siren call; elusive oddities that speak quietly to the perceptive. In the numbers and scribbles across my notebooks, I'd noticed an alarming one. It revealed the magnitude of what was at play—for keeping elephants in captivity, at any cost. And it reinforced what I believed was the true motive behind the planted stories.

For nearly two decades following Packy's birth, there were no other successful* elephant births in the United States outside of Portland. Yet, the Oregon Zoo had a virtual baby boom.

Between 1962 (the year Packy was born) and 1980, a staggering *eighteen* elephants were born in Portland. It wasn't even until 1978, sixteen years after the birth of Packy, that a single baby elephant born anywhere else, lived past the age of one. During all that time, the Oregon Zoo was the country's exclusive source of baby elephants.

Although five died shortly after birth, thirteen survived. Of those, five were taken before their first birthday purchased by circuses or other zoos. Four more were sold at age two, and one at four. The separation of those young elephants was noted by the

---

* A "successful birth" is defined as a baby elephant that survives to the age of one year.

keepers as traumatic and distressing to the mothers. It was hardly surprising considering that in the wild, elephant calves aren't fully weaned until around five. Females stay together for life, while males disappear for short bouts, leaving the herd altogether by their late teens. Yet, studies show they remain in contact with their maternal herds most of their lives.

Oregon had developed a product that, for the first time, allowed any zoo with an elephant to move from financial hardship into prosperity. Prior to this, most zoos could barely keep their doors open. But once elephants entered the picture, the game changed. The more product they produced, the faster handlers separated them from their mothers, and the sooner everyone got paid. The breeding wars had begun.

Belle, Morgan's first elephant, had only one baby, Packy. But Pet matched the record set by Oregon's original elephant Rosy. Both exceeded expectations by having six babies each and, remarkably, did so by their thirties.

Pet was impregnated by Thonglaw by age seven, ten, thirteen, and fifteen. Then again by Packy at twenty-two and thirty-one. Rosy, by the age of ten, thirteen, seventeen, twenty-one, twenty-seven, and thirty. And Portland's third female, Tuy Hoa, was pregnant at seven, eleven and thirteen years old.

It proved to be quite a feat, considering there are no examples of wild elephants giving birth to so many so young. It revealed an alarming trend and one that had all the hallmarks of a puppy mill, driven solely by profit. Because it most certainly wasn't for the benefit of the elephants.

The Oregon Zoo stood unrivaled as the foremost breeder throughout much of the 20th century, earning the title of the "elephant breeding capital of the world." Then they introduced a second revolutionary concept: the first breeding and leasing contracts, ensuring payments on their valuable investments for years to come. They incentivized the entire operation, and it made them rich.

I'd noticed what I thought was a discrepancy when Kenneth sold Tunga to the zoo as a breeder, in the months following Morgan's death. Later, I realized it was one of the first contracts of its kind.

Several reports stated Tunga was sold for $5000, while others listed the price at $15,000. Upon discovering the true nature of the error, it became clear that it wasn't a typo—both were actually correct. The zoo paid Kenneth a down payment of $5000 for Tunga with "the option" to own the first baby he sired.

After the one-year-old calf (Sabu, later renamed Look-Chai) was taken from its mother Hanako, Kenneth was given a choice. He could either claim the baby and do with it as he pleased, or waive his ownership rights in exchange for a buyout payment of $10,000. In the end, that's what he chose, receiving a total of $15,000 for the sale of Tunga.

During that first year, Look-Chai was put on display at the zoo and ticket sales skyrocketed. Once again, massive crowds gathered to view the newborn, generating a staggering profit compared to what they paid to Kenneth.

To enhance their proceeds even further, they then sold Look-Chai just before his second birthday to the Ringling Bros. Circus, substantially boosting their earnings. They could also keep every baby Tunga sired for themselves and lease or sell those offspring too, though he never had any more calves while he remained in Portland.

When Warren Illif, the zoo's director at the time, called the sale of Tunga "a steal," he wasn't kidding. It was more like the steal of a century. And it hinted at another motive for why baby elephants were taken from their mothers at younger ages than anyone fully realized.

In 2013, a similar arrangement came to light, shocking those who believed the public would support such deals. An elephant bull named Tusko (formerly Sobik), who many thought was owned by the Oregon Zoo, was actually on loan as a breeder. In reality, he was the property of a private company, Have Trunk Will Travel. The owners, Gary and Kari Johnson, leased their elephants for events like commercials, fairs, birthday parties, circuses, and zoos.

The Johnsons were both raised in the circus, their father's renowned elephant trainers. Kari is the step-daughter of Smokey Jones, who trained Buddha and The Tuskers of Thailand—adding yet another twist to an already bizarre coincidence.

The Oregon Zoo paid them to lease Tusko, while the contract's fine print gave the couple ownership of the second, fourth, and sixth baby he sired. This compelled the zoo to breed Tusko with as many females as possible to maximize their profit. The more babies they could produce, the more they could keep, breed, lease or put on exhibit.

When someone secretly alerted *The Seattle Times* that the Johnsons were about to take Portland's beloved, a one-month-old elephant named Lily, the situation descended into chaos. And when the training tactics of Have Trunk Will Travel were exposed—videos online of Gary and Kari beating and shocking the elephants in their care—all hell broke loose.

At first, the zoo denied the existence of such a nefarious agreement, and did whatever they could to duck and jive each bomb being thrown at them, anything it seemed, to prevent the public from learning the truth. But the pit bull press (who had grown wise to the zoo's propaganda) had them by the throat until the slow drip of leaked information turned into a gushing flood and within days, the entire contract was exposed in its entirety.

With their backs against the wall, the zoo finally admitted—it was all true. They switched from defense mode to damage control, doing whatever they could to divert attention from the growing scandal. Instead, they began fundraising, begging the public and their rich donors for money to buy Lily out of her contract.

Two weeks later, the Oregon Zoo paid the Johnsons the staggering sum of $400,000 for the sale of Lily and Tusko. It exposed the sheer level of profit these kinds of legal agreements generated: from the mere $15,000 paid to Kenneth in 1983 to nearly half a million by 2013. Similar contracts existed between Have Trunk Will Travel and various zoos, proving these dealings were neither unusual nor unique.

If zoo officials were so confident they weren't doing anything wrong, then why hide it, why deny it, why go to such lengths to keep it a secret? Maybe people wouldn't object. Either way, we had the right to know, regardless of whether we accepted it or not. As a publicly funded institution, they at least owed us that.

Ultimately, the transaction turned out to be a rather expensive disappointment. Tusko sired no more offspring and died within two years of tuberculosis, while Lily succumbed to a deadly virus when she was just six. Even so, the zoo smashed attendance records due to her birth, softening the financial loss.

An object dropped onto my windshield, startling me. Curious, I opened my door to investigate and discovered it was a small acorn. After a brief examination, I placed it on the dashboard to admire it. It had flair, boasting its own French-style beret—a stylish touch for a seed.

A cloud momentarily blocked the sun, leaving me chilled. It reminded me of another somber moment in history: In the early 1970s, the Portland Zoological Society took control of the zoo from the city, which led to a major staff overhaul. Most of the longest serving employees were forced out, including Doc Maberry. They hired new personnel focused on one primary mission: to produce as many elephants as possible, no matter the cost.

In the years following, six elephants were conceived through inbreeding, and it shed light on just how desperate those men were for more. As word spread, the practice faced increased scrutiny, with *The New York Times*, among those condemning it. Though eventually phased out, four of the inbred calves died shortly after birth, and only one survived past the age of three.

Several keepers spoke out about the harm inbreeding caused, seeing it as a desperate and cruel act. Yet their complaints went unanswered. Although the zoological society's reign lasted just a few years, the damage inflicted had a lasting impact.

Over his last few months, Morgan grew disillusioned with the decisions being made at the zoo, as he shared in the letters he wrote to Shana. Occasionally, he suspected another veterinarian was experimenting on one of his elephants and raised hell. But like a conductor of a runaway train, he was powerless to regain control. All he wanted was to be the first to produce a baby elephant in captivity. And to keep his herd together, which he believed, was the key to their happiness. However, times changed faster than he ever could have imagined, spurred on by the desire of others to replicate Oregon's monumental breeding success. This rapid shift, along with the sudden death of Eloise, likely deepened his depression in the final stages of his life.

I found myself once again drawn to the delicate acorn—so

much hidden potential inside such a little seed. One day it could grow into a massive tree. I gazed into the branches of the large oak, imagining what it must have gone through to get to where it was. Perhaps that's what Buddha's story symbolized: a seed capable of growing into something spectacular. At that exact moment, the clouds parted, and my entire car was illuminated by the sun. I smiled. Finally, my higher power was making herself known.

I placed the small, elegant acorn in a nook next to my steering wheel, where it would serve as a reminder of greater things to come. There was some reason Buddha had chosen me to learn his story. I simply had to trust that the purpose of knowing it might reveal itself in time. Though I was still wrecked and uncertain, there was also a slight glimmer of hope.

I started my car but instead of going home, it drove me to Sauvie Island, to a little slice of paradise just outside Portland where two members of my herd waited. Whenever I showed up unannounced, they knew there was trouble. They did what good elephants do: they wrapped their trunks around me, shoved me into the middle of a safe space, and offered comfort when I needed it the most.

CHAPTER 20

They said in my early days of sobriety that if I wanted to remain sober, I needed to do two things: change my playground and change my playmates. At first, I wasn't on board with that theory at all. I couldn't imagine giving up Pennie and Dave. We were so close that I simply could not picture a world without them.

We met in 1994, right after my twenty-second birthday, at a monthly event called Last Thursday in the Pearl District in Portland. All the art galleries threw open their doors to attract the 'who's who' of society. It was fun to dress up and mingle with that crowd, but I went primarily for the alcohol served at each one, most of it free.

It was by pure chance that the three of us found ourselves at the same bar in the back of a gallery after a rather boring evening. When I arrived, a woman was the only other person there, though I hardly noticed. Irritated at having to pay for my own drink, I considered the night, up to that point, a total bust. As soon as the bartender handed me a glass of wine, the stranger leaned in.

"They call this wine," she whispered, "but it's just grape juice flavored with regret."

Her choice of words made me giggle. "Great," I said, with a loud sigh. "A perfect end to a fucked-up waste of time."

"This Last Thursday sucked, didn't it?" she asked.

"It was so lame."

That's when I noticed how well her bright red lipstick worked with her pale complexion and red hair. Only someone who knew the art of make-up could have paired a color like that. Dressed in black from head to toe (my favorite), complete with a long, leopard-print coat, she exuded a fierce, confident style and I liked her immediately. When she rose to grab a napkin, I couldn't help but admire how tall and elegant she was.

"What's your name?" she asked when she sat back down.

"I'm Debbie. Debbie Ethell," I said, extending my glass for a toast.

She clinked hers with mine. "Well, it's nice to meet you, Miss Debbie. I'm Pennie."

Then a charming man with a shock of white hair slid in next to her. He was in his mid-forties, like Pennie, and wore a navy blue suit jacket with a pair of jeans and smart leather shoes. His face had all the lines of someone who enjoyed life, but it was his broad, contagious smile paired with an equally infectious laugh that endeared him to everyone.

"That's *Penny Lane* if you please."

"Oh, Dave!" Pennie squealed, giving him a hug.

"Miss Debbie, you have to meet Dave!"

I liked him instantly, too. When he bought us another round, I liked him even more. Their connection seemed close—a familiarity one develops over time—but I was surprised to learn they had met only a few weeks earlier. It was obvious they adored each other, but there wasn't anything romantic between them, just the beginning of a deep and enduring friendship.

Pennie explained that Dave was a photographer and had traveled to nearly every country in the world, winning awards everywhere he went. In fact, he was among the most successful photographers in Portland, though far too humble to ever admit it. Pennie raised horses on a farm in the stunning Sauvie Island region, a few miles north of the city, where she also worked as a marketing executive.

"Hey, why don't you girls come back to my loft? I have plenty of wine and you can stay for as long as you like," Dave suggested.

He didn't have to ask twice as we abandoned our posts and followed him across the street to an old brick building that had been converted into luxurious two-story lofts. We quickly realized that Dave's was one of the most popular hangouts in town—a chill atmosphere where people came to meet new friends, unwind, and party. There was always a celebrity or two flitting around; directors, artists, actors, and models were everywhere, popping in after their fashion shows.

The far side of the gorgeous loft was Dave's photography studio, and the other had a beautiful wood-carved bar with over-sized stools surrounded by couches and lounge chairs. Veda, an Egyptian Basenji dog with no bark, ruled the palace and Dave bent to her every whim. Everyone who visited knew the rule: *Veda was Queen*. People stopped in around the clock because Dave, a consummate night owl, never slept before dawn. When we weren't mingling with the "society" at his loft, we were at Pennie's farm on the island. The contrast between the two couldn't have been more different.

Pennie and I both had a farm-girl spirit, so when we wanted something more laid back, we went to her place and lit a bonfire. Hers was more of an 'invite only' affair, and she was picky about who came. But that crowd was always interesting, too. She invited the incredibly wealthy and mixed them with blue-collar workers: waiters and delivery drivers, people she met in the world that she liked. She had this innate ability to recognize unique personalities and combine individuals from totally different societies, who would never cross paths any other way. And it worked. I watched an award-winning film director talking with a bus driver for hours one evening while Pennie smiled and toasted me from across the fire. The two became friends that night and have remained so since. It was pure magic.

Later, as we relaxed in front of one of Sauvie Island's legendary sunsets, Pennie turned to me and Dave and said, "I think it's about time for you both to get Lyman-ized."

We had no clue what that meant, but we jumped into the seats behind hers on the big tractor as she drove it across a large field to an ordinary house. Dave handed me a joint while we leaned back and waited for her to come out.

Soon, an older gentleman appeared wearing overalls with a stern look on his face. He walked over and began examining us from head to toe like a drill sergeant looking for a wrinkle. Our giggles quickly turned to silence while Pennie stood behind him, as grim as I had ever seen her.

The man halted abruptly at the base of the tractor, his voice erupting with the force of a thunderclap.

"What are you trying to do to my daughter?"

The sheer force of his words jolted me upright, my heart pounding as the weight of his fury filled the air. I was so stoned I could barely speak.

"I—ah—ah—I—I—I—"

Dave stifled a nervous giggle, offering no help whatsoever. Suddenly, the man's laughter exploded, reverberating through the air with the ferocity of a wolf howling at the moon. I couldn't tell if Dave was shaking from laughter or fear as he cowered in the seat next to me. The man turned to Pennie.

"Jeez Pen, are your friends so gullible they don't know I'm kidding? Come on in, you guys, let's have a drink."

Dave immediately cracked up, apparently aware it was a joke the entire time. I, on the other hand, took several minutes to gather my composure and steady my nerves. Pennie ushered her father back into the house, then returned with a wide grin.

"You should have seen the look on your face" she laughed, as I shook my head still trying to process what had just happened. Finally, I slipped out of my seat and followed them inside.

The truth is, Lyman scared the living hell out of me, stoned or sober. We found out later that not everyone survived being "Lyman-ized," but once I understood his wicked sense of humor, I came to appreciate the unique and colorful character he was.

Pennie, Dave, and I took several trips together and as our bond grew, so did my drinking. They both practiced something unheard-of for someone like me: *moderation*. That word wasn't even part of my vocabulary then. I did everything to excess, and my disease blossomed.

The first time they bailed me out of jail, it was funny. Dave brought me back to one of Pennie's bonfires and all her guests leaned in as I told them in great detail what had happened. The second time still had a ring of humor to it, but by the third time in as many weeks, hilarity was replaced by concern. I realized then I needed to cover my tracks, hide how much I drank, and pretend I actually had the ability to slow things down.

I hid bottles of alcohol around Pennie's farm, so whenever I left to go to the bathroom, I caught myself back up. At Dave's loft, there was always someone who could discreetly get me a few lines of cocaine to reverse the effects of the alcohol and make me feel normal again.

A few years after we met, Pennie began building a home for herself on her property. I spent my days helping her and Lyman working around the farm. She operated the large tractor while I handled the smaller equipment. In the evenings, we sat on her newly poured foundation and played "house."

"Let's go have a drink in your bedroom," she said, giggling.

"Ohhh, good idea!"

We picked up our chairs and moved a few feet over an orange string. We toasted with red plastic cups, admiring the spectacular view from each room. Pennie bought a camper trailer for me to stay in, likely to reduce the risk of my getting arrested again for driving home drunk. I was an expensive friend.

One afternoon, while working on her farm, she left to take a phone call.

"You'll never guess who that was," she said when she returned.

I had no clue. When it came to Pennie, it could have been anyone.

"Cameron Crowe," she continued.

I stopped what I was doing and stared in disbelief. "The famous director? That Cameron Crowe?"

One year earlier, another film he had written and directed, *Jerry Maguire,* had won two Oscars, propelling him to the top tier of Hollywood's most sought-after directors.

"Yes! And you'll never guess what he asked me," she continued.

"What? What is it?" I could hardly imagine.

"Well, I don't think it's that big a deal—"

"Would you stop? What did he say?" I hated it when she downplayed a momentous event.

"It was interesting because he said he had written a new script about how we first met, and—I guess he wants to turn it into a film. He asked for my permission to use my name."

"What? What do you mean, 'it's not a big deal'?"

"That's what it sounded like to me," she defended. "Besides, who would want to watch a movie about that, anyway?"

"Oh sure," I said, rolling my eyes. "I think people would watch just about anything he touches."

Pennie laughed and shook her head. Although *Jerry Maguire* was Cameron's biggest hit, he had already achieved cult status for his films: *Fast Times at Ridgemont High*, *Say Anything*, and *Singles*. I knew bits and pieces of her past, but had learned that since Pennie didn't find it particularly interesting, she assumed others wouldn't, either. As usual, she was wrong.

Growing up, her life revolved around horses and music. It was during a ride on her beloved Quarter Horse, Lady, that the two unexpectedly collided. During a competition at the State Fair in Salem in the early 1970s, a relatively unknown musician wandered into the horse barn. Captivated by Pennie's skill and grace, he introduced himself and the two became friends. Later, he would recall her quick wit and hilarious sense of humor. Her magnetic personality quickly made her a favorite in the local music scene.

That unknown musician, however, wouldn't stay that way for long. When his first hit catapulted him into mega-stardom, Pennie found herself in the eye of the storm. Soon, she was surrounded by the rising royalty of rock and roll—musicians, managers, and the people who made things happen behind the scenes. She was never star-struck, and her talent for being able to mingle with anyone, regardless of who they were, made her a steady anchor in the stormiest seas of fame. When she left Oregon for California full-time, she became known in their circles as the one and only *Penny Lane*.

Eventually, Pennie, her best friend, known to everyone as *Marvelous Meg*, along with a few friends, found themselves immersed in the iconic music scene of the 1970s. With her keen marketing instinct, Pennie christened them "The Flying Garter Girls," a name destined to make its mark upon the chambers of celebrity. They weren't groupies, at least not in the stereotypical sense. They had no interest in the spotlight or fleeting thrills—but were muses—friends of the musicians without ever stepping into the public eye. Their discretion is what set them apart. The Flying Garter Girls never named names about who or what they saw. They didn't write books, give interviews, or reveal any secrets about their famous friends, unlike traditional groupies who thrived on exploiting their associations for fame.

Pennie had a way of making any situation, no matter how ordinary, into something unexpected and fun. Even at her farm, when rich (and sometimes) famous people showed up, she handed them a raw hot dog to toast in the bonfire: there was no five-star service waiting for them. And they absolutely loved it. With that much success, no one ever thinks to serve the rich and powerful a hot dog—except for her.

Long before Cameron became a world-renowned director, the two had crossed paths. At just fifteen, shortly before he became a freelance writer for *Rolling Stone* magazine, he attempted to gain entry backstage for a show at The Old Globe Theater in San Diego. Although the headliner was up-and-coming, they were already creating a stir across the music scene. When the security guards turned him away, Pennie stepped in and let him through. That one simple act not only opened the door for him to get close to the band, but to a friendship that has lasted ever since.

A few weeks after Cameron's initial phone call, Pennie informed me that the script he had written, that she was convinced would be nothing more than a small indie film, had already been purchased by none other than Steven Spielberg's production company, DreamWorks—the biggest powerhouse in Hollywood. Things were about to get a whole lot more interesting.

By the following year, Pennie's world had turned upside down. Kate Hudson was cast to play her in the movie and invites to the most exclusive events—from Portland to Los Angeles—began pouring in.

Meanwhile, I was living in Ojai, California with *Marvelous Meg*, just before I entered a drug treatment facility in Oregon. When I got out, Pennie invited me to join her at those parties, but since I had only recently left rehab and was staying in a halfway house, trying to learn a new way of life, I turned down every invitation—except for one.

Pennie hosted a spectacular "Secret Garden Party," in a forest on her property complete with bands, fairies, peasants, and visually stunning acrobats in glowing costumes swinging from the trees. Storm Large, among Portland's more famous musicians, headlined the event, and hundreds of people converged onto Pennie's fifteen-acre farm. Her fields were a sea of tents and campers as far as the eye could see.

Dave, my sister Carrie, and I arrived dressed like peasants. I convinced myself that in their presence, everything would be fine. Meg had flown in from Ojai, and it was the first time I'd seen her since leaving rehab. She was concerned about my well-being in a sea of temptation. Alcohol was everywhere, and it was harder than we thought to get access to anything else. Using every ounce of my willpower, I clung to my sobriety, which hung by a thread. Shortly after arriving at the party, I realized I was definitely not fine and left.

Instead of going home, I drove to my sponsor's house, where she reminded me once again that most of us needed to change our playgrounds and our playmates if we had any chance of remaining sober. After some difficult conversations with several people from my past, I called Pennie and Dave. I knew what I had to do, and I removed myself from both their lives.

"How long?" Pennie pleaded when I told her.

"I don't know. I have no idea," I said over the phone.

"Well, can we at least talk to you?"

"No. It's hard to explain, but I just need to pull back from everything. From you, from everyone," I cried.

She didn't understand, and I couldn't blame her—I barely understood it myself. How could I convey that certain people, including her and Dave, were a trigger. Simply being in their presence made me feel so lighthearted and full of energy that I wanted to indulge in drugs and alcohol to excess. They rarely got drunk, and neither had any real idea how out of control my drinking had become, since I'd gotten so good at hiding it. The recurring arrests were the sole indication that all was not quite as it seemed. Yet something deep inside knew my sponsor was right, no matter how much I resisted. Disappearing was my only chance to survive. And so I did. For *ten* long years.

I often say it took me ten years before I truly felt normal in my skin, sober. It took at least that amount of time before I stopped noticing those drinking around me—strangers in restaurants who left their drinks unfinished, something only alcoholics like myself pay attention to. There is another part to that story, though: one's world gets quite small when lived one day at a time. Days turn into weeks and months into years before the passage of it all is fully realized. And once so much time has passed, even a tiny phone seems too heavy to lift. Did I need ten years not to see my friends? I don't know. Maybe. But as I look back now, I am convinced that everything happened exactly the way it was supposed to.

A few years after my disappearance, Dave tracked me down to inform me that Lyman had died after a long illness. I imagined how devastated Pennie was, as the two had always been close. He invited me to the funeral, but I declined. Despite my admiration for Pennie's father, I didn't want to make that day about me. It needed to be about him and his legacy. Anything else would only be a distraction, so instead I stayed home and lit a candle. I missed the death of Dave's dear Veda, too, and lit another candle for her. I felt like an awful person for not being there for either.

I remained in minimal contact with Dave over the next several years and though I loved hearing his voice, I was still shy, too afraid that the cravings I had fought so hard against would return, even after so long. My sobriety was the most precious thing I had. Given the chance to reflect on how drastically my life had changed and how far I'd come, I was terrified of going back.

Every so often I called Dave, and he always answered his phone as if we'd just spoken yesterday. I loved him all the more for that. There was no judgment or animosity, only kindness and love. Eventually, I started wandering further from my shell to meet with him in person. I was relieved to learn he had moved to a new residence, that was no longer Portland's most popular hangout.

One day, he insisted we go see Pennie together. Ten years was enough. By then, I was terrified of what she would say. A decade is a lifetime not to speak to someone. He picked me up, and we made the familiar journey to her home on the island. As we pulled down the long driveway, and came to a stop, I was flooded by memories.

Pennie was unaware I was with Dave, and when she stepped outside to welcome us, failed to recognize me. She greeted us politely as she did with all her guests, and then looked at me with a puzzled expression. Suddenly it registered, and without saying a word, she threw herself into my arms and sobbed. For a moment, I froze. It wasn't the reaction I expected, but I was deeply grateful. And just like that, I was back in the fold of my long-lost herd.

Pennie and I spent hours talking about all the things I had missed. Cameron's film, *Almost Famous*, became another cult favorite. By the time it hit theaters, I had already lived in my halfway house for over a year.

While waiting at a bus stop one rainy afternoon, the title caught my eye on a marquee outside of a movie theater. Although it was released months prior, I could not bring myself to watch it until I saw that sign. Without thinking, I crossed the street and bought a ticket. Then I witnessed the journey of my friend unfold on the screen. Once it ended, I was overcome with emotion. It was *beautiful*. Kate Hudson had captured Pennie's essence brilliantly.

Instead of taking another bus home after it was over, I walked. It was a wet, rainy day, and the gloomy weather mirrored how I felt. Watching her story made my heart ache. It reminded me of how much I had missed my friends. Yet there was also an acute awareness that I had done the right thing by stepping away. Had I stayed and embraced the chaos of Pennie's newfound fame, I never would have survived, let alone remained sober. And I hated every minute of that feeling.

I told her how I'd watched, from the living room in my halfway house, as Tom Cruise handed Kate Hudson a Golden Globe for her performance as "Penny Lane." And a few weeks after that when Tom Hanks presented Cameron Crowe with Hollywood's most prestigious award—an Oscar for Best Original Screenplay.

I saw Pennie on television occasionally after that. Due to the film's success, she became Portland's most famous muse. Images and videos captured her attending events across the globe, while the internet was flooded with photos of her posing alongside a variety of actors, actresses, and music royalty.

Soon, ten years felt like ten minutes, and the three of us picked up right where we left off, as if we had never been apart. It was a powerful lesson, and a gift. I did what I had to do to take care of myself, even if it meant giving up the friendships that were everything to me.

When I arrived on Sauvie Island after the long afternoon spent with Violet at the secret museum, Pennie and Dave immediately sensed something was wrong. Instead of asking questions, they put me to work in the kitchen as Pennie made one of her wonderfully prepared home-cooked meals. It was a reminder of the comfort and solace found in the simple act of sharing food between close friends. Rather than pressing me for answers, they gave me the space I needed, knowing that I would eventually share what happened.

Pennie handed me a glass of sparkling water, and Dave offered me a blanket as I took my seat in a lawn chair between the two, in the shadow of Pennie's beautiful home. We turned to face the sun just as a golden light swept over the breathtaking landscape. I felt myself begin to relax and let go of the day's earlier struggles. As long as I had my closest friends—those who put me back together and lifted me up again—I could handle whatever was coming, no matter how hard or awful.

"Let's make a toast," said Pennie.

"To Imenti," she motioned to Dave.

"To Aitong," she nodded at me.

"To Emily," she lifted her own glass.

The three of us paused, smiling at one another, before we yelled in unison.

"To ELEANOR!" We clinked our glasses toward the magnificent bright pink sky.

"To Eleanor," Pennie said quietly before taking a sip.

Eleanor wasn't just the first elephant who had inspired me all those years ago. It was also the name of her beloved mother, who passed away the year before I met her, and one more reason we were bonded for life.

CHAPTER 21

The darkness of morning was interrupted by a soft rustling, followed by two quiet knocks. As I emerged from a deep sleep, the sound floated across the blurred line between dream and reality. After a few moments, I heard it again—*knock, knock*. I sat up, squinting in the dim light, and traced it to a murky blob outside one of my bay windows. The glow from my phone revealed a large woodpecker hugging the screen.

"Hey there," I said, as it watched me closely. "Are you stuck?"

The window didn't open and was too high off the ground for me to set the bird free. The only way to reach it was with a tall ladder. I'd have to wait until later to borrow one from a neighbor. In the meantime, I lit a few candles and eased into the quietest part of morning.

The woodpecker continued watching me, swiveling its head as I scooped coffee grounds into my French press. Then it cocked to one side while I poured the boiling water, as if learning how to make the perfect cup. I wrapped myself in a soft blanket and settled into my favorite chair to read a few passages from my favorite meditation book. But this time I did so out loud, to share the wisdom.

As the sun began to rise, I noticed the woodpecker's beautiful color. Its belly was covered in spots and there was a trace of brilliant red under one of its wings, with a matching red mustache—the telltale sign of his sex. He was a full-grown Northern Flicker, about the size of a crow. I wondered how a bird that large had gotten stuck to my screen when he could have easily landed on the wide ledge of the windowsill below.

Situated less than two feet away, he twisted his head each time I made an especially good point about something and proved himself to be a great listener. The wildlife around us slowly woke as the soft glow of dawn painted the sky pink while I finished my first cup of coffee, then my second.

After an hour or so, he pecked my window twice—*knock, knock*—and then he flew away, leaving one delicate feather behind, evidence perhaps that he wasn't a figment of my imagination. I was stunned and wondered how he'd gotten himself unstuck. When I examined the screen, there was no sign of what had held him there; no tears, no apparent reason whatsoever. I scanned the yard, wondering if he was injured and fell into the grass, but my attention was drawn to a tree where I could hear his distinctive bird call. Bewildered, I sat and watched him for the rest of the morning until he disappeared.

That was the first time I met the woodpecker, but he showed up every few days after that. He wasn't stuck to my screen, but purposefully attached himself to the only window with a bird's-eye view into my apartment. Sometimes I was already awake and other times still asleep, but each time he knocked quietly, as if trying to get my attention.

After several appearances, I looked forward to his random visits. When I thought about what I should call him, I was listening to one of my most cherished albums: Johnny Cash's *Live at San Quentin*, recorded inside San Quentin Prison. At the moment the woodpecker appeared, Mr. Cash began to sing a particular favorite, "A Boy Named Sue," answering my question in real time.

Over coffee I told my friend Tina, a Reiki Master and a life coach, about Sue and his regular visits. As we caught up, I couldn't help but notice how the sun accentuated the blonde streaks in her hair and how the color in her sweater brought out the deepest blue in her eyes. We were both still grappling with the awful news of Leslie's diagnosis, since Tina was also one of her closest friends. The woodpecker story provided a much-needed reprieve, complemented by the peaceful vibe of Ava's—a quaint coffee shop with large plants and strategically placed fountains that offered privacy from nearby conversations.

"Let's look up the spiritual significance of a woodpecker," Tina suggested. I hadn't considered that, and waited while she pulled it up on her phone.

"Ohhh," she said, scrolling slowly.

"What is it?"

She handed the phone to me. "I think you'd better read it for yourself."

The symbolic meaning of a woodpecker was a sign of significant change, a shifting of perspective, and a warning to pay attention. The sound of Sue knocking on my window represented the knocking of an opportunity.

"I wonder," Tina said, as I passed the phone back, "if learning the identity of that elephant skull indicates a change in course or a new direction."

"Buddha?" I asked, slouching in my chair. "I don't know how."

For weeks, I felt trapped inside a stale, poorly decorated hallway, lined with locked doors to the outside, leading somewhere I could not reach. Buddha's story, his fate, pressed down on me like a firm hand on my shoulders, insisting that I confront the past, *his* past. Yet, I still didn't understand why.

Days marched on in relentless succession, each one leaving me more exhausted than the next. My depression deepened, and my world shrank. I tried to find my bearings, but each prayer was met by more crickets.

Tina appeared, just as she usually did, at the exact moment I needed her. When she'd called and asked to meet, it felt like a break from bad weather—a ray of sunlight peeking from behind a cloud.

"Where did you used to go to feel inspired?" The weight of her words hung heavy in the air, and I had to think hard to remember.

"The secret museum was always my favorite, but now it just reminds me of him and what happened. It feels dark and ugly, and I don't like to go there anymore ..." my voice trailed off, as I took a deep breath. "I used to love the science building at Portland State, where I performed necropsies."

The large, green science building was like an enigma to me when I first arrived on campus. Gaining entry required a special pass, and those were only issued to students enrolled in the advanced science classes, which I was not. Until then, I would have to wait. But I'd stalked that building like a burglar and found a secret way in. I walked the hallways illegally and read the walls, which were covered in dissertations of emerging science on all sorts of creatures: frogs, salamanders, dolphins, and whales. No one ever questioned what I was doing there, and once inside, I pretended to blend in.

For two years, that building taunted and inspired me. Once the day finally arrived, with my long-awaited pass firmly in hand, I sprinted across campus and swiped my card to enter through the front door the way I was supposed to—*legally*. Unable to hide my exhilaration, I flopped down on one of the couches on the second floor, where I stared straight up into the belly of a whale. The wait had been worth every minute.

"Why don't you go back there?" Tina suggested. "Let the room embrace you again, have a look around, rest your eyes on the things that used to make you happy, and see what happens."

It was an odd suggestion, one I never would have come up with on my own. Though I no longer had a pass card to enter the building, I knew enough people who worked there to be let in. But when I thought about sneaking back in like the burglars did, I felt the first twinge of excitement I'd had in weeks.

Later that afternoon, I flopped down on the same couch and stared into the belly of that whale. I smiled as my spirits lifted. Tina was right—I did feel better. The skeleton, meticulously constructed on the ceiling above, was massive even though it was just a baby. A full-grown Humpback was longer than the entire science building. The skull alone could reach nearly twenty feet, and the only skeletons of those existed in real museums, large enough to hold such things.

Each flipper bore a striking resemblance to a human arm, yet with notable distinctions between the upper and lower sections. It even had a wrist and a hand, four extremely long fingers, and a single bone in place of a thumb, offering surprising dexterity for gripping objects. The scapula, or shoulder blade, allowed each powerful flipper to move independently, with a wide range of motion similar to the way we move our own arms. From the outside, it appeared to be nothing more than a fin. I smiled, thinking about how much I loved peeling back the mysteries of science.

The haunting melody of a whale song suddenly echoed through the lobby. I recognized it as I slowly sat up and looked toward the source. I distinctly remembered the first time I'd heard it. When I was seven, *National Geographic* magazine released an edition I couldn't wait to get my hands on. The issue was dedicated to whales and included an actual album, neatly pressed into the middle crease. Titled "Songs of the Humpback Whale," it was produced and recorded by Roger and Katy Payne (she would go on to make the groundbreaking discovery that elephants, like whales, also use infrasound to communicate over long distances). I listened until it became too scratched to play.

In 1979, that recording sold over 125,000 copies and went multi-platinum. Thanks to the foresight of the Paynes and *National Geographic*, we finally had context where none existed before. That album brought whales into our living rooms, and allowed us to understand them in ways we couldn't before. For the very first time, the public gained a deeper appreciation of the world's largest marine mammals. People who would never study whales suddenly saw them in a new light, connecting with them on a personal level.

I walked down the hallway, enchanted by the operatic symphony, and peeked through a crack in a door. The professor stood quietly in front of her class, allowing the students to absorb each section of music. It was an advanced marine mammal biology class that left a lasting impression. Not only did she play the album I hadn't heard since childhood, but it also deepened my fascination with elephants.

Both the largest marine mammals and the largest land mammals—the whales and the elephants—share common traits. Each possesses a large brain, complex social structures, long lifespans, wicked intelligence, and the ability to communicate across vast distances using infrasound. When researchers set out to study a new species, they often start by looking at a similar one: a method known as comparative anatomy.

A photograph on the overhead projector displayed the skulls of a whale and an elephant, side by side, cut in half. The interior of each shared a common structural pattern: an intricate network of air sacs resembling a large, exaggerated honeycomb. Though it's presumed they're related to infrasound, no one is certain.

Then the professor dropped her first bombshell.

"Each year, a different Humpback whale composes the first verse of a new song …"

Confused murmurs filled the classroom. I smiled, knowing what she was about to reveal.

"In the Southern Hemisphere, a male Humpback begins a new song in the breeding grounds of the French Polynesian islands."

She pointed to a map on the wall.

"The first singer composes the first verse before another comes along, sings it exactly as he heard it, and composes the second. Then a third male sings those two verses, note for note, before adding a third. This continues with each whale, creating a new section of a song until they decide it's complete. Each song typically contains several verses and can last anywhere from thirty minutes to several hours."

A hand shot up in the air.

"Are you calling it verses because it's a block of similar sounds, or are you saying it's actually a 'verse'? I'm also a music major, so I want to understand the distinction," the student said.

The professor smiled.

"I was hoping someone would ask that question. Roger and Katy Payne, who discovered that whales were in fact *singing*, were also accomplished musicians who understood the laws of music before they redirected their focus to biology. Due to their unique background, they recognized a familiar pattern in the whale song, as it contained the essential components of a human song.

We call each section a 'verse' because, according to the rules of music, that is precisely what it is. Each segment of a Humpback whale song has a recurring pattern of sounds, and they exhibit striking similarities in structure and repetition.

Each song contains multiple parts, such as melody, harmony, repetition, and rhythm. The Paynes recognized a highly sophisticated level of organization that even includes rhyme. Rhyming is one of the ways humans remember long passages of text, and it appears, whales do it too. What's more surprising, is they tuck their breath between notes, just like human singers, never interrupting the actual performance of the song."

The entire room fell silent. Everyone seemed as shocked by the information as I was when I'd first learned it.

"I don't get it," another student said. "How can anyone possibly tell all that just by listening to whale sounds?"

"Because of this," the professor said, plunging the room into darkness. Illuminated on the wall was a digital image. "This is a spectrogram—a visual representation of sound on paper."

Two side-by-side graphs revealed similar wave patterns, each featuring a Time Axis labeled "sound duration" and a Frequency Axis ranging from the lowest to the highest frequencies. Unbeknownst to the class, the graphs were a comparison between a whale song and a human song.

"It's when we look at recordings of sound—even the silent sound waves of infrasound—that we can see the underlying patterns," the professor continued.

She directed the class's attention to the first graph, where she pointed to a bright red letter 'A.' With another click, a group of letters emerged, scattered across each wave, pinpointing peaks and valleys and unveiling clear and distinct letter combinations.

Once the class saw each sound, or a unique wave marked with a specific letter, the pattern was obvious. Then it was easy to track the beginning of a new verse or a new combination of letters. When a sequence like AABCCD appeared again later in the graph, it signified the repetition of an earlier verse. The professor then revealed that one graph represented a human song while the other was a whale song, highlighting remarkable similarities between the two. The class was stunned.

She then explained that once the humpback aria was complete, it would then cross the entire Southern Hemisphere, almost always traveling in the same direction, from east to west.[*]

"Each male maestro sings the identical song throughout the rest of that year," the professor continued, "rarely missing a single note. Think about that for a moment. Not only does each whale remember the individual notes of a song after hearing it just once, but they also retain the harmony and melody that goes along with it. How many humans do you know that have a memory capable of that? Imagine someone who, after hearing a song just one time, can then sing every note exactly as they heard it."

The class buzzed with excitement as a door to a hidden universe cracked open, offering a glimpse into a world they had yet to explore. I quietly observed as my favorite professor planted the

---

[*] Due to a land bridge, the Southern Hemisphere whales are isolated from their Northern Hemisphere counterparts, resulting in distinct songs for each group. As a result, two unique songs—one from the north and one from the south—circulate the globe annually.

seeds of inspiration, just as she had done with me, nurturing each student like a master gardener. Little did they know it was but the beginning of a much larger story.

Mimicry, the act of repeating another's sounds (like the songs of the Humpback), is also at the heart of human language. The ability to mimic requires a variety of cognitive skills, as well as an outstanding memory. That is why any species caught doing so is deemed exceptionally intelligent. Imitation serves as an essential process through which knowledge, behavior, and tradition are passed down and preserved within a society.

Human babies mimic the sounds of their parents. Initially, simple words such as "ma-ma" mean nothing, but once that word is associated with their mother—then the phenomenon of vocal learning occurs. In other words, vocal imitation is the first brick in the foundation of human language.

When anthropologists began exploring the origins of human language, they also made another fascinating discovery; language, art, and culture emerged simultaneously in the human brain. Whenever scientists find one of those three elements in an animal species, they look for the other two. And that is exactly what happened with the whales, suggesting we may have a whole lot more in common than anyone previously realized.

At first, researchers thought humpback whale songs were related to breeding, but further investigation has challenged that theory. The intricate and diverse nature of each song suggests a deeper, more complex purpose, beyond ordinary mating rituals, and why many in the scientific community have begun to classify whale songs as a form of art, hinting at the potential for sophisticated language. This led scientists to dig deeper, searching for evidence of culture within whale communities.

One such discovery was bubble-net feeding, a fascinating example of how humpback whales practice cultural behavior—a technical skill that is passed down socially, with individuals teaching each other.

Researchers observed one experienced whale diving deep while a group of younger humpbacks stayed close to the surface, watching and learning, like students in a classroom. The skilled whale would blow a complex pattern of bubbles, forming a large circle—or underwater net—to trap schools of fish, allowing the entire group to feast. The younger whales then tried to create their own bubble-nets, but left huge openings that allowed the fish to escape. Over time, with the older whale's guidance, each member perfected the technique.

This behavior shows their remarkable ability to cooperate and coordinate through practice. The presence of both art and culture in whales—two fingers of the three-pronged fork—suggests that complex languages also exist, similar to how these traits evolved in the human brain.

The next series of scientific grenades dropped onto those unsuspecting students revealed that scientists have already discovered twenty-one separate "codas" (individual patterns of clicks similar to letters in our alphabet) used by Sperm whales. That alone implies they can create all the combinations of language that we can with our own twenty-six letter system.

For years, scientists have known that dolphins call each other by name, a behavior also observed in orcas. And dolphins have languages that contain at least 60,000 separate words, surpassing the vocabulary found in any spoken by people. Orcas, which are also a dolphin species, exhibit another unique trait found only in humans and birds. They possess a wider range of dialects than any human language on the planet, with each individual pod having its own.

They speak a familiar language but with an accent, in the same way that Irish English sounds different from Australian English. A distinction so pronounced that if a baby orca is captured and put into a tank after learning its family's dialect, scientists can use that to identify every member of its wild family—no matter what ocean they live in around the world.

After turning on the lights, the professor resumed her speech, allowing the students a moment for their eyes to adjust to the brightness.

"Five million years before the first humans appeared," she said, pointing to the far side of an evolutionary chart. "For five million years longer than we've been here, whales and elephants were already developing skills like sonar and infrasound. They were also creating complex dialects and learning advanced ways to communicate, similar to human languages."

And with that, the minds of the class were officially blown. I grinned to myself as I walked back down the hallway to my couch, contemplating the profound lesson of the day. Since humans were given the gift of hands, we focused our evolutionary energy outward into the things we could build. But whales and elephants harnessed the power of their minds and developed all of that same energy inward.

As I thought about the future of our world, I couldn't help but wonder what it would look like in another five million years. Considering that whales and elephants have had such a long head start on us, I think it's safe to assume we've barely scratched the surface of what they can do.

Within elephant societies, culture had already been established—when they revisit a site where a loved one died, or they practice social and cooperation skills. Yet mimicry—the gateway to sophisticated language—had never been discovered.

That is, until two remarkable individuals got caught whispering something nobody had heard before. At just the right moment, a scientist who'd studied elephant communication—and one of the few capable of recognizing its significance—took a listen for herself. She uncovered a hidden aspect of elephant behavior and a secret primed for revelation.

It was a discovery that hinted at far more to come, poised to reshape not just our understanding of elephants but perhaps the very concept of intelligence itself.

CHAPTER 22

*T*he Kenyan sun dipped below the horizon, transforming the landscape from day to night within minutes. Along the equatorial belt, dusk swiftly gives way to the rising moon. In a seamless transition, the invisible hand of Mother Nature transforms her canvas from warm, rich colors to a deep indigo backdrop with a single stroke of her brush.

The keepers, who had just tucked the elephants in for the evening, sat on a short cement wall, reflecting on their day as the full moon cast a silver glow when Jill emerged from the shadows. Her frequent visits to Voi were a welcomed sight by both the men and the elephants.

Jill Woodley had spent much of her life immersed in the Kenyan wilderness and few were more familiar with the sounds of the night. As the eldest daughter of Daphne Sheldrick, she grew up alongside Eleanor, rescuing orphans in Tsavo National Park. There, her stepfather, David Sheldrick, managed one half of the expansive preserve, while her father, Bill Woodley, oversaw the other.

On that evening, she heard a sound unlike any other, echoing through the still night air.

"*Ulisikia hivyo?*" *Did you hear that?* She whispered as she approached the keepers, illuminated by the soft light.

"Yes," a husky voice answered in the darkness—unmistakably Thoni, short for Gathoni.

Jill paused, listening for the sound again, *"Umewahi kusikia kabla?"* she asked quietly. *Have you ever heard it before?*

"Ni tembo wanaotoa sauti hii," Thoni continued. *It is the elephants who make this sound.*

"Tembo ... kweli?" The elephants ... really? Jill squinted toward the elephant enclosure. "I have never heard them make that *sauti* before."

Then, as if on cue, they heard it again.

"How long have they been doing that?"

"Muda mrefu," Long time, Thoni replied. *"Nitakuonyesha."* I will show you, he said, slipping off the wall.

Jill followed him down the moonlit path, accompanied by several keepers. He opened the gate to the night stockades with care, so as not to disturb its occupants. Once inside, he switched on a flashlight, casting just enough light to see the elephants closest to them.

As they wound their way through small groups of sleepy orphans scattered across the large, open space of the modest barn, the air was thick with the scent of elephant dung—a pungent blend of freshly cut grass and earthy notes. The floor, cushioned with soft hay, offered a cozy resting place for the elephants to sleep, while leafy branches were distributed throughout for those who craved a midnight snack.

Jill and the keepers stayed still until they heard it again, this time closer. Although they couldn't tell which elephant was making the sound, there was no question it was coming from inside that room. After listening to it for a while, they stepped back outside. Jill was astonished—certain it was a call she had never heard the elephants make before.

Upon returning to Nairobi, she contacted Dr. Joyce Poole, who was conducting a long-term research project on wild elephant communication in Amboseli National Park, a hundred miles south. While intrigued by what Jill described, Joyce initially thought they were simply one of the many unique sounds she had heard elephants make before. However, Jill's insistence that this was different prompted her to investigate further.

In December 1998, Joyce arrived in Voi with her recording equipment, to determine whether the elephant call Jill heard was indeed familiar. She set up inside the elephant stockades to capture the full range of their nocturnal activity. To her surprise, the elephants repeatedly produced a sound unlike anything she had encountered before.

Joyce adjusted her earphones to focus more closely when she heard the distant rumble of trucks traveling down Mombasa Road, over two miles away. A few hours after sunset, the truck noise carried farther during a temperature inversion—the ideal time for low-frequency sounds to travel the greatest distance, as the heat of the day gives way to the coolness of night.

At first, the distant truck noise blended with the soft calls of the elephants, making it difficult to distinguish between the two. By removing her earphones, she was able to separate the sounds more clearly, sharpening the distinction.

While she listened further, Joyce noticed a striking resemblance. She wondered if the elephants were mimicking the truck-like sound. The idea that they could replicate a mechanical noise seemed almost implausible, but the possibility couldn't be ignored. She listened intently as the deep, rhythmic tones of the elephants' calls intertwined with the distant hum of the trucks, leaving her with more questions than answers.

Between December 8th and 18th, Joyce recorded the truck-like calls made by the elephants 118 times. Of those, 108 were produced by Malaika, and four by Imenti. The remaining vocalizations couldn't be traced to specific individuals, yet the pattern was undeniable.

Although Joyce confirmed to Jill that it was something she had never heard before, she hesitated to share her findings with the world, since no one had ever documented elephants practicing mimicry before. Then, out of the blue, an unexpected message arrived from a researcher wanting to know if it was possible that elephants could mimic sounds from their environment.

Dr. Angela Stöeger-Horwath was studying communication in captive elephants when she recorded an African bull doing something unusual. Calimero, housed with two Asian females at the Basel Zoo in Switzerland, seemed to mimic their chirps, a vocalization completely unique to the Asian elephant species. Since African elephants had never been recorded making similar noises before, this was a surprise.

It was then that Joyce realized—they were definitely on to something. She contacted whale biologist, Peter Tyack, who along with his colleague Stephanie Watwood, analyzed each of their recordings. They confirmed that in both instances, the elephants were imitating the sounds of their environment, just as Joyce suspected. It was a moment that hinted at the unexplored depths of the elephant mind, but more would soon come to light.

Shortly after their groundbreaking research was published in 2005, whispers surfaced that an Asian bull elephant at a zoo in Kazakhstan mimicked the speech of his human trainers. Allegedly, he repeated words in both Russian and Kazakh—the languages spoken by his two favorite keepers. Unfortunately, he died before this could be proven. However, a short time later, rumors of a similar case involving another male Asian elephant, Koshik, surfaced.

Angela and her team traveled to the Everland Zoo in South Korea where they recorded Koshik's interactions with his keepers. They concluded he could actually speak five Korean words, including "annyeong," which means "hello" in Korean. Even more surprising was that Koshik didn't just mimic his trainers after they greeted him—he initiated it. And he produced a novel method of sound production that no scientist had ever encountered before in *any* species.

Since the elephant's upper lip is fused with its nose (or its trunk), it cannot produce certain vowels such as the letter 'u'. But Koshik discovered a way to overcome this anatomical limitation. He inserted his trunk into his mouth and expertly manipulated the airflow, replicating our own vocal tract without altering his own. When this discovery was published in 2012, scientists were floored. Koshik's ability to mimic human speech and use it to communicate with *us* remains unprecedented.

Dr. Michael Pardo (known as Mickey) made the next startling revelation. By supplementing his own recordings of elephants in Kenya along with vocalizations collected by Joyce Poole since the 1980s, he discovered they produced a unique sound to identify and address specific individuals in a herd. It offered the strongest evidence yet that elephants *also* call each other by name. While research on dolphins exhibiting this behavior is far more extensive, supported by decades of data, Mickey's 2024 paper pushed the boundaries even further. As the first of its kind, it has undoubtedly opened the door for many more to follow.

Each scientific breakthrough inched closer to an extraordinary possibility: that elephants could use a hidden language so vast and complex it challenged our very understanding of what that could mean. In less than two decades, our comprehension of animal intelligence had expanded beyond what we once thought possible.

The sudden chime of a text message snapped me back to the present. Still lying on the couch on the second floor of the science building, I sat up and dug through my bag until I found my phone. It was Jason.

"Do you want to go to a meeting?"

I looked up at the whale and hesitated, torn between spending the rest of the peaceful afternoon remembering the science that inspired me, and the call to join my people.

With a deep breath, I typed, "Which one?"

"You decide."

When I realized what day it was, I agreed to meet him at my first and favorite meeting. Due to my work schedule, it was held on a night I hadn't been able to attend in months. Reluctantly, I peeled myself off the couch and said goodbye to the baby whale.

As my foot touched the first step, a thought struck me. For a moment, I froze. It was the perfect solution to address KOTA's stance on keeping elephants in captivity—I couldn't believe it hadn't dawned on me before then. I checked my watch and realized I had just enough time to make a stop at the library. I rushed across campus, filled with quiet certainty that the answer which had eluded me for so long was suddenly clear.

CHAPTER 23

"Welcome back, kiddo!" Bobbo said with outstretched arms, as I entered the front door.

He stood in the same spot, in the entryway of that fellowship hall, for what felt like a lifetime. As we embraced, all my nervous anxiety melted away. I crossed the room, hugging friends I hadn't seen in months, and settled into a chair beside Jason. It felt good to be back where my recovery began at Sunset.

The speaker sat at the front table facing us, waiting for the meeting to begin. It was the same table where women had gathered stacks of free clothes for me when I was newly sober, after noticing I showed up each week in the same white T-shirt, black sweater, and dark green cargo pants. After all of my belongings were stolen from my homeless shelter, I was left with nothing but what I was wearing. If I'd known it would be another nine months before they got replaced, I might have made a more careful selection.

As the chairperson began the meeting, I settled in, surrounded by newcomers with less than thirty days sober and veterans with decades. Amid the familiar faces, many of whom had been there since the beginning, sixteen years ago, I couldn't help but disregard the statistics I'd heard about how few alcoholics find lasting sobriety. At nearly every group I attended, there were people I had met when I first came in. If so few of us ever got sober, then how did I know so many who were?

Toward the end of the meeting, a sliding glass door opened, and a stranger stepped inside. The person sharing paused and a quiet hush slowly spread across the room. I turned to see who it was, but the man's face was obscured by someone hugging him tightly. He appeared tall, skinny, weak, and wobbly.

One after the next, people rose from their chairs and held him warmly, like a Viking returning home after a long journey. Soft thumps echoed as he worked his way down the line. When he finally took a seat, I got my first good look. He wasn't immediately recognizable, but after a moment, I realized who he was. My heart pounded in my chest. It was *him*—it was Hugh.

I turned back to the front to gather my composure. Jason, equally surprised, muttered a quiet "Oh my God" under his breath. He knew Hugh well, too. It had been over two years since anyone had seen him, and we all prayed he'd survived. When no news came, I realized the chances of him making it out alive were slim. He looked gaunt and pale, a stark contrast to the muscular, radiant presence of the man he once was. Jason and I exchanged a look—it was obvious Hugh's last relapse had nearly killed him. I hated what addiction did to people, reducing them to a sliver of the person they once were, and sometimes not even that.

While in the treatment center, I'd learned that the disease of addiction affects my brain, my body, and my spirit. It is progressive and grows even when I'm not feeding her. Hugh was the first to teach me this. My counselor compared addiction to a fatal disease that simply goes in and out of remission, which sounded about right.

I was certain, however, that our ghost was deeply cunning, and always hungry. It lies in wait for the moment I let my guard down like a wolf stalking from the shadows of a dark forest while its unsuspecting prey, an innocent deer, grazes in an open meadow. But once that deer ventures too far away from its herd, and gets too close to the edge—too close to the darkness—life as she knows it quickly comes to an end.

If the deer survives, everyone questions why she continues taunting the wolf, why she keeps wandering so close to a monster. But the deer can't answer that question. She is unable explain that the pull to wander toward darkness is far more powerful than anything else. Unless ... *unless* ... she remains embedded deep in the middle of her herd. That is her only protection against the big, bad wolf.

Hugh had thirteen years of sobriety when I first met him at Sunset. At the time, just weeks sober, I was skittish, quiet, and terrified of most people, especially men. Physical abuse had been a recurring theme in almost every relationship I'd had. Although the bruises healed, the emotional toll it took on my soul didn't. I was determined to avoid all men until I understood why I was attracted to the dangerous ones to begin with.

One night, after Sunset, I waited at the bus stop across the street and watched everyone smoking and hanging out in the parking lot, for what they called "the meeting after the meeting." I desperately wanted to be a part of it, to laugh and feel like I belonged—but I was too new and too scared. Besides, the last bus left shortly after the meeting ended, and I had a curfew at my halfway house.

The crowd dispersed, and when no one was left, I realized the bus was either *really* late, or not coming at all. As the knot in my stomach grew, a bright red truck pulled up next to me.

"Looks like you got stood up," Hugh said, rolling the window down. While he waited for my response, my thoughts raced, searching for an alternative. "Look, it's obvious the bus isn't coming. I can give you a ride home."

I hesitated, uninterested in getting into any vehicle driven by a stranger. "It's okay," I muttered. "I'll just walk to the next stop."

Even as I said it, I knew it was too late. The last bus of the night would have already left there, too.

"Listen pal, I get it. But it isn't like you have a lot of options here. Let's call Shelly and tell her I'm taking you home." Hugh extended his phone.

Shelly was my sponsor—my mentor in recovery—and Hugh was her boyfriend. Even that fact didn't make me want to trust him any more than necessary, but I called her anyway.

"It's okay Deb," she said. "He's safe. Call me when you get home." Reluctantly, I handed the phone back and got into his truck.

"Where am I taking you?" he asked.

"Do you know how to get to Felony Flats?"

"Of course I know it, who doesn't?" He laughed, then stopped and looked at me sideways. Apparently, he thought I was joking.

Felony Flats was a region on the outskirts of Portland and a landmark in the city's underworld. Every addict knew where it was, especially if you wanted hard drugs. It was also notorious for the brutality of its Asian gangs, skyrocketing crime, and a murder rate that far surpassed anywhere else in the city.

"Wait, *that's* where you live?" Hugh's truck momentarily drifted across the center line.

"Yes," I sighed quietly. I hated talking to people. We drove in silence for the next several miles before he spoke again.

"I know you," he said.

I squirmed, unsure where this was going.

"I've seen you and watched how hard you work with Shelly.

And I get it. I get the whole *I want to stay the fuck away from people* thing. I understand because I used to be just like that."

I showed no reaction, stared straight ahead, and listened carefully as he continued.

"But I want you to know something. There are safe people here who know what you're going through. You just keep showing up, keep working with Shelly, and you'll see, one day you'll feel your old self return."

I gave him nothing, no indication I had heard him, let alone that I was touched by his words. I couldn't fathom that what he said was true—that I could return to the person I always thought I was—happy and outgoing. I wondered if she ever even existed to begin with. Perhaps it was just a disguise created by the drugs and alcohol, and the real me was no more than a scared, shy wallflower invisible to the rest of the world.

"This is it," I said a half hour later when we arrived at my house.

"*That's* your house?" he asked, hitting the brakes harder than in-tended.

From the outside, my halfway house looked quite inviting. The 1960s home had a quaint, almost whimsical appearance. Painted stark white with a light blue trim that highlighted the windows, it even had a charming white-picket fence surrounding the front yard.

It stood in contrast to the rest of the neighborhood, a street scarred by blurry chalk outlines of gunshot victims, left behind after the authorities removed the bodies. The yellow police tape, draped haphazardly across bushes and trees, clung to the surroundings like leftover, tattered Halloween decorations. It was a stark reminder of the street's relentless violence.

"Yeah, what's the big deal?" I asked.

Before Hugh could answer, a massive pit bull flew by his door, vanishing into a gap between two houses further down the street.

"Holy shit! Did you see that? Don't get out of the car." He grabbed my arm as I went to open the door.

"That's just Chunk." His overreaction made me smile.

"You know him? That's his name?" Hugh's gaze darted frantically between the rearview mirror and his side window, as if expecting to see a pack of pit bulls appear at any moment.

"Yes, he lives around here somewhere. He looks like a massive chunk, so that's what I call him."

The first time I saw Chunk, he scared the hell out of me, too. It was four in the morning, and I was on a sidewalk halfway between the bus stop and my house when he emerged from around the corner, charging straight at me. With nowhere to escape, I closed my eyes and braced for the hit, but he didn't even acknowledge my presence as he whizzed by. With chiseled muscles spread across a massive frame, Chunk reminded me of a jacked-up kangaroo, with a body as sturdy and compact as a well-built tank. Clearly, he wasn't a fighting dog, but was owned and cared for by somebody. Despite seeing him almost every day, I had no idea where he lived or why he ran at full speed everywhere he went. Each time he passed I said, "Hey Chunk," as he sped by, going wherever it was he needed to go.

"Okay," Hugh said, his voice growing increasingly alarmed. "I don't feel comfortable leaving you here."

"Oh, relax," I said, getting out of the truck. "This is where I live."

"Seriously, Deb—"

"Seriously. Thanks for the ride," I interrupted, slamming the door.

Hugh waited while I stood on the front porch, digging out my keys. The faint sound of his car doors repeatedly locking made me giggle. The truth wass, the crime-ridden neighborhood didn't bother me, despite how much time the nightly news dedicated to segments about the street I lived on. In a way, it mirrored my own inner turmoil, and I was never afraid, nor did anyone disturb me. Instead, I was left in peace to come and go as I pleased—even by Chunk, who never seemed to notice my existence. And that suited me just fine.

After that first night, Hugh made *me* his service commitment. He gave me a ride home each week after Sunset and introduced me to his closest friends there, Steve and Leo, who turned out to be two of the funniest men I'd ever met. The four of us hung out in the parking lot with people I used to watch from across the street. Sometimes they joined Hugh and me for the drive home, and we continued "the meeting after the meeting" in Hugh's truck, laughing all the way. It was the most fun I'd had since I could remember and gradually my former self returned, just like Hugh said.

It was during those rides that they shared fragments of their past. Leo was a professional pool player who'd lost everything due to a severe cocaine addiction. He was short and reminded me of a gay mobster, although he wasn't gay or a mobster. His thick glasses framed his face, his teeth looked slightly too perfect to be real, and he was the only man I knew who wore a pinky ring. His deep, scratchy voice brimmed with humor and wit, and he often turned himself into the butt of a joke—something that delighted both Hugh and Steve, who teased him at every opportunity.

Steve owned a business fixing dents on cars and had been in more treatment centers than I could count. He didn't have a particular drug of choice; anything would do. He was the typical tall, dark, and handsome gentleman with kind eyes, a sweet soul, and a soft spot for desperate women who believed a man or marriage could save them from the demons of addiction. More than one of his exes died trying to achieve that goal.

Hugh effortlessly blended into any crowd, standing tall alongside Steve—the two shared a talent for witty banter. As a steel broker who traveled the world and earned an obscene salary, Hugh had only one drug of choice: alcohol, and as much as he could get.

During my first year of recovery, with my family estranged, Shelly invited the four of us to spend the holidays together at her home. It was a world away from the previous winter when I'd spent Christmas alone in a treatment center. I couldn't help but reflect on the contrast. Surrounded by booming, raucous laughter and a table overflowing with delicious food, I was struck by how dramatically my life had changed in such a short amount of time.

One night Hugh wasn't in his usual seat at Sunset, which the three of us found strange. After the meeting, Shelly pulled us aside and told us why. Several days earlier, Hugh had relapsed and disappeared. Her words completely knocked the wind out of me. At the time, I didn't realize such a thing was even possible—that one could relapse with over *thirteen* years of sobriety.

Within weeks, Hugh resurfaced when he was admitted to a hospital for acute alcohol poisoning. When we visited him, he assured us he was "done" and came back to the meeting. But just as we breathed a sigh of relief, he relapsed again and the whole ugly cycle was repeated.

Soon Hugh's relationship with Shelly ended, he was fired from his job, and within a year, he'd lost everything. There was nothing we could do to stop it. He checked into multiple treatment centers, detoxes, and hospitals, but none of it worked for longer than a few weeks before he disappeared again.

To make matters worse, Steve also relapsed within months and the hilarity from those early days turned to horror fairly quickly. I learned just how expensive relapse is. When you love someone, as I loved them, one pays a very high emotional price agonizing over what happened to them once they're gone.

When an addict disappears, it feels especially painful and cruel. Nobody puts up posters because even though we may not know their exact location, we know where they are. Even if we could force them back into recovery, we've realized how fruitless those efforts can be. All we could do was wait for them to ask for help. Until then, we clung to hope for their safe return.

Each week, I stared at the empty chairs at Sunset and felt the void of the missing. Leo and I grew closer, as the years passed. Hugh and Steve showed up occasionally, sometimes for months at a time, before relapsing and disappearing again. Hugh detoxed on my living room floor numerous times while we waited for a bed to open at yet another detox. Every so often, a mutual friend who was a doctor slept on my couch, monitoring Hugh's alcohol intake in order to keep him stable. We knew all too well the dangers of alcohol withdrawal—it can easily prove fatal if the person isn't properly weaned. By then, Hugh suffered from severe grand mal seizures whenever he attempted to quit "cold turkey."

After several years, he vanished onto the streets of Portland, a drunk living in a tent under a bridge. He changed the way I thought about the homeless. How many had someone who loved them as we loved Hugh? Probably quite a few, if I had to guess. I bet there are lots of good people out there who were suffering from a disease that came roaring out of remission—one that kept the strangers who passed them on the street from seeing what amazing human beings they once were, and could be again.

Eventually, Steve found his way back to long-term sobriety and moved away. He married a woman unaffected by addiction, started a successful business, and now, years later, continues to lead a fulfilling and stable life.

Leo spent so much time with my family, he was like the brother I never had. He traveled to Vietnam where he met his future wife, Lek, and I stood next to him not as his "best man" but as his "best friend" when they wed. His career took off and things got busy. We grew apart, but I thought it was because his life was rich and full until the day I received a call from a number I didn't recognize.

"Debbie," said a quiet, scratchy voice.

"Yes. Who's this?"

"Debbie, come on now. It's your old friend Leo." His voice sounded weak and strange, almost a whisper, and much deeper than I remembered.

"Leo! What are you doing? Why do you sound so strange?"

"I need your help. Listen, just … can you come and get me?" he asked.

"Yes, of course. Where are you?"

I scribbled the cross streets on a piece of paper. When I arrived at the address, I was met with a scene that felt utterly surreal. Leo's wrecked car was wrapped around a telephone pole. He stood on the sidewalk, amid the wreckage, engaged in conversation with a group of people whose laughter filled the air. Nothing about the situation made any sense.

"Oh, thank God you're here," he said, as he climbed in. "Bye, everyone. Thank you, I'm fine," he waved to the crowd. "Go! Go!" he hissed. "Let's get the fuck out of here before the cops show up."

"Leo, what happened? Are you okay?" My heart pounded against my chest.

He seemed spacey and out of it. We drove a few streets over before I stopped and confronted him. That's when I noticed he was grabbing his side.

"Let me see," I said, lifting his shirt before he could stop me. A deep purple bruise was already forming.

"It's nothing," he muttered, brushing my hand away.

"It isn't nothing, Leo," I snapped furiously. "What the fuck just happened?"

He started laughing, but it was a strange cackle, not the familiar belly-laugh I was used to.

"Calm down. Jesus. I'm fine. Just take me back home and Lek will take care of me."

Everything about his demeanor seemed off. Instead of taking Leo to his apartment, I drove straight to the nearest emergency room. He dozed off, oblivious to my rising panic as I maneuvered through traffic and skidded to a stop in front of the hospital's sliding glass doors. Before I ran for help, I locked him inside, hoping to delay his attempt to get out. The moment he realized where we were, he fumbled with the door, but fortunately, the medical staff arrived before he could escape. They strapped him to a gurney and once he was safely in their hands, I contacted Lek.

Leo had suffered from severe internal bleeding as a result of the crash, due to not wearing a seatbelt. The doctor said that if he hadn't received immediate medical attention, he probably wouldn't have survived. But there was something even deadlier. Leo had also overdosed on methadone, which no one knew he was taking. And it was likely the cause of the accident. Luckily, they were able to catch both in time, and he made a full recovery.

Two weeks after Leo was released from the hospital, Lek found his lifeless body in the hallway of their home. The doctors had prescribed him painkillers, which he had accidentally mixed with a lethal dose of methadone. I like to think that he died peacefully in his sleep.

After Leo's death, I retreated once more into solitude, grappling with the incomprehensible loss of yet another dear friend. I struggled to make sense of what was happening to us: to my friends, to addicts like me. Why were some spared while others endured such tragic outcomes?

Jason placed his hand on mine just as the meeting ended, snapping me back to the moment. He squeezed it, a gentle reminder of where we were, what we had survived, and how far we'd come. His gesture made me smile. There was an understanding between us—alcoholic telepathy.

"Thank you again," I said, as we stood in line to put our chairs away.

"For what?" he asked.

"For suggesting a meeting … for bringing me back here." I hugged him before he left, then turned to greet the Viking. Hugh didn't recognize me at first, but when he did, he gasped.

"I'm so glad to see you," he whispered in my ear as gave me a deep hug.

There was nothing left to say that hadn't already been said. I gave him a ride home that evening, just as he'd done for me so many years ago. Only this time, we pulled up outside his halfway house and not mine.

Hugh was finally brought off the streets by the Salvation Army. In exchange for room and board, he worked in one of their stores and he loved it. Though I wish I could say it was his last relapse, it wasn't, but something had changed. He embraced recovery in a way I hadn't seen him do before, reached out to new guys, and lived a life of true service. When his boss tried to promote him as a manager, impressed with his remarkable people skills, Hugh refused. He wanted nothing more than to continue exactly as he was, since it worked.

Hugh no longer had any interest in owning a car. "Riding the bus allows me to see the world and the people in it," he shared. I understood that. It was an amazing transformation from the man I'd first met, who was once consumed by wealth and could never have imagined himself riding a bus, let alone choosing it over the freedom of driving his own expensive car.

I looked at sobriety differently because of Hugh. I learned to focus less on the amount of time someone had sober and more on the quality, once they were freed from the chains of addiction, even if only temporarily. Hugh was also my family. When he suffered, I suffered. But I would not follow him when he left the quiet peace of that meadow to taunt the monster at the edge of darkness again. He would have to make that journey on his own, and he did many times.

I returned home that evening, overwhelmed by gratitude. In just one hour, I had remembered who I was and where I came from. I was reminded of how those of us in recovery are like elephants. We speak a language that nobody understands but us. Only an alcoholic can truly understand another alcoholic in the same way that only an elephant can speak the language of another elephant.

CHAPTER 24

"I've made my decision," I said, as I stood facing KOTA's board members. They stared at me from across a long wooden table, their expressions a mix of curiosity and anticipation.

"I'm finally prepared to take a formal stand *against* keeping elephants in captivity."

"Just to clarify, you mean KOTA taking a stance publicly?" Jason asked.

"Yes," I continued, "publicly. And this is the documentation we can use to support why."

I unzipped my backpack and placed two large piles of paper on the table.

"This is from my library research—use it as a reference. We need to stick to the facts because taking this position will create enemies for KOTA."

I pushed the first stack toward Jason, who distributed them to each member. As they scanned the documents, I carried on.

"These are separate court cases. The transcripts of each one describe how zoo officials and elephant keepers have admitted, under oath, to the horrific treatment of several elephants in captivity."

"This is good," Jason grinned, flipping through the first few pages.

A stillness settled over the room as everyone delved into the information.

"Can I ask a question?" Debra said, breaking the silence. "It says here that the Oregon Zoo is ranked as one of the ten worst zoos for elephants in the country."

She flipped to another page.

"For the *eleventh* time. Do you know what criteria they use?"

"That's an annual report from In Defense of Animals, which uses several factors to determine which facilities make their list," I explained. "They dig into government and veterinary records on mistreated elephants, including fines given, elephant deaths, and more. It isn't grounded in opinion, as some might think."

I paused, letting the information settle.

"When the USDA issues a fine, it's typically the result of an inspection or investigation that found violations of the Animal Welfare Act, which can include gross mistreatment, inadequate care, or unsafe conditions for the elephants."

Carolyn leaned forward. "What about zoo renovations? What kind of difference does a larger exhibit make, if not an improved life for them?"

"Those are done mostly for the paying public," I said.

"I don't get it," Aimee interjected. "How is that better for people?"

"Because it's all about the aesthetics. It makes visitors feel good to see visually pleasing exhibits."

I pulled a book from my backpack and set it on the table.

"This is *Jumbo Ghosts* written by Dr. Michael Schmidt, a veterinarian who spent over thirty years working at the Oregon Zoo. He explains why the size of a zoo exhibit matters little to the elephants while easing the conscience of the people who paid for it."

Suddenly, the rustling of papers stopped as if the room's weight shifted with the turn of a page, and all eyes turned toward me.

"He pointed out several startling things. Most zoos, including Portland, have elephant keepers on duty only eight to nine hours a day. Despite multi-million-dollar renovations, elephants are still confined to stalls, rooms, or chained for up to sixteen hours each night—just as they were before the renovation. Since nearly all elephants across the country are kept indoors overnight, the time they spend outside hasn't increased, no matter how large the new exhibits are. He makes a compelling case that elephants belong in sanctuaries, where they can live more independently. Every U.S. sanctuary is hundreds of times larger than any zoo, and most importantly, the elephants have real autonomy."

"How exactly is autonomy defined in that context?" Aimee asked.

"In a sanctuary, elephants have the freedom to make their own decisions without human intervention or control. They aren't confined by enclosures or keepers' schedules. While they are fenced in for safety, most provide hundreds of acres of space (per elephant) to roam freely. And they aren't bred. In zoos, when a female is in estrous, she isn't allowed to wander far—they need to keep her close so they can inseminate her every few hours. But in a sanctuary, the elephants come and go as they please, night or day, and interact with others whenever they choose."

"So, if I'm understanding correctly, elephants in zoos can spend no more than eight hours outside?" Carolyn asked.

"Exactly," I said. "But it's even less than that."

"What else affects how much time they spend outdoors?" Jason said, curious.

"Lots of things," I continued. "Every elephant must be cleaned each morning to remove the waste that accumulates overnight on their legs, feet, and bodies—a process that can easily take another hour or more. Most also require foot care and medical treatments, which further reduces that time.

Weather is another constant challenge, especially in colder regions where elephants—adapted to warm climates—cannot tolerate low temperatures. In Portland, for example, elephants can't be left outside for long during the winter because it's simply too cold for them. Realistically, six hours outdoors is likely the maximum, and *only* during the warmest months. Since most elephants aren't fed at night, or receive very little food, they must also use their limited time to eat as much as possible, rather than roaming around a large exhibit. In the wild, they'd spend almost their entire day, eighteen to twenty hours, just foraging and eating."

"Oh, wow," Debra said, as she and the others digested the information. "I never even thought about any of that."

"It's so disturbing," Carolyn added, shaking her head, "and misleading. But it makes so much sense when you think about it that way."

After several minutes, Pennie muttered to herself, "I can't believe this is happening to an endangered species."

In the film version of her life, she headed to Morocco. But in reality, Pennie went to Kenya, where she completed her marketing degree at a university in Nairobi. While there, she spent time with a Maasai tribe, learning about their culture and the wild elephants who lived nearby. She fell in love with Kenya and its people but knew very little about elephant behavior until I began sharing their stories. Once she understood the challenges they faced, Pennie joined KOTA, and her cat Pitbull became our most favorite mascot.

In front of her was a devastating court case that involved an elephant named Rose-Tu, the granddaughter of Portland's original elephant Rosy. In April 1999, the head keeper at the zoo, Fred Marion, showed up on his day off, drunk and angry. Armed with a sharpened bullhook, he stabbed her over 176 times (according to the puncture wounds they counted on her body), and ripped out part of her anus.

The attack sparked an uproar across the city. But the cover-up that followed garnered even greater attention. When the keepers finally separated the young elephant from the drunken Mr. Marion, they refused to call the vet, though his office was just steps away.

Instead, they took it upon themselves to administer medical treatment. Believing they had done an adequate job—according to the testimony of the then zoo-director, 'elephant expert' Mike Keele—they were shocked when she collapsed in her stall three days later from her injuries. As various accounts and witness statements emerged, they shed light on the true events of that day and offered a bit more insight into why the Oregon Zoo consistently made IDA's Top Ten Worst Zoos list year after year.

The elephant keepers' failure to inform medical staff revealed a kink in the system. Veterinarians are required to report abuse or suspicious injuries to protect their licenses. Their findings are filed with the USDA, which means they are also made public. It was this fact that exposed the real risk: a detailed account accessible to anyone could devastate a zoo's reputation.

There was incentive to keep the whole unfortunate situation quiet—*especially* from the vet. By keeping it a secret, the Oregon Zoo staff stayed in control of the narrative and thought they had avoided yet another scandal. But when Rose-Tu collapsed, they had no choice, since a dead elephant would pose far greater legal risks than just a severely injured one.

In the end, the veterinarian on duty alerted the authorities, and the zoo was given the maximum fine of $10,000. And as everyone feared, the entire episode was made public. Lawsuits were filed, new legislation was proposed, and Mr. Keele attempted to fire the drunk keeper. However, the union to which he—and all the elephant keepers—belonged to prevented him from doing so. Instead, he was put on "paid leave," receiving his full salary for the next two years until his record was expunged, according to the terms of his union contract.

As a result, Mr. Marion was free to seek employment at any other zoo without disclosing his violent, abusive past—one that revealed Rose-Tu was not the first elephant who had met the end of his sharpened bullhook. It exposed another flaw in the system. Even when zoos tried to do the right thing, such as thoroughly investigate prospective employees, there was nothing they could do if there was no record to find. They were powerless to uncover the truth once the union erased a bad keeper's disciplinary history.

I could see the pain on Pennie's face and wondered if this was more than she had bargained for when she agreed to join KOTA's board. As she continued reading, my thoughts wandered to the plight of Morgan's elephants, and how the culture of secrecy had its roots buried deep in the past. With each new eye-opening incident, the public clamored for reform, demanding change in the system. But as I observed the cycle unfolding over time, it seems zoo officials simply grew more skilled at concealing the truth. The painful reality became clear once I learned the tragic outcome of Portland's elephants and Morgan's beloved herd, who all died from severe, chronic foot disease, except for one.

By sixteen, Tuy Hoa was already having trouble walking. Within a few years, she relied on her trunk as a crutch as she hobbled around the exhibit. She endured advanced arthritis and bacterial infections that began in the cracks of her hind toenails from constant exposure to her urine.

In the wild, elephants avoid letting their feet come into contact with their waste because of the damaging effects it has. Natural behaviors, such as walking through dust and dirt, help clean off any residue. In captivity, however, they don't have this luxury. Due to its highly corrosive nature, their urine is so potent it can actually cut through metal. If left unattended it eats through the elephants' toenails, causing cracks and open wounds that are prone to infection. And the reason they all have to be washed first thing each day.

As elephants expel hundreds of pounds of waste in their stalls overnight, they have no choice but to lay and walk in it until morning, especially if they're kept on chains. They have to wait until the keepers begin their shifts and can clean both their bodies and confined spaces. Unfortunately, the conditions inside a ball of elephant dung provide the perfect environment for bacteria to thrive. When combined with an open wound—well, that's like giving an alcoholic access to an open bar—it doesn't take long for all hell to break loose.

The painful infections slowly ate away at all the elephants' feet, but Tuy Hoa was the youngest to be put down, at just twenty-eight. By the time Rosy was euthanized in 1993, she hadn't been able to lie down for years. The arthritis in her legs was so severe according to her vet records, that she couldn't get back up. Instead, she leaned her body against a wall and slept when she could.

Belle, like Rosy, didn't lie down for over a decade. In 1997, she died from a similar foot infection that had taken Tuy Hoa's life. Both Belle and Rosy had been diagnosed with a severe vascular deficiency, which not only led to significant loss of their eyesight but also, due to poor blood flow, likely worsened their infections.

A new veterinarian, Dr. Murray Fowler, was brought in to operate on Belle's badly infected toes, but all he could do was remove two and hope it was enough. While she healed, Belle was held in a sling, unable to walk for weeks. A second surgery confirmed their worst fears—the infection had entered her bloodstream and spread up one of her legs. There was nothing more they could do; she was only forty-five.

In the end, Pet outlived them all, but couldn't escape the deadly foot disease that claimed the others. At fifty-one, Morgan's last elephant, the pigeon-toed gentle giant, was also euthanized in 2006.

There are times when I wish the elephants would just let me be—my heart can only take so much. But long after I had moved on and put this story aside, the ghost of Tuy Hoa paid me a visit.

While working on a research project having to do with tranquilizing drugs used to disable large animals in Africa, I stumbled across a scientific paper with a title so packed with complex medical terms that I was unable to pronounce a single one. What it revealed left me stunned.

∞

Tuy Hoa arrived at the Oregon Zoo as a nervous baby. At just one-year-old, she was given as a gift by Portland engineer, Orville Hosmer. He helped rebuild an irrigation system in Tuy Hoa, Vietnam, the capital city of Phu Yen Province on the central coast. As a token of their appreciation, they gave him a baby elephant.

Rosy, the zoo's only other elephant at the time, seemed relieved to have company. At just five years old, she adopted Tuy Hoa as her own. From then on, they were inseparable, often seen sleeping side-by-side with their trunks tightly intertwined—a behavior reminiscent of the close bond between Belle and Pet. Whenever they were separated, Tuy Hoa's anxiety spiraled out of control, which is why she remained by Rosy's side and the two were rarely kept apart.

As Tuy Hoa's arthritis worsened, making walking difficult, Rosy and Pet were often seen comforting her and bringing extra food. She was a regular on the nightly news due to a pair of specialized boots constructed specifically to ease her pain. Scientists and veterinarians from across the country studied her to try to understand why she suffered from such severe foot deterioration at such a young age. But Tuy Hoa also became famous for an entirely different reason.

While Katy Payne was at the Oregon Zoo conducting research on the elephants—where she discovered they communicated using infrasound—she witnessed something extraordinary.

In 1982, Tuy Hoa's oldest daughter, Hanako, rejected yet another of her offspring. While the keepers frantically tried to get Hanako to nurse, milk formed in Tuy Hoa's breasts, despite not having had a calf in over a decade. It was she, the baby's grandmother, who gave him the life-saving colostrum he needed to survive. Such acts of spontaneous lactation are incredibly rare in the animal kingdom. It served as a testament to Tuy Hoa's remarkable skills as a mother, even when the baby was not her own.

Mike Keele, the head of the elephant keepers at the time (years before his promotion to zoo director), delivered a heartfelt eulogy for Tuy Hoa in *The Oregonian* following her death.

"It was a difficult decision," he said. "She was a great elephant and we'll all miss her very much." It was comforting to realize that she was surrounded by those she loved in the end. When a reporter asked if the rest of the herd knew she was gone, Mr. Keele replied, "Not yet ... but they're all very close. In time, they'll know."

But that research paper I stumbled across suggested that the last hours of Tuy Hoa's life were anything but peaceful. The notes, published as part of the study, described an experiment conducted from 9:48 a.m. that lasted until 4:11 p.m., detailing the truth of what really happened behind closed doors.

Tuy Hoa was given four large doses of an experimental tranquilizer over that six-hours, followed by two antidotes. They sedated her, then woke her up, adjusting the amounts of both drugs while recording the results. Throughout the ordeal, Tuy Hoa struggled to stand and collapsed several times. Once she was finally able to get herself upright, she leaned her body against a wall for hours, despite her visible weakness and instability. Since the zookeepers and veterinarian knew she was about to be put down anyway, they performed a final experiment on her before they did. Back then, it wasn't so uncommon. Today, it's illegal.

The elephant barn was so small that Tuy Hoa was separated from the rest of the herd by only a single stall, with Rosy in the one closest to her. Their communication was noted multiple times, with loud calls exchanged between them. Although they weren't able to physically touch, there is some solace in knowing that during Tuy Hoa's final, harrowing hours, Rosy was still there, comforting her and calling out until the very end.

Back then, elephant barns were small and cramped, which made it impossible for large equipment—such as a tractor capable of hauling an animal the size of a small truck—to fit. Apparently, no one thought about how to get a full-grown elephant out once it was stuck in. The only way to remove a dead one was to do so piece by piece. So when that reporter asked Mr. Keele if the other elephants knew that Tuy Hoa was gone, I think it's safe to assume that the sound of chainsaws and the grim reality of what followed gave them all a pretty good idea. There are many ways elephants are traumatized by captivity, but to me, this ranks among the highest.

It was not until 2015, with the renovation of Elephant Lands at the Oregon Zoo, that a redesign allowed for large equipment to handle the removal of a dead elephant more humanely. Thankfully, zoos that have updated their facilities in the 21st century have learned from past design mistakes. However, for those that have yet to renovate, I can't help but wonder how their elephants continue to endure such trauma.

Thonglaw was the only one of Morgan's elephants who died before he did. In 1974, after he returned from a long run of performances with *The Tuskers of Thailand*, he found his elephant barely clinging to life. Since no one could take care of Thonglaw's basic needs, other than feeding him, nobody did. In order to clean out his tiny stall, it meant the keepers would have to move him, but they were under strict orders not to. Instead, Thonglaw's waste piled up around him as everyone waited for Morgan to return.

To reduce the overwhelming buildup, zookeepers cut back on the quantity of food he was given. A full-grown elephant typically requires at least four bales of hay per day, not including additional supplements. Yet Thonglaw received only an eighth of that at just half of a single bale. This time, they went too far. Based on Morgan's description of the awful scene, it was clear they'd nearly starved Thonglaw to death.

Once Morgan dug the elephant out from the massive pile of waste, he realized that starvation was the least of his problems, as two of Thonglaw's feet had practically rotted off. Morgan was furious that his beloved elephant had been treated so poorly, but was unable or unwilling to see how he had put that ball in motion. At just twenty-seven years old when he died, Thonglaw is still considered one of the oldest bull elephants ever held in captivity.

Both of Thonglaw's hefty 40-pound tusks disappeared within hours after his death. Locked away in a storage room for safekeeping, they vanished without a trace. Surprisingly, the authorities failed to identify the thief. With only a forty-five-minute window in which the valuable ivory could have been stolen, and only a select few with a key, suspicion pointed inward. One tusk was eventually recovered, though the police never disclosed its location or the identity of the culprit. Instead, they concluded the obvious, the perpetrator was most likely a zoo employee.

Pennie came up beside me and touched my shoulder, causing me to jump.

"Whoa," she said. "Are you OK?"

"Yes, sorry," I mumbled, embarrassed. "I was just lost in thought, and you startled me."

"Do you want to go get some lunch?" she asked.

Everyone else was fully engrossed in the material before them, quietly flipping pages. Since it wasn't an official board meeting, we were free to leave whenever we chose.

"I would love that," I said.

We excused ourselves and walked in silence to my car, the weight of the day still heavy. I could tell the group was tired and emotionally exhausted from having to read through the awful content. I didn't feel like going home and being alone after that either.

After a quiet lunch, Pennie and I visited Target, where we often enjoyed wandering through every section. As I approached the front entrance, I noticed she was no longer by my side. Glancing around, I spotted her heading toward the back of the building, where the inventory trucks were lined up.

"Pennie," I yelled. "Where are you going?" She stopped and looked up, suddenly realizing where she was.

"Oh," she said, turning and smiling.

"What are you doing?" I asked, with a mixture of confusion and humor.

"I was heading backstage," she giggled, shaking her head. "You know, old habits."

"What—?" I erupted in laughter, an unexpected release of the tension I hadn't realized I was holding.

The awfulness of the earlier part of the day manifested not as sadness or anger, but near hysteria. I sat down on a patch of grass on a nearby curb, laughing uncontrollably. Pennie joined me, and soon we were both in tears. Shoppers in their cars stared at us, likely assuming we were stoned out of our minds, which only fueled our delirium. Finally, our laughter subsided.

"That was an intense day, wasn't it?" she asked.

"No doubt," I sighed.

"All those horrible elephant stories," Pennie started giggling again as she said it.

"Oh no, stop," I begged. "Please stop." But it was too late. We were engulfed by yet another wave, only now our hilarity was laced with shame.

"We're going straight to Hell," I managed at last, wiping away the tears of our morbid amusement.

"Wasn't it Mark Twain who said, *You go to Heaven for the climate, but Hell for the company?*" she asked.

"That it was," I said quietly, calm once again.

Pennie knew how much I loved Mark Twain. She extended her hand, and we helped each other up. After a long, meaningful look, she gave me a heartfelt hug. Without saying a word, we walked back to my car hand-in-hand. Although we had planned to shop at Target, we never made it inside.

As we drove away and the sky cleared, the setting sun cast a golden light across the city. In that moment of serenity, I was reminded of my favorite Mark Twain quote:

"The two most important days in your life are the day you are born, and the day you find out *why*."

CHAPTER 25

My heart pounded. I ran even faster, frantically looking over my shoulder. Each step propelled me forward, a desperate plea for safety in the dark. His presence clung to me like a suffocating shadow, a lurking menace.

The distant wail of sirens signaled that help was on the way. I just needed to hold on a little longer. Fear, panic, terror—each stride was a battle against their unyielding grip as I darted between houses, praying that they caught me before he did. The sirens grew louder. Survival was within reach. Just when it felt like I couldn't go on, I stopped in the middle of the road and waited for rescue. As the emergency vehicles got closer, I waved my arms but quickly realized they weren't slowing down but speeding up. Panic seized me again, when I unexpectedly heard the sound of my own voice drowning out the noise of everything else.

No one is listening. Nobody cares. You're just a voice swallowed by the void. Alone.

I bolted upright, clutching my throat as a piercing ring cut through the still night. It took a moment before realizing I was in my own bed. With a quick glance at the clock—2:52 a.m.—the sound of sirens morphed into the ring of my cell phone. Fumbling in the darkness, I wondered who was calling me at this hour. The covers tumbled to the floor.

"Hello?" My voice was hoarse as I tried to calm my beating heart. It was a number I didn't recognize.

"Hey, it's me. Did I wake you?" Leslie asked quietly.

"No … I mean yes, but it's okay. Oh my goodness, it's so good to hear from you! How are you? *Where* are you?" I was instantly alert.

Leslie had been taken to the hospital several days earlier. I knew she was admitted, but had no clue where. I'd desperately tried to reach her, but the only information I had was that she was taken there by someone I didn't know. The friend, we later learned, had transposed one digit of my phone number, so all her messages were left unanswered. Leslie wondered what had happened since I was her medical power of attorney and always there, usually within the hour. Once we had resolved the confusion, the nightmare faded, and I calmed down.

None of the breast cancer treatments Leslie tried had worked. Her quarter-size tumor had grown to the size of a golf ball. When they removed that, they found more golf balls deeply embedded across her body. Her team of doctors was able to get her into an experimental trial with new drugs and immunotherapy, along with heavy, bone-chilling doses of chemo and radiation. All kinds of side effects emerged, and Leslie was repeatedly admitted to the hospital managing those.

"Can you come over here?" she asked. "I would really love to see you."

"Of course! I'll be right there. Do you need me to bring anything?" I quickly rifled through a pile of clothes, searching for something to wear.

"Just some lotion, if you could. My hands and feet are so dry they hurt."

"Got it," I said. "I'm on my way."

Leslie gave me the name of the hospital and her room number; it was one of the few places I hadn't checked. The roads at that early hour were tranquil and empty. The brisk fall air cut through the night, keeping me alert as the stars twinkled across the sky like a handful of scattered diamonds. My excitement and relief at seeing her overwhelmed me to the point that I couldn't care less what time it was.

At the hospital, I stood outside Leslie's room for several moments and focused on my breathing, in order to regain my composure after sprinting from the covered parking area. I wanted to present myself as calm, exuding an attitude that whispered, "Everything will be all right."

"Hello," I said quietly as I opened the door and stepped inside.

Leslie was awake and smiled at me, looking smaller than before—weaker and frail. I sat on the edge of her bed and gave her a hug. After explaining what new side effect had brought her there, she assured me that, thankfully, she was stable and comfortable. Then she paused and looked at me steadily for a long moment.

"I'm ready to talk about it," she said quietly.

"Are you sure?" I knew what she meant. I had a feeling it was time.

"Yes, I would like to. I'm ready now."

I've always made an effort to assure my friends, whether they were grappling with the loss of a loved one or facing their own devastating diagnosis, that if they ever wanted to discuss the topic of death, I was willing.

After a tragic accident involving my friend Stephanie's son, who was struck and killed by a bus when he was just fourteen, I noticed people avoided the subject, likely fearing it might trigger her intense sorrow. Perhaps they believed it was simpler to ignore the situation and act as if it had never occurred. But when I first asked Stephanie if she wanted to talk about Austin, she burst into tears. Despite the immense difficulty, she craved the comfort of his memory more than anything, and we talked about him for hours.

It often strikes me as surprising how discussing death, whether our own or someone else's, instills so much fear in people. I've long found great fascination in exploring the topic—the mysteries of the unknown and the profound serenity described by those who have been there and come back.

"What do you think it will be like?" Leslie asked.

"Peaceful, I imagine. Perhaps it starts like a good acid trip—at least I hope so—all rainbows and tunnels." I giggled. "I find comfort in thinking it's true what they say, that we're surrounded by those we love, the people and the pets who've gone before us."

"I would really like to see my parents again," she said. "I never had the opportunity to apologize for my awful behavior. They never knew that I got sober."

"They know," I said, rubbing her hands with lotion. I took a deep breath, feeling the weight of the moment before she broke the silence.

"What would you want to see … if you could go back in time as a wandering spirit?"

I thought about it for a second.

"I wouldn't mind hanging out with Cleopatra for a week or two, see what she was really like. Or the Turkish ruler Mehmed the

Conqueror, and how he took power away from the Roman Empire? I'd love to be a fly on the wall during that pivotal moment in history. Then there are figures who appear so striking in old photos, like the pianist Chopin—he actually seems pretty hot, but I wonder if he really was. You know how history distorts how some people are seen. Maybe he was gorgeous, but a total prick. Or others who weren't that good-looking, but their personalities made them hot as fuck."

Leslie giggled. "I've thought about that, too."

We entertained ourselves for a while, imagining how various historical figures, often depicted as magnificent and influential, might actually have been unassuming and ordinary. Then she got quiet and serious.

"I'm so scared of leaving my girls," she said.

Leslie had two grown daughters, one in California and the other in Tennessee. I'd known them since they were young and had watched them grow up, as Leslie learned how to live life sober.

"What if we do still get to see the people we love, just on a different plane," I said. "Like maybe, once we cross over, we can see them, but they can't see us."

"I hope that's true," she said. "I can hardly bear the idea of never embracing them again. Of not meeting my grandchildren."

Her oldest daughter had recently announced she was pregnant with Leslie's first grandchild. We talked long into the night about death and dying and laughed more than we cried. When she was done and all her fears were laid out in the open, Leslie looked happy and relaxed.

"Thank you." She grabbed my hand.

"For what?" I asked.

"For letting me talk about this. For making me laugh. I feel so much better."

"That's what friends are for." I squeezed her fingers. "Where you go I go, remember?"

"That's right," she said. "I'll save you a seat in the big meeting in Heaven."

"Not if I get there first," I said, as she smiled. "I'm actually quite looking forward to seeing so many of our friends in Valhalla. Must be an incredibly large meeting with that many slain warriors in the same place."

Suddenly, Leslie's laughter filled the room.

"What? What is it?" I asked.

"Do you remember our greatest sin? Our Great. Cardinal. Sin? When we pledged our souls to the devil—"

She burst into laughter again, unable to finish the sentence.

I rolled my eyes.

"Yes, I remember. It was not one of my finer moments."

Though it was a favorite of hers, apparently. It was true. Together we had committed an act so grievous we knew it would likely take us both straight to Hell. We started out with the best of intentions, but as usual, we fell from grace like birds who'd lost their wings. But that was the thing about friendship—the fall didn't seem so hard when you had someone willing to take the plunge with you.

∞

The auditorium was filled to the rafters with religious people yelling *Hallelujah* and *God Bless You*. Every week for the past several years, Leslie and I listened faithfully to the sermons of Joel Osteen, a non-denominational Christian who runs one of the largest churches in the United States—Lakewood, in Houston, Texas. He had a weekly podcast and his Sunday sermons were broadcast on television. One day, Leslie caught me watching his show when she came over.

"When the hell did you become so religious?" she asked.

"I'm not," I giggled, "but I love listening to him."

"You've got to be kidding me," she said, raising an eyebrow in disbelief.

I made her sit down and watch the rest of it with me. By the end, she was hooked, too. We both thought it was funny because neither of us was religious. I had nothing against anyone who was, but knew that any form of organized religion would never be my calling. I was definitely spiritual, however, and believed in something greater than myself. Joel tapped into that without making me feel uncomfortable.

He always shared real-life accounts about people who'd overcome incredible challenges. Sometimes he wove them into stories from the Bible, but ones I could relate to, not the kind where a whale ate somebody. Hearing the truth about enormous obstacles others overcame gave me faith in myself, the same way I felt after learning about the elephants.

One night before a meeting, Leslie and I joined our close friends Steve and Tucker for dinner, as we did each week. While checking in, Steve shared a problem he was facing.

Once he was finished, Leslie blurted, "No weapon formed against you shall prosper," taking a line directly from one of Joel's sermons. It was a mantra we repeated any time we encountered trouble. Then she paused, looked at me playfully, and added, "You know ... as they say."

I thought Steve and Tucker's eyes were going to bug out of their heads. In unison they toasted, "JOEL OSTEEN!!!"

We had no idea they were "secretly" watching him, too. Joel

would occasionally take his show on the road, so we each agreed that if he ever came to the Pacific Northwest, the four of us would go. A few months later, when his upcoming tour was announced with Portland as one of his stops, we bought tickets.

At the event, as we searched for our seats in the massive auditorium, Steve whispered, "What happens if they find out you aren't religious?"

"Shhh—" Leslie giggled, whacking him with a flyer as we all sat down.

The cheap seats placed us high, near the top of the MODA Center. Soon the show was underway, with choirs singing songs and guest preachers. By the time Joel took the stage, I was already tired since it was late and we had been there for hours. I willed myself to pay attention as he shared several inspiring stories, just like we'd seen him do on television. Somewhere along the way, I zoned out. The next thing I remember was Joel telling us to "Stand up!" so I did.

A woman, who sat on the other side of me lightly touched my arm and said, "God bless you," catching me off guard. That's when I realized no one else was standing. As my eyes desperately scanned the auditorium, I noticed a few other people had also stood sprinkled across the massive arena, but not many. I was instantly on high alert.

Then I heard more *God Bless Yous* and *Praise the Lord*s echoing from seats all around me—all directed *at* me. I looked down at Leslie and could see the whites of her eyes over the rim of her red glasses. Steve, obviously noticing my confusion, turned bright pink as he covered his mouth to hide his erupting laughter. He hit Tucker's arm repeatedly, saying between each breath, "She doesn't know. She doesn't know," as tears streamed down his face.

Doesn't know what? What the fuck is going on? Why am I standing? Why am I standing? I frantically scanned the room, searching for a clue.

And then my face appeared on several giant screens across the arena. Leslie covered her mouth and whispered, "Oh my God." Steve gasped so loud I thought he was going to have a heart attack. Both he and Tucker were hysterical, pointing at the large monitor directly in front of us.

Then Leslie jumped up, startling me, cheering loudly, which took me totally by surprise. The crowd, applauding and whistling all around us, got even louder when they saw her standing next to me. And now we were both on the big screen.

"What the fuck is going on?" I whispered.

But Leslie screamed with her arms over her head, as if our team had just scored a goal.

Finally, she stopped and said through clenched teeth, "Look at the camera and smile. You just got yourself pre-ordained."

"What?!?" My mouth dropped open.

Apparently, this was the part of the service where non-religious people stood to publicly declare Jesus Christ as their Lord and Savior—when we officially embraced religion and were touched by the Spirit.

"Jesus …" I said quietly, as the shock set in.

"Exactly," she giggled. "Don't worry," she grabbed my hand and lifted it into the air, "friends don't let friends get pre-ordained by themselves." Then she cheered, "Woo-hoo!" as the *God bless yous* and the *Amens* blended in unison all around us. Joel, seeing Leslie and me on the massive screens, pointed in our direction.

"Man, we got us some big believers in God up there."

And the crowd went nuts. They assumed Leslie was so inspired by my decision to get pre-ordained that she decided to as well, believing they had just witnessed a miracle. "We were definitely both miracles," I reflected to myself. "But not for the reasons they thought we were."

"God bless you too," Leslie replied to every person who came up to us after it was over, each time playing her part to perfection.

Even when I committed what I considered was an enormous sin, she never let me walk alone. Leslie stood next to me, toe-to-toe, sin-for-sin. We were in it together or not at all.

I finished washing her face and wrapped her hands and feet in warm towels. She had finally drifted into a peaceful sleep. Dawn was just about to break, and the sky hinted at a magnificent sunrise. Rather than leaving immediately to beat the early morning traffic, I moved a cushy chair in front of the window and curled under a blanket, intent on witnessing the brilliance. Instead, I dozed off before the masterpiece was complete, dreaming about Kenya and the elephants who lived there.

CHAPTER 26

A white van, full of tourists, careened down a dusty road in Tsavo, its blaring music cut through the serene atmosphere. A keeper mending a fence nearby watched as it sped past. With a sense of urgency, he ran to his jeep and shouted into the radio.

"Joseph, do you copy? There is a speeding van heading in your direction!"

But it was too late. He and the other keepers lagged too far back. The elephants had already begun crossing the road, directly in the path of the fast-approaching vehicle.

Emily sensed the danger first and raised the alarm with a deafening trumpet call. Aitong immediately shoved the younger orphans from behind, trying with all her strength to move them out of harm's way, but there were too many. As the van closed in, the men watched in horror, helpless to stop the tragedy unfolding before their eyes.

All of a sudden, the enormous frame of Imenti materialized in the middle of the road. He raised his head, spread his ears wide, and squared off with the danger barreling toward them, positioning his massive body between the threat and his herd.

The vehicle screeched to a halt, disappearing into a large plume of red dust. The pulsating music went silent as Imenti's scream cut like a knife. He waited for a moment, then lowered his head and charged, with Emily right on his heels.

"No, no, NO!" the keepers yelled, still racing to the scene.

The tourists shrieked as the driver slammed the van into reverse, backing up as fast as he could, but the two elephants advanced with alarming speed. A charging, angry elephant can outrun all but the fastest humans. Even a vehicle going full-speed in reverse had little chance of escape.

Imenti's posture gave away his mission—to attack. He swiftly narrowed the gap and, without hesitation, rammed both tusks right through the windshield, missing the driver by a hair. With the van stopped, Imenti withdrew and slid them under the front bumper lifting the vehicle and its occupants high off the ground.

Mishak shuddered knowing that a full-grown elephant could easily flip a large truck packed with people with little effort if it chose to. The tourists screamed as their lives flashed before them.

"Imenti—Imenti! *KOMESHA!*" *STOP!* yelled the keepers.

With a loud, hard thud, Imenti obeyed, and the van dropped. The two elephants stood side-by-side, motionless, and glared at the whimpering driver who lifted his hands in surrender—as if either elephant knew what that meant.

Together, they formed an intimidating presence. The sobbing, terrified tourists covered their mouths and remained as quiet as possible, fully aware their lives depended on the elephants' next step.

Mishak, out of breath, stopped within a few feet of Imenti and extended his arm toward the angry elephant.

"*Ni sawa. Ni sawa,* Imenti." *It's OK. It's OK.* He tried to slow his breathing while speaking gently to his friend.

"Stay where you are and don't move," another keeper whispered to the driver and the cowering tourists through the open windows.

Terrified eyes peeked over the edges as they watched the scene unfolding before them. They could hardly believe that the men were standing so close to the dangerous, wild, angry elephants who'd almost killed them—and still might. They didn't know that these were orphans raised by their human caretakers.

Imenti used his front foot to kick a large cloud of dirt toward the vehicle. Tiny pebbles struck the metal frame as a swirl of red dust followed—a sign of his disgust. Then he turned to face Mishak, who reached out, lightly touching Imenti's trunk. The elephant took a deep breath and exhaled long and hard.

"*Vizuri mvulana,*" *Good boy,* Mishak said, reassuring him as he nudged Imenti in the opposite direction.

Emily didn't need to be coaxed. Once the danger was over, she turned and ran back to Aitong and the terrified herd while the rest of the keepers surrounded the tourists to make sure there were no injuries.

"*Njooni* Imenti, *hapa, njoo,*" Mishak beckoned. *Come on* Imenti, *this way, come.*

The elephant followed, turning back every few moments to be certain the threat had passed. He trumpeted one last time, as if warning the driver, before he shook his massive head, slapped his ears, and rejoined the rest of his herd. Mishak jogged close behind.

The keepers were relieved that there were no injuries to anyone except to the vehicle itself, but the situation represented a growing problem in Tsavo. Tourist operators wanted their clients to have "an experience to remember." Getting a photograph of an elephant charging at them certainly did the trick, so some got too close and even tried to provoke the elephants. It was a pattern seen in every country and park across Africa where wild herds roamed, though some cases were more troubling than others.

Occasionally someone was seriously injured, or worse, and charges were filed. The elephant that attacked was always killed, but the tourists were left with their precious photo and a riveting story to share with friends. Meanwhile, their drivers, who were to blame for the chaos in the first place, often escaped accountability.

From then on, anytime Imenti spotted a white van, he charged at it. The keepers had to remain extra vigilant, ensuring they arrived before pandemonium ensued. Though he never attacked again, his reaction to white vans specifically never changed—he blocked their path, stood firm, and delivered a stark warning.

Every driver Imenti encountered stayed still and wisely cut their engines, anything to avoid provoking him further. However, the park authorities grew concerned. They told Daphne that if Imenti didn't knock it off, they would have to remove him one way or the other.

Over the next few months, tensions escalated. In hindsight, Mishak realized the elephants' peculiar behavior hinted that something was amiss. Yet it wasn't until he pieced together each event that he recognized the first signs of trouble had emerged long before anyone understood the full extent of the growing problem.

On the morning of May 16, 2001, Dika and Ndume appeared out of nowhere just outside the Voi stockades, marking the start of what would soon become a much larger crisis. The two bull elephants, which hadn't been seen in months, were practically inseparable during their upbringing at the orphanage in Nairobi. After several years, they integrated into a wild herd.

Their sudden appearance at the stockades took the keepers by pleasant surprise, but when they realized the reason, alarm quickly followed. Dika had a wire snare wrapped around one of his massive legs, cut deep into his skin. The trap, designed to capture large animals as they walk through a loop, tightens with the slightest touch. When the animal moves, the snare constricts, restraining it and preventing escape. Fortunately for Dika, Ndume was there to help set him free. Despite the many years they'd spent in the wild, the bond between them remained strong.

While the keepers began the task of removing the twisted metal and tending to Dika's wound, which appeared to be minor, he repeatedly touched one side of his face with his trunk. Standing over ten feet tall, Dika towered over the men, making it impossible to see what he was trying to show them.

Mishak grabbed a ladder to get a closer look and discovered a painful, infected abscess in the elephant's cheek, requiring a thorough cleansing and more antibiotics. They couldn't determine the cause of the wound: whether it was from a spear thrown by a poacher or if Dika had accidentally cut himself, leading to an infection. It was Mishak's first inclination of the trouble that lay ahead.

While the men tended to the elephant's wounds, Ndume enjoyed several of his favorite snacks. Once Dika had received the proper treatment, the two bulls vanished back into the bush, disappearing together just as they had arrived.

Nearly three months after his last appearance, on August 3, the keepers returned from a day out with the younger elephants to find Ndume waiting for them inside the night stockades. This time he was alone. He had never ventured into the orphans' quarters before, not since his return to the wild years earlier.

"Ndume," Mishak whispered as he approached.

The elephant didn't extend his trunk as usual. Instead, he curled it to one side, revealing a long streak of blood. Mishak gently grabbed it, fearing the worst as he turned it over. His dread was confirmed when he saw the broken end of a spear tip embedded deep within.

Panicked, he raced outside. *"Piga simu Nairobi!" Call Nairobi!* he yelled, instructing them to get a vet there now.

The men sprang into action, alarmed at the urgency in Mishak's voice. His unusual panic raised everyone's anxiety. Once they learned of Ndume's injury, they quickly understood why.

Sometimes poachers used unpoisoned spears or arrows, but it was much more common to find the tips coated in the toxic sap of the Acokanthera plant, otherwise known as the Arrow Tree. Once the poison entered the bloodstream, quick treatment became vital. Their only hope was that it had diluted over time, since the fresher it was, the more lethal it became. Mishak wondered if that was why Ndume had ventured into the orphans' night enclosure. Perhaps the elephant realized that when he inevitably collapsed, he would at least be safe and surrounded by those he trusted most.

Joseph joined Mishak inside the stockades after he made the urgent call to Daphne for help.

"There's no chance of getting the vet here before dawn," he said. "But they will come at first light."

All they could do was wait and pray there was enough time. Mishak stayed with Ndume during that long night, making sure he had plenty of water and his favorite treats. But when he woke in the early hours, Ndume was gone, slipping out after he'd fallen asleep.

That morning, a plane arrived, and they conducted an extensive search by air and on the ground, but there was no sign of the wounded elephant. Mishak pushed aside panicked thoughts of Ndume collapsing somewhere in the bush, all alone as the poison took hold.

"We'll find him," Joseph said reassuringly, as darkness forced their retreat.

For the next two days, they searched by land and air but found no trace of him. At 4:00 a.m. on August 6, a loud rumble jolted Mishak awake. He rushed outside to find Ndume waiting for him. The vet was awakened, and by sunrise an operation was underway. They successfully extracted the spearhead, administered a massive dose of antibiotics, and hoped they'd gotten it out in time.

Once Ndume was back on his feet, he stayed within the fenced perimeter of the sanctuary instead of venturing into the bush as usual. Over the next three days, Mishak cared for him just as he had when the large elephant was a baby. While the poison wasn't strong enough to kill, it was sufficient to make Ndume quite ill.

On the fourth day, Edo arrived at the stockades along with a younger bull he favored, Lewa, eager to see their friend. Ndume joined them in the afternoon, but returned to the safety of the stockades by nightfall. The two elephants continued to visit over the next several days, until finally, a week later, Ndume was well enough to leave with them.

At the end of that same month, on August 28, a keeper called out from his rock perch overlooking the orphans.

"*Tembo wawili wanakaribia!*" *Two elephants are approaching!*

The men stood, eager to see who they were. Through his binoculars, Mishak made out the unmistakable figures of Ndume and Lewa. And then he saw more blood.

Imenti squealed as soon as he recognized them and ran to engage Lewa in a bout of play. But they walked right past him, straight toward the keepers. Mishak could see that Lewa had a deep, bloody gash on his back. This time Ndume was his escort.

Once again a vet was summoned and Lewa was tranquilized while they cleaned and dressed his wound.

"What is it from?" asked Joseph, already suspecting the alarming answer.

"Probably a *panga* thrown from high above," the vet said as he made a throwing motion. The deep gash across Lewa's back was much too broad to have been caused by an arrow. Instead, it matched a large, machete-like knife with a wide blade, commonly used for cutting through thick vegetation. Everyone knew it would take a long time for an injury that deep to heal.

Later that evening, Mishak spoke with Joseph in hushed tones outside the dorms. He shared his fear that something felt wrong and wondered if their elephants were being deliberately targeted.

"Yes, I feel it too," Joseph responded, just as concerned.

"*Lazima tuwafuate,*" *We should follow them,* Mishak suggested.

The two devised a plan. If someone was targeting the former orphans, they could at least defend them and—if luck prevailed—identify who was behind the attacks.

The following day, Ndume was seen leading Imenti into areas beyond the protected park boundary. It offered an important clue. The men were able to get in front of the elephants and chase them back.

A few days later, they spotted Ndume again, in the company of several wild bulls. When the group came upon one of the many electric fences that separated the safe zone from danger, Ndume leaned into a post until it collapsed beneath his weight. Then he delicately walked on the fallen log to get to the other side without getting shocked, and the others followed.

It was both brilliant and scary to the men who witnessed it. Elephants had been spotted all over the park, discovering various methods to bypass the system that kept them safe. But if electric fencing couldn't prevent them from going into dangerous zones, then what could?

Days later, a report came in that a group of wild bulls were seen at one of the many lodges rummaging through a garbage pit. Even though open garbage pits are illegal in Kenya, some establishments—particularly those owned or connected to untouchable government officials—ignored the regulations. The idea was to lure elephants closer for the tourists, but unfortunately, it almost always ended in tragedy. And once they got used to this kind of behavior, the elephants usually wandered into other areas they weren't supposed to. As a result, they either came too close to people, and were killed for that reason, or they ingested things their bodies couldn't process, like glass or plastic, and died an even more excruciating death.

Daphne asked Joseph to gather a few men to investigate which elephants were at the nearby lodge, see if any were theirs, and report back. Armed with binoculars, Joseph and the keepers parked a short distance below the garbage pit and watched until their worst fears were realized as the familiar figures of Ndume, Edo, Imenti, and Lewa came into view, accompanied by several unfamiliar large wild bulls. While three of their elephants entered, Edo hung back.

"What is he doing?" a keeper asked Joseph. "Why is he waiting outside?"

Joseph watched Edo and smiled to himself.

"His mother was killed in one," he said quietly. "He remembers."

Edo lost his mother when he was a baby after she swallowed a chunk of glass from a garbage pit in Amboseli. At the time, he was still milk-dependent and forced to watch her suffering for several, agonizing days before she died.

ELEPHANT MOUNTAIN

The keepers realized the orphans' wayward behavior was most likely the cause of the sudden increase in elephant injuries. Poachers weren't targeting them; rather, it was the elephants themselves who were behaving recklessly. It was more probable they were entering other restricted areas and being chased away by responsible lodge owners trying to protect their guests.

It was not the scenario Joseph had hoped for. Elephants rummaging through garbage pits or being the target of poachers still produced the same result: both ended in tragedy. He called Daphne and informed her that at least three of the garbage raiders were their own.

"I was afraid of this," she said, sounding worried. "We have to move fast before the authorities intervene. I'll make some calls. Please let me know right away if there's trouble."

It didn't take long before there was. On September 22, an elephant suffering from a severe injury was spotted by a plane on the outskirts of the park, barely able to walk and alone. Their hearts sank when they realized the injured one was Ndume. Again. Another frantic call was placed to the vet.

By the time they reached him, Ndume was too weak to make it back to the compound and the safety of the night enclosure. The vet anesthetized him and discovered a poisoned arrow deeply embedded in his left thigh. After it was removed and Ndume regained consciousness, Mishak and Joseph set up camp next to him.

They watched over their friend as he fell gravely ill. Over the next several days, his strength began to return, and despite the potency of the poison, he pulled through. When he had enough energy to walk to the stockades on his own, Ndume stayed close to the keepers and the compound until he once again regained the stamina to rejoin his wild friends.

Daphne knew that to have any chance of saving the rebels, they had to act fast. It was only a matter of time before park authorities identified the group as "problem elephants," and that would demand that they be shot.

On October 4, Daphne shared some news with the keepers: she'd found a safe place for Ndume to go. They all breathed a sigh of relief. However, it was the second part of her announcement that stopped them in their tracks. He would not be going alone.

CHAPTER 27

I'm calling to arrange a time to speak with the President," a smart voice said at the other end of the line.

I ignored the call when a number I didn't recognize appeared on my phone. After the third attempt in as many minutes, I thought it might be important.

"The ... President?" I asked, trying to get my bearings.

"You spoke at his Rotary Club a few days ago, of which he is *the President*. Can I schedule you for this afternoon?"

"Ohh, yes, of course." I laughed softly, realizing how ridiculous it was to think she meant *that* President. "What is this regarding?"

"Does three this afternoon work? The President is very busy and stressed that time is of the essence."

"Sure, I can do that."

I wondered why she kept referring to him as "the President" instead of using his name or if she was just joking. Still, I was intrigued.

The large Rotary Club in an affluent suburb of Portland had booked me to speak more than a year in advance, due to its considerable size and popularity. I thought back to the brief interaction I'd had with *the President*, but nothing obvious stood out.

He was a tall, older gentleman with a splash of white hair, dressed in a fine, tailored suit, with well-manicured nails and soft hands, which I noticed when he shook mine. When I arrived to set up, he was among the first people there to greet me, and the only reason I remembered him.

"Hi, Debbie, this is *the President*," he said, calling precisely on time. It was so strange to hear someone call themselves that and sound as serious about it as he did.

"How can I help you?" I asked.

He rambled on about my presentation and how much he'd enjoyed it, specifically a section where I talked about the Bonobo, one of the four species of Great Apes. *The Bonobo?* His comment surprised me. I paused for a moment before realizing that, though I mentioned them, it was only in reference to the similarity of our DNA.

"No one's ever said that before," I giggled. "Usually, they like the part about … the elephants."

Apparently, he was also the president of a major financial institution with locations around the world. I listened patiently as he listed his conquests and accomplishments, including the fact that he had once owned the most expensive home in Oregon. I knew the one. Not because of its enormous price tag, but because it kept getting called out by the *Willamette Week*, a local newspaper, as one of Oregon's most egregious "water-wasters." As he droned on, I wondered what any of it had to do with me.

" … and this brings me to what I would like to discuss with you," he said finally. I sat up, curious where this was going. "My company selects five nonprofits that we finance in full, but recently we had to make a tough decision to let one of them go."

"OK," I said, waiting for him to continue.

"I've already discussed it with my board, and we all agree that KOTA is the perfect fit to step into the open position."

"Uh, wow. I—I think that's great ... but I'm not sure what that means exactly."

A mix of excitement and uncertainty washed over me, as the implication of his words sank in.

"When's the last time you went to Kenya?" he asked.

"Last year."

"I imagine you could make significant progress if you were able to go back more often. We would cover all expenses for any trips you need to take, including all of KOTA's business costs. We have several office buildings in the Portland area, so we'd like to offer you space in one of those free of charge as well. Your passion really came through in your presentation. You have exactly what I, and our company, are looking for."

I could hardly believe what I was hearing. All I could say was, "I'm sorry, I'm at a loss for words."

As if he hadn't heard me, he continued. "I would also be happy to donate front page ads in all the local newspapers and magazines to bring in more donations and help build a larger audience for your organization."

It took me a moment to fully process his generous offer. Simply put, it was beyond my wildest dreams. I had never imagined that such proposals even existed. *And all because I'd worked so hard on that presentation.* Those early mornings and sleepless nights and every minute spent crisscrossing the state had finally paid off in the most spectacular way.

At KOTA, we made a conscious decision to operate entirely as volunteers—including myself. For us, this approach felt important because so many organizations on both sides of the elephant debate are financially invested in their positions: zoos receive funds to keep elephants in captivity, while advocacy groups raise money to keep them out. I believed that, for our work to be as objective as possible, it was essential that we remain free from financial incentives. It also ensured that all of our donations went toward our projects, without benefiting anyone associated with the foundation.

Jason had expressed his concern, wondering how long I could continue balancing a full-time job while continuing to run KOTA, which was growing bigger by the minute. As a result, the board decided that hiring external contractors for specific tasks could be considered if necessary. This unexpected opportunity sounded like the solution to most of our problems. I could hardly wait to share this exciting news with him.

"Listen," the President said, "I have another meeting I have to jump into, but I'd like to meet in person to discuss your nonprofit's needs in more depth. I have to leave the country first thing in the morning, so would it be possible to get together this evening?"

"Ah … yes," I said. "I can make that work."

"Excellent. Bring a list of everything you need. Sound good?"

"That sounds great!"

"I'll have my assistant, Samantha, send you the details. We'll see you tonight and again, nice job!"

"Thank you," I gushed, brimming with excitement.

Shortly after I hung up, I received a text with the time and location. I was thrilled to learn that we were meeting at Ox, recently crowned "Restaurant of the Year." Since then, getting a reservation was next to impossible. Besides, a single dinner was way more than I could afford. Pennie was fortunate enough to get in, and couldn't stop raving about it.

A few hours later, I found a parking space down the street. The car I drove was a total clunker and there was absolutely no chance

I would allow it to be parked by a valet at such a nice restaurant. The outfit I chose was elegant and stylish, perfect for blending in with the upscale clientele, but my vehicle was a dead giveaway to my financial situation.

A young man held open the door, and as I entered, someone called my name. I turned to find the President standing behind me.

"Was that you walking up the street?" he asked. "Why didn't you park your car with the valet?"

"Oh, I found a spot so easily, there was no need," I said, eager to change the subject.

The entire restaurant was bathed in red light, giving it a dramatic, almost Chinese-inspired ambiance and not what I expected. The President diverted my attention by peppering me with questions about specific topics from my presentation, and I became so engrossed in our conversation that I hardly noticed one of the hostesses leading us to our table.

As we walked through the dimly lit dining room, an eerie sensation washed over me. Each server stopped until we passed, nodding at the President, then at me. At first, I dismissed the attention, assuming it was just some fancy restaurant protocol. I'd worked in the industry long enough to know that each establishment had its own set of rules. The moment we were seated, a young woman handed us our menus.

As her fingers struggled to uncork a bottle of champagne, she said enthusiastically, "Happy Valentine's Day!"

My face drained of all color. Valentines Day. That explained why the restaurant was lit in red. *Fuck, fuck, fuck, fuck, fuck, fuck.* How had I had missed such a crucial detail? Since I was single, I didn't pay attention to holidays meant for couples. Even when

I was in a relationship, Valentine's Day wasn't an occasion I'd celebrated or cared for. But to have overlooked it for a business meeting felt like a monumental mistake. Embarrassment tinged my cheeks. I was thankful for the crimson lighting, which offered a discreet camouflage to my growing discomfort.

While the President kept the server busy with questions about the menu, my mind raced. *Was this a date?* Then I remembered—he was departing the next morning, the very reason for our urgent meeting. I took a slow, deep breath to center myself. *Just be cool.* My inner calm slowly returned. The server uncorked the bottle and went to pour champagne into my empty glass.

"Ah, none for me, please." I said, placing my palm over the rim. "I don't drink."

"Don't worry," the President said lightly touching my hand. "I took the liberty of ordering non-alcoholic champagne."

Alarm bells rang again. How did he know I didn't drink? While my glass was being filled, it suddenly occurred to me that I had shared a snippet of my recovery journey during my presentation. Relieved, I settled down. *See? All fine.*

As the President scanned the menu, I wondered how he'd secured a reservation—at the last minute. And on a holiday that must have been booked for months. Casually, I looked across the expansive, red-lit room. There was nothing but romantic couples as far as my eye could see. When he called for a toast, I lifted my champagne flute, concentrating to keep my hand steady.

"To what I hope is the beginning of a new partnership," he said.

"To a partnership." I clinked my glass with his.

I was grateful for my past life as an actress and the years of acting classes that came with it. Just then, an appetizer we hadn't ordered appeared on our table. When I tasted a bite, a burst of flavor exploded in my mouth, transporting me to a new dimension. It was unlike anything I had ever tasted before.

"We'll take another one of these," the President said to our server.

I nodded vigorously. It took every ounce of self-control to refrain from groaning with pleasure after each delicious bite.

Before long, I noticed something peculiar happening with the servers at our table—they were hovering, and it was becoming annoying. Whenever I sipped even the smallest amount of water, a server swooped in to fill my glass. When I dropped my napkin, before I could bend down to retrieve it, a fresh one appeared. The President and I barely exchanged a word before yet another interruption. Finally, I'd had enough and needed to find out what was going on.

"If you'll excuse me," I said, flashing a bright smile and using my best manners. "I need to go to the ladies' room."

I waited in the hallway, hoping to catch one of the people stationed at our table. Instead, a hostess saw me and approached.

"Can I help you with something?" she asked. "Oh, Debbie, hi!" I didn't recognize her at first. "It's me, Layla. I know ... the hair, right?"

"Wow," I said as it registered. "It looks great dark."

We'd attended the same recovery meeting downtown for years until I moved to West Linn. I was accustomed to seeing her as a blonde, like myself.

"How are you?" she asked, giving me a hug.

"I'm doing well," I said. "How long have you worked here?"

"A while," she grinned. "But *you* ... are you enjoying your Valentine's Day?"

"That's what I wanted to ask about," I whispered, leaning in. "Confidentially, of course." I looked around her, back to my table.

"I don't have much time." Layla nodded in the direction of a closed door, and gestured me to follow.

"What is it?" she asked as we entered a small closet.

"I'm curious how we … I mean, the President and I—"

"The President?" Layla asked, raising her eyebrows. Then she used his first name and rolled her eyes. "He makes us all call him that too," she said. "It's so weird."

"Isn't it though?" I shook my head at the absurdity. "But first, do you know how he got a table here at the last minute? And why are so many servers hovering over us?"

"He comes in here all the time," Layla whispered. "How long have you two been together?"

"Oh, no," I said, correcting her. "We're only friends—we just met, actually."

"Must be some friend," she murmured under her breath, peering through a crack in the door. Then she turned back, reached into her pocket, and presented five, crisp one-hundred-dollar bills.

"He gave it to all of us to make sure we took great care of your table. He said that he was coming in with someone *really special*," she added, making air quotes.

"What?" I was shocked.

"We bumped another couple off the schedule in order to get you in. He must have pulled some strings because we've never done that before. At least not as long as I've been here."

"So that's why everyone is staring at us." The realization hit me as Layla nodded.

"I can ask the servers to give you some space at your table if you'd like."

"Yes, thank you," I said. "I have to go, he'll start wondering where I am, but it was great to see you!"

We hugged again before we calmly exited the closet and went our separate ways. With each step, my anxiety rose. I took a deep breath before diving back into character, one that exuded calm and confidence. But my insides churned.

Just as I settled into my seat, another delectable appetizer arrived, and I was plunged once again into a state of total bliss, unable to think or concentrate on anything else.

"Let's get down to business," the President said at last. "Did you bring the list?"

"Yes," I replied, feeling a wave of relief. Partly because he'd asked when my mouth wasn't full, and partly because I was eager to delve into the details.

I took it from my purse and passed it across the table, catching sight of a paper partially hidden beneath his napkin. After glancing briefly at what I'd given him, he pushed the concealed document toward me.

"I think this should cover just about everything," he said.

It appeared to be a formal, legal contract. The first few paragraphs were standard until the text opened to a section of bullet points that began with:

- The Contractor hereby agrees to walk on the back of the Client, while naked and wearing high heels, at the Client's full discretion.

Before I could fully comprehend what I was reading, the President leaned in.

"You should know," he said in a hushed tone, "that this contract not only covers all of KOTA's expenses, but also comes with an apartment and a vehicle for you. Think carefully before you decide."

Then he shoved a whole empanada into his mouth, looking thoroughly pleased with himself, as if this were a normal contract on a normal day. For him, it probably was. It made me hate Valentine's Day more than I already did.

I paused after reading the document in full, each bullet point more sadistic than the last. Finally, I steeled myself and stared directly into his eyes.

"Do you think you're the first guy to proposition me?" I struggled to keep my voice steady.

"Nope," he said without flinching. "But I certainly hope I'm the last."

I wish, in that moment, that I'd told him to go fuck himself. I wish I'd thrown my drink in his face and stormed out of that restaurant. Then he said what I already knew was coming. He said the thing guys like him always say.

"You do realize I would not enter into this type of contract with someone I did not have fully vetted. I know who you are. I know where you come from."

"You've looked into me?" I asked. Goosebumps prickled down each arm. "We only met, what … a few days ago?"

"Oh, I checked into you before then," he said with a smug grin. "I noticed your name on the schedule as one of our upcoming speakers and had you … *surveyed*."

Surveyed? It was such an odd choice of words. I stayed quiet and forced myself to remain calm. Our servers had all disappeared just when I would have done anything for an interruption. I kicked myself for asking them to leave us alone.

"If you so much as whisper a word about this to anyone, I will bury you. Do you understand?" And there it was. The threat I already knew was coming.

"Is this what happened with the last nonprofit? She wouldn't follow the rules?"

"Let's just say, she didn't honor the agreement she signed."

"How many?" I asked.

"How many what?"

"How many of these do you have set up? How many women do you have stashed in apartments around town?"

"A few. Almost enough. But I have room for one more." His wedding ring glistened in the light.

"Well, I'm not interested." I slid the contract across the table.

I would rather live the rest of my life in abject poverty, yet free, then be confined to a cage, no matter how gilded.

"Have you two decided?" Our server finally appeared.

"I don't think—" the President said as he closed the menu.

"Yes," I interrupted him. Before he could object, I ordered the most expensive thing available.

He looked at me with a twinkle in his eye and said, "I'll have what she's having."

My decision to stay and finish what I'd started may not have been popular or even right, but I didn't care. The food was extraordinary. At the very least, he owed me that. The President was a consummate professional who thrived on the thrill of the game. I was quite familiar with his kind. Yet, after we ordered, he surprised me with polite conversation, making the rest of dinner much less awkward.

On my drive home, I thought about guys like him: the groomers and the predators. I'd encountered more than my fair share and had hoped that with age, it would dissipate. I was no longer the naïve girl I once was, and not by choice.

During eighth grade, my once-flat torso transformed into curves that felt like an unwelcome betrayal. As an athlete, I was horrified by the new development and began taping my chest—anything to make them disappear. Despite my limited knowledge about sex, I was acutely aware that the way men looked at me had changed. *Significantly.* And I didn't like it. Things were never the same again after that.

Over time, I came to recognize the lingering gaze of a predator and took measures to avoid that kind of attention. I started noticing anyone who went too far out of their way to help me. I hated being that person—always questioning, looking for hidden motives, unable to take someone at their word. Although occasionally, I let my guard down and caught more than one knife by the blade. I'd learned it was usually safer to expect the unexpected.

I grew increasingly enraged with these selfish kinds of men, the ones who sullied everything they touched and whose motives only ever served two purposes: sex or power. The President's proposition hurt more because it affected something I cared about so deeply—the elephants.

The freeway was dark and nearly empty as I drove home. When I changed lanes, I noticed a car behind me doing the same a short way back. At first, I was lost in thought and brushed it off as a coincidence. But when I switched lanes two more times, and it followed, I felt a rising sense of unease. With so few cars around us, it was strange. I tried to remember what to do in this kind of situation and exited into a well-lit area. Thankfully, the car kept going. As it passed above on the overpass, I managed a brief glimpse. It was a white, four-door BMW.

The President had driven away in a dark-colored Range Rover, so I knew it wasn't him, although it made me wonder if he was still having me "surveyed." I sat at the bottom of the exit for a few light cycles before rejoining the freeway.

I continued on, but just when I convinced myself my paranoia was winning, I spotted the same vehicle sitting on the shoulder of an on-ramp with its lights on. It pulled out and merged behind me as I passed, maintaining a safe distance. Once again, my nerves tightened as I watched it nervously in my rearview mirror.

Part of me was gripped by terror, while the other believed I was still overreacting. I got off at my exit, but the large curve leading up to it obscured my view of the car trailing me. I skidded through the red light, hoping the officer who normally sat on the corner would notice. Unfortunately, he wasn't there. Being new to the area, I didn't even know where the police station was.

I took a different route home, driving through a nearby park instead. The entrance was at the bottom of a long, steep hill, which led to several small parking areas and a boat ramp by the river. From there, it would be easy to spot someone approaching from a distance. Though the park was closed, a lesser-known back road ran parallel to the water, passing right in front of my secluded apartment.

I accidentally hurled over a large speed bump, nearly giving myself a concussion. "Settle down," I said out loud, but it was no use. I screeched into a space in one of the smaller lots, then ran across a larger, empty parking area where I took refuge next to a hidden entrance to the trail I walked daily. Not only was it a perfect vantage point to see a vehicle coming down the hill, but I could easily remain unseen in the dark forest.

While I stood among the trees and absorbed the stillness, my shoulders relaxed for the first time in what felt like hours, and the tightness in my body eased just a little. I couldn't help but recall how much I'd missed sneaking around at night. In my childhood, long after everyone had gone to sleep, I often climbed out my bedroom window. I loved roaming the streets of my small town in the dark, skipping from one shadow to the next.

Suddenly, a pair of headlights pierced through the trees—a car was coming down the hill. My pounding heart echoed in my ears. "It's probably just a local," I whispered to myself, willing my composure to return. The car advanced slowly, still too distant to identify its make or model. I crouched low to observe it without being seen. It crept toward a stop sign before turning in my direction, its lights sweeping over the top of my head. When it stopped behind my car—the only other one in the park—I held my breath and inched closer to get a better view.

It was the same white BMW that had followed me on the freeway. I covered my mouth, desperate not to make any sound. A man got out holding a large flashlight. He approached my car, shining his light into the driver's seat before trying the locked door handle. Then he walked to the front and placed his hand on the hood checking to see it was still warm. The beam of his light swept into the forest, pointing away from where I was hidden. After a brief pause, he climbed once more into his car and drove down the secret back road, heading toward my house.

Silently, I jogged beside him along a trail several feet below, grateful for its smooth, paved surface and the flat shoes I'd wisely chosen for dinner. As he turned left onto my street, he stopped in front of my unmarked parking spot, a chilling move since the main driveway was on the opposite side. The driver lingered while I watched, frozen in place.

Then he pulled away, drove up the hill, and disappeared, leaving me alone in the darkness. I exhaled and walked a short distance down the trail to my favorite bench by the river, letting the surge of adrenaline pass, certain that the stranger was a warning.

Of course, the President knew where I lived. Whoever he had tailing me obviously wanted me to be aware of his presence, since I'd noticed him so easily. His words hung in the air—a haunting reminder that he was still watching me and intended for me to know it. I felt drained from the roller coaster ride. Why couldn't this just be about the elephants?

The river was tranquil and serene, a stark contrast to the turmoil of the night. Hours ago, I had been on such a high, feeling as though all of my hard work had finally paid off. And now this.

"Nothing has changed," an inner voice whispered.

This was yet another rich, entitled asshole who expected the world to bend to his will. That's all. I had grown accustomed to them over the years. In truth, I was exhausted by these types of men. I was exhausted by the patriarchy.

"No," I thought. "This changes nothing."

I would keep moving forward, even if only one baby step at a time, just as I always had. Despair was not an option. My focus had to stay on the elephants and bringing their extraordinary qualities to light.

After a while, I steadied myself and walked back to my car, feeling less shaky. The cool air had replaced the heat of adrenaline. All I wanted was to go home, crawl into bed, and forget any of this had ever happened. But when I stepped through my front door, my confidence to keep moving forward wavered and I was pulled to the bookshelf. Suddenly desperate for a sign, I turned to the elephant stories, hoping to reignite my spark. I needed to find something to assure me that my purpose was higher than what this night suggested and that I hadn't lost my way.

CHAPTER 28

*T*he men gathered for an important announcement. Daphne had called from Nairobi and as they listened, their faces were etched with anticipation. An investigation was already underway to identify which elephants were raiding the garbage pits. The authorities were closing in and once they targeted the individuals to kill, there was no turning back.

David Sheldrick's original philosophy extended to all the animals in their care. He believed they deserved the right to make their own decisions, just as we did. Therefore, none of the orphans—whether elephants or zebra—were kept longer than necessary, no matter how fond their human caretakers became of them. Instead, every animal was given the chance to choose its own path, and ultimately they all did.

After David's passing, the Kenya Wildlife Service allowed Daphne to continue releasing orphans into Tsavo. But only if the elephants and other animals stayed away from people. If the authorities discovered that her orphans were not only part of the problem but leading others out of the safety of the park, it could ruin everything they had worked so hard for and jeopardize the entire organization.

"I've found somewhere safe for Ndume to go," Daphne said. "However, he won't be going alone." Mishak and Joseph looked at one another as she continued. "He will be sent away with Lewa ... and Imenti."

As she issued further instructions, Mishak's heart sank, even though he understood it was their only chance to save them. He had known Daphne for years and recognized this wasn't a decision she'd made lightly. Imenti was already on thin ice with his charging-every-white-van-he-saw behavior. Once the park officials learned he was also one of the garbage raiders, it would be his last straw—and the keepers knew it.

Lewa would go along to keep them company, since Ndume and Imenti had protected and adored the younger elephant for years. Daphne hoped the three would form their own mini-bachelor herd. The keepers wondered how Edo, Lewa's adoptive surrogate parent, would react to his sudden departure. It was a truly unique case, being the sole documented instance of a bull elephant adopting a baby as his own.

Lewa had been the favored orphan of Malaika, the former matriarch. After she collapsed during labor, he seemed confused when she couldn't get back up. He tried desperately to lift her. When he was unable, he laid down next to her, refusing to leave the side of the only mother he had ever known. The keepers had to make the heartbreaking decision to end Malaika's suffering. But when Lewa heard the gunshot that ended her life, he panicked and fled. The men searched for him late into the night, worried about his safety since large predators roamed nearby.

The next morning, Ndume and Dika arrived escorting the younger elephant, back to the safety of the stockades. This time Lewa refused to enter. Perhaps his memory of Malaika kept him from going inside. Too young and small to survive alone and still dependent on milk, he posed a problem the keepers had never encountered before. Unsure how to protect Lewa if he remained alone, the men were at a loss.

Edo, who had also returned from the wild just before Malaika died, seemed to sense the situation. At night, he stayed close to the stockades with Lewa, as if he were protecting him. Before long, Edo took on the responsibility of raising the young calf himself. When his bachelor herd of bulls moved on, including Ndume and Dika, Edo chose to stay behind with Lewa instead of rejoining them.

Each day, Edo brought the young calf to the keepers for his twice-daily milk feedings. At night, the large and powerful elephant, guarded and protected Lewa just as Malaika would have. Considering her close relationship with Edo, it seemed natural that he would become the little bull's caregiver, filling the void left by their beloved matriarch.

As Lewa got older and became less dependent on milk, he began venturing further afield with other young bulls, away from Edo's protective eyes, although he was never far from the young elephant's side. Since Lewa was also among the elephants identified raiding the garbage pit, including him in the relocation would allow Daphne to plead her case if park management put one, two, or all three on a kill list. This proactive measure would, at the very least, buy them all time.

The night before the transfer, Mishak spent most of the evening inside the stockades surrounded by Emily, Aitong, and Imenti. They knew something was wrong; elephants were too perceptive not to sense it. How could he explain they had no other choice? Mishak wondered if they would ever forgive him for what he was about to do.

At dawn the following morning, the keepers stood by as the two matriarchs led the orphans on their daily walk, hoping the absence of Imenti bringing up the back would go unnoticed. They assumed it would give them enough time to remove him before any of the elephants realized he was missing.

Ndume shrieked when he was hit with the biting sting of the tranquilizer dart, running a few steps before he fell to the ground, while Lewa and Imenti were subdued with little effort. Just as the keepers loaded their limp bodies into crates and onto the backs of three waiting trucks, Emily and Aitong came charging back, scattering the men. Mishak was the only one brave enough to stand in front of the massive, furious elephants barreling toward them. He held his hands high, but they swerved around him to get to their friend.

"*Rudi nyuma,* Emily!" *Stay back!* "Aitong, NO!"

But it was no use. They shoved their trunks inside the three crates, carefully inspecting each sleeping elephant. Then they surrounded the truck holding Imenti, gently touching his body as if looking for the reason the men were taking him.

Finally, Emily stood back, her gaze fixed on Mishak, while the other keepers observed from the safety of their trucks. With a swift motion, she lifted her front foot and kicked a swirling cloud of dirt in his direction. He turned his back, shielding himself from the onslaught of pebbles that pinged against the trucks. Aitong stood quietly next to her.

Before he climbed into the cab next to Joseph, Mishak stopped.

"*Nasikitika,*" *I'm sorry,* he said to the two, praying they understood.

As the trucks pulled away, he watched their giant frames disappear in his side mirror, overtaken by a large plume of dust as they pulled away. All he could do was hope they would eventually understand that removing Imenti from the park was their only option to save his life.

After driving a short distance, the men saw the rest of the herd in the care of one of their nannies. Several elephants in the group lifted their trunks in the convoy's direction before disappearing in the distance. Joseph glanced briefly at Mishak as they drove on, the loud sound of the engine filling the silence between them.

Hours later, the three trucks entered the Mtito Andei gate in Tsavo West, in the heart of Ngulia Valley. Daphne believed it was their best option since it was managed by her ex-husband and close friend, Bill Woodley, whose staff of park rangers were friendly toward elephants.

There was also no path to get back home. Ngulia Valley sits next to Chyulu Hills National Park, a large protected area with several wild herds. Years ago, they would have migrated between Voi and Chyulu, but now human settlement blocked their passage in every direction.

John Mbulu was waiting for them when they arrived. Mishak got out of the truck and greeted him with a wide, sweeping hand slap—a Kenyan handshake. It had been a long time since they'd seen each other. John used to be a keeper at the Nairobi orphanage and was there when Ndume and Malaika were rescued. He had witnessed the two recover from their devastating wounds and knew them well. Now he worked as a driver for tourists at a local lodge, and offered to keep an eye out for the three.

"*Habari rafiki yangu wa zamani*," *Hello my old friend*, he said, reaching into the elephant's crate.

Ndume had awakened during the journey and seemed less than enthusiastic; he was restless and wanted out. As soon as a keeper opened his door, Ndume shot into the bush. Unable to tell if he was disoriented or furious, Mishak chased after him with a bowl of his favorite treats, but he wasn't interested and vanished into the heavy underbrush. His sudden departure suggested he wanted nothing more to do with humans for the moment.

Soon, Lewa and Imenti got out of their crates and stood together. Lewa seemed jumpy and scared and clung tightly to Imenti's side while Mishak gave them Ndume's ration of treats. When it was time to leave, Mishak approached the elephants and offered a few words of parting encouragement. Imenti touched him with his trunk and rumbled as temporin ran down the sides of his face. Mishak couldn't explain to him what was happening or why.

"*Unabaki kuwa jasiri,*" *You stay brave*, he said, quietly rubbing his large head.

Imenti watched Mishak closely as he climbed back into the truck, then lifted his trunk as they pulled away.

"*Mlinzi juu yake,*" *Watch over him*, Mishak shouted at Imenti as he pointed toward Lewa.

John waved them off and agreed to report on the elephants' progress as soon as he was able. The last thing they heard was Imenti's thunderous rumble, but Mishak couldn't bear to look back again.

Weeks passed, and neither Daphne, nor the keepers received any updates. John searched daily and though he spotted small bachelor herds, he failed to locate any of the three. They could only hope the elephants had gained enough knowledge from the matriarchs to survive on their own.

Early one morning, Mishak and Joseph climbed high on a rock overlooking the orphans, as was their usual routine. The sun shone bright, yet still carried a hint of desert chill. An Agama lizard emerged from a shady recess, walking in slow motion before it leisurely flopped down in the open sun right in front of them. They smiled at how unafraid it was. Before its cold blood turned warm, the lizard moved at a glacial pace. But once its temperature rose, it darted faster than a bolt of lightning.

"Ahh," Joseph said, taking a seat. "Let's enjoy the rainbow."

They watched as the Agama's muted color came alive, slowly awakening with the warmth of the sun. Its head shifted from a pale gray into a shade of brilliant orange, then to the brightest hot pink, while its body transformed from the color of sand to a stunning neon blue, highlighting rings of previously unnoticeable white stripes down its long, skinny tail.

The two men were still fixated on the marvel when a loud scream pierced the landscape. Startled, they leapt to their feet. In the distance they saw Emily and Aitong charging and trumpeting as they rushed toward something.

The keepers closest to the commotion looked through their binoculars to identify the danger before they called for help. Just then, a large elephant appeared from behind a massive rock.

"Who is it?" Joseph asked, in a hushed tone.

Mishak peered through his binoculars, then, taken aback, lowered them as he stared at the elephant.

He quietly murmured, "It's Ndume," echoing the shouts of the distant keepers.

"But how—"

Joseph reached for the binoculars to look for himself.

It wasn't a mirage, Ndume was back.

Emily and Aitong could hardly contain their excitement while the men watched in quiet astonishment. The large elephant kept his distance, including from Mishak, which was unusual. His behavior echoed that of Emily and Aitong when the keepers returned from Ngulia Valley without Imenti. Both elephants seemed disgusted by the men's presence. Instead, Ndume stayed in the company of his elephant family, who draped their trunks across his body and showered him with affection.

Once the keepers returned to the stockades, Mishak called Daphne in Nairobi and shared the news. She could hardly believe it. He then reached out to John to see if he had heard or seen anything. The only way Ndume could have made it all the way to Voi was by walking through towns and villages that hadn't seen an elephant in years. Surely, someone must have noticed something. If they did, everyone would have heard about it. But there was nothing. John was just as shocked as they were by Ndume's reappearance.

When Mishak walked into the men's dormitory later that evening, he found the keepers arguing, huddled tightly around several maps spread across their food table. The men talked over one another, trying to figure out which route Ndume took and how he did so without being seen. The deeper they looked, the more intrigued they became.

Ndume would have had to cross several rivers. If they were too swollen, as many were that time of year, bridges were his only option—something elephants typically avoided, though no one understood why. Perhaps the water's vibrations against the bridge pillars made them nervous. Or maybe the space was too narrow, leaving no escape if danger emerged from the front or behind.

However Ndume accomplished the passage, it was nothing short of remarkable. On November 5, 2001, he returned to Voi, twenty-seven days after being relocated, nearly seventy-five miles away. The mystery of how he found his way back home, navigating between the human world and his own, remains an unexplainable feat.

Imenti and Lewa's fate remained uncertain, leaving everyone to wonder if they, too, might reappear. Until Daphne and the keepers heard otherwise, they could only hope for their safety.

They wouldn't have to wait long. Soon they would find themselves at the center of one of history's most remarkable episodes, a story so compelling it would be chronicled in books, newspapers, and films for years to come.

CHAPTER 29

"Where are you?" the text demanded.

I was standing backstage, getting ready to be called up, when I felt the buzz in my pocket. A friend of Leslie's had set up a list of people to check on her. I had signed up for 1:00 p.m., it was only ten. Luckily, the person on stage introducing me was taking her time.

"I'll be there at 1:00," I typed frantically.

"You're supposed to be there *now*."

I knew it was a mistake since I'd scheduled this speaking engagement months ago, and would not have overlapped the two.

"I'm just getting ready to get called onstage," my thumbs tapped furiously on the screen, half-listening to the introduction in the background. "I will be there as soon as possible. What's going on?"

"No one has heard from Leslie since Monday. She's not answering her phone, and we need someone to check on her immediately."

Alarm bells rang. *Since Monday?* It was Wednesday. I was told that several people had signed up to go to her apartment every few hours beginning on Sunday after Leslie returned from a trip to her daughter's.

"Can you go?" I asked, as desperation took hold.

"No, I'm working," the friend said, as if I weren't.

Suddenly the audience applauded, waiting for my entrance.

"I'll be there ASAP," I quickly typed before stepping onto the stage.

Despite my efforts to remain focused during the presentation, my mind was elsewhere. I couldn't think fast enough to just drop everything and run. Besides, if Leslie's friend thought it was an emergency, why didn't she call the police or someone who could get there faster? Still, I was unnerved.

As soon as my presentation was over, I told my handler I had to leave due to an urgent matter. Sprinting to my car, I knew if I pushed the speed limit I could be there in half an hour.

After pulling in next to her Jeep, I willed myself to stay calm. Outside, in the middle of her driveway, I dropped to my knees and prayed. As I made my way to the sliding glass door that led to Leslie's studio apartment, I begged the angels to stay close.

Thankfully, it was unlocked. I brushed aside the curtains and stepped into the darkened space. The television blared so loud I could hardly hear myself think. I swiftly turned it off as my eyes adjusted to the dim light.

"Leslie?" I called out, scanning the cluttered room. The bed was strewn with debris—clothes and mail scattered everywhere—making it impossible to tell if anyone was tucked underneath. Suddenly the comforter shifted, and an arm emerged from below the pile.

"Hello? Who's there?" she asked weakly.

"Hey," I cleared away the mess that nearly buried her. "It's me."

Leslie peeked out from under the covers.

"Thank you for coming," she said. "And for turning off that damn TV."

I sensed something was very wrong, but was unable to pinpoint what.

"Yeah, why was it so loud?"

"I couldn't find the fucking remote."

When she lifted her arm, I noticed it was attached to the underside.

"This one?" I asked, peeling it off.

"Where was it?" she asked. "I've looked everywhere."

"Let's look underneath your other arm and see what we have there," I giggled, half-joking. "Well, there's your phone," I said, peeling it off too. There were hundreds of missed calls, and I felt a wave of panic.

"I've looked for that everywhere, too."

"How long have you been here by yourself?"

"Since I got back from San Diego."

Concern deepened in my voice. "Weren't you supposed to have someone with you when you returned?"

"I thought so, but no one showed up."

I wasn't familiar with the friend who supposedly coordinated people to check on her. If I had known that hadn't happened, I would have canceled everything to have been there myself. Fury bubbled just below the surface, but I forced myself to concentrate on the situation at hand.

"Oh my God, your medication," I said, looking at all the pill bottles stacked on her bedside table. "How long has it been since you took any?"

"I can't remember," she winced. "I'm in a lot of pain."

I went to the kitchen and grabbed a protein shake from her refrigerator. While she drank, I rounded up all of her prescriptions and set out a handful of pills.

Part of me was grateful she hadn't been left alone longer. The other wanted to commit murder. After she had taken all of her medication, I picked up her phone, and headed for the door to make some calls.

"Wait," Leslie clung to my arm. "Don't go."

"Oh sweetie, I'm not leaving," I assured her. "I need to call your girls and tell them you're all right. They've been really worried about you."

"Lay with me for a moment," she said, "just until the pain killer takes effect. I don't want to be alone."

"Of course." I settled beside her, my hands shaking from both terror and rage.

As soon as Leslie dozed off, I got up and went out onto her back patio. First, I texted her girls to let them know I was with her, but didn't share anything more until I'd spoken with Leslie's medical team. Next, I called her favorite nurse, Sarah, who thankfully answered right away. After I described what I'd walked into and answered all of her questions, she fell silent. The pause stretched on for so long I wondered if the call had dropped.

"Hello? Are you there?"

"Yes, sorry, it's just ... things have changed so fast, and we need to focus on comfort now," she said quietly.

It was then that I knew. Leslie loved Sarah because of her ability to tell the hard truth. Having worked as a hospice nurse, she talked about death in a way no one else on the medical team did.

"This is it," I realized, as it sank in. "We're at the end?"

"Yes," she replied, without skipping a beat. "Your main focus right now is to manage her pain and prepare her girls."

"But how?"

"First, call an ambulance to take Leslie to the hospital. They will make her comfortable."

"What about her daughters?"

"Do whatever you can to get them here as soon as possible. We don't have much time."

"Okay," I bit my lip. "Then what?"

"Let me know what ER they take her to, and I'll meet you there."

I hung up and immediately dialed 9-1-1. With the phone still clutched in my hand, Alan, a close friend of Leslie's, appeared around the corner, worry etched across his face after he too had failed to reach her. His timing couldn't have been more perfect. We quickly gathered her things, just as the paramedics arrived.

At the hospital Sarah greeted us warmly while they were checking Leslie in. Her friendly smile and calm demeanor belied the seriousness of the situation. She leaned in and whispered something in Leslie's ear that made her laugh, and I understood why Sarah was her favorite.

Later that afternoon, once we were settled in a room with a view on the top floor, a wave of exhaustion washed over me. When we finally had a moment to ourselves, the stark reality set in. The doctors had explained no further treatment was possible, and the end was near. Her daughters were grappling with the shock of her sudden decline and making plans to come as soon as they could.

"Is there anyone you want to see?" I asked. "I mean, before your girls get here?"

She paused. "My family at Sunset."

I went into the hallway and called everyone on her list. Within the hour, a long line of people in recovery showed up to pay their respects. Given the large number of visitors, I requested they do three things: go in groups, spend only five minutes with Leslie to allow her to conserve her strength, and to please hold it together while they were in her presence. She was a natural caretaker, always focused on others' pain, but this—the end of her own life—needed to be *only* about her.

"Woah," Sarah said when she saw the crowded waiting area. "I don't think I've ever seen so many visitors for a single patient. She must have touched a lot of people."

I looked around the packed room. "More than you know."

Later that evening, after everyone left and Leslie drifted into a light sleep, I noticed Tina standing in the doorway. When I'd called her earlier, she wasn't sure she had the strength to say goodbye in person.

"That was the longest elevator ride of my life," she whispered when I greeted her in the hallway. "How did it go today?"

"There were so many people. It was really touching, and Leslie loved every minute."

"Does she have energy for one more?" Tina peered around the corner into her room.

"Of course. I'm sure she would love to see you. Go sit with her. Even if she doesn't wake up, she'll know you're there."

"OK," Tina said, her voice wavering. "I can do this."

With a deep breath, she stepped into the dimly lit room and settled on the edge of the bed while I observed from the doorway. Tina held Leslie's manicured hand, and she stirred. Her eyelids fluttered open, and a broad smile spread slowly across her face as she recognized who it was. I'd shared with her that Tina might not be able to come for a visit, that she'd been out of town. I didn't want her to know how difficult it was for us to say our final goodbyes.

The image of the two of them is seared into my memory. Leslie radiated happiness, and Tina, true to her nature, brought much-needed serenity to that space. It was a beautiful parting gift they gave to each other.

I returned to the empty waiting room and took a seat on one of the many couches. As I waited for Tina, my mind dwelled on the striking similarities between us and elephants: how we grieve for our loved ones, comfort the dying, and offer what solace we can to those nearing the end. But there is a notable distinction: elephants don't get cancer.

With my legs tucked underneath me, I stared out the large window and wondered what would happen if Leslie received the same diagnosis twenty years from now and if elephants held the secret to the cure, as some predicted. And wouldn't it serve us right if they actually did, as we systematically decimated every last one from the planet.

It was always assumed that larger mammals with significantly more cells than humans, would also have higher rates of cancer. However, Richard Peto, an epidemiologist, discovered that the opposite was true. While a few developed the disease (including one elephant in captivity), the occurrence was so low that it became known as Peto's Paradox.

A pediatric oncologist at the University of Utah, Dr. Schiffman, wanted to understand specifically how elephants evaded cancer. He, like many other scientists, presumed that their healthy white blood cells had found some secret way to repair themselves after a deadly attack, therefore preventing the spread of the disease. But that is not at all what they discovered.

Both human and elephant white blood cells have a hidden weapon—a protein called P-53. When a healthy white blood cell is attacked by a cancer cell, it unleashes a small army of P-53 warriors hidden inside who defend it to the death. Yet if they are overcome, and the aggressor wins, the attacker then moves inside the healthy cell and makes itself at home.

Cancer cells feed on the healthy cell from the inside out, gaining the energy it needs to generate its own army of mutants. The white blood cell doesn't die right away, but deteriorates gradually. Once it succumbs, the cancer army spreads and attacks more healthy white blood cells. And with the death of each one, they gather strength in numbers.

An elephant white blood cell, however, pulls a move nobody saw coming, straight out of a Japanese Samurai playbook. They perform a ritual act of suicide—the Harakiri—perfected by the noblest of all warriors. Once a healthy cell is overcome and the army of P-53 Samurai realizes there is no hope, they kill themselves in a mass suicide, which in turn also kills the white blood cell. Since there is no longer a home available for the invader to live in or food to sustain it while it mutates, the cancer cell starves to death, therefore preventing any chance of it spreading.

It was fucking brilliant. Researchers implanted those same elephant cells into humans and were astonished to discover that, in a few cases, they actually activated inside a human cell and triggered some of the same responses. A cure, though, seemed light years away and Leslie was out of time.

"Hey," Tina whispered quietly.

I looked up and saw her image reflected in the window.

"How did it go?" I asked, turning toward the door.

"Don't worry," she said through tears, as she took a seat next to me. "I kept it together for her but, um, I can tell it's close, she's … she's close."

"I'm so glad you came. And that you got to see her one last time."

"So am I," she replied. "How are you doing? How are you holding up?"

"OK … numb, mostly. Too exhausted to feel anything. My only concern is getting her through with as much ease and comfort as possible. Then I can focus on my feelings. Just, not right now."

"I understand. Are you leaving or are you gonna stay?"

"I need to stay," I said. "I would like to sit with her in case she needs anything. Hopefully, she'll be able to rest. Her family should all be here tomorrow, and she should save the energy she has left for them."

We hugged goodbye, and I walked back to Leslie's room. She was asleep, and I set up camp beside her on a lounge chair and looked out over the city's twinkling lights. After a while, I glanced at her and saw her eyes wide open, staring at me.

"BOO!" she shouted as I flew off the recliner.

"Jesus Christ!" I howled.

"I'm sorry," she laughed hysterically, "I don't know what got into me. I just couldn't help myself."

With a steady dose of fluids and painkillers, Leslie's devious personality had made a welcome appearance.

"God, you scared the hell out of me," I smiled, grabbing the blanket off the floor. "How are you feeling?"

"Tired," she said. "But I can't sleep. I think it's all the drugs they've given me."

"Did you enjoy visiting with so many friends today?"

She grinned and thought for a moment. "Yes, I did. I really did. What about you? You did a lot, wrangling all those people."

"I'm fine. I enjoyed seeing everyone as much as you did."

Leslie rolled onto her side, facing me. She appeared more alert, though weaker than before. I decided it was now or never and began the speech I'd carefully constructed in my head.

"Tomorrow will be a busy day, and we might not have time to talk. I wanted to tell you, that um—"

"No," she interrupted. "We don't do goodbyes Debbie Ethell. Let's just say … I'll see you soon."

"OK," I smiled.

After a long pause, she said, "Since you're here and I can't sleep, I want you to do something."

"Of course. What is it?"

"You need to share the end of Imenti's story. I have to know what happened to him."

With a twinkle in my eye, I grinned. "You got it."

The elephant stories were our escape. They dulled the sharp edges of Leslie's pain and offered a flicker of hope, just like they did for me. Each chemo session became an opportunity to share a new tale and when Leslie learned about Emily, Aitong, and Imenti, she was as riveted as I was. That night we went on our final journey together, exploring the extraordinary life of one of the greatest elephants I've ever known.

CHAPTER 30

On Christmas morning in 2001, Mishak and Joseph brought their jeep to a halt and cut their engine just beyond the main gate. In the oppressive heat, beads of sweat formed on their brows. With wary eyes, they scanned the area, hesitant to leave the safety of the steel-reinforced cab. The noise of the trucks' engines could alert the rogue elephant, potentially escalating the danger. As they quietly opened their doors, Joseph waved at the keepers stationed in the large transport vehicle behind them.

"You stay here while we go to the lodge," he whispered loudly. The driver gave a thumbs up.

The two men turned and focused their attention on the long entrance road leading to the Kilaguni Serena Safari Lodge, a good distance away. The manager, urgently seeking assistance, had contacted Daphne about a rogue elephant that had taken over the premises and held everyone hostage. She dispatched a team of her most experienced keepers to help defuse the situation.

Mishak and Joseph exchanged a nod as they walked toward the establishment, their expressions tense as they sensed nearby danger. If the elephant they were searching for caught them out in the open, there was nowhere to hide. Their strategy was to approach with extreme caution, keeping a safe distance from the wild elephant's last known location. With each step, they braced themselves for the unknown.

Hotel guests gathered on their balconies, adorned with twinkling Christmas lights, while they observed the scene below. The rooftop deck and adjoining restaurant, with its sweeping view of the savanna, was buzzing with patrons and staff. Their lively chatter faded as they observed the pair approaching from the far end of the long road. Mesmerized, they watched the keepers draw near, the display of courage leaving them speechless. Though they knew of the men's mission to confront the enraged elephant that had held them captive for days, the absence of visible weapons added an unnerving element to the already tense situation. All that could be heard was the rhythmic crunch of their boots on the hard-packed earth as they approached the lodge.

A short time earlier, Daphne received an urgent phone call from John, who'd learned from a fellow driver in Chyulu Hills that inside the gates surrounding Kilaguni was a large, agitated elephant. Then came a pressing request from the hotel manager asking for her help. To ensure their safety, guests were instructed to remain inside the protected areas of the building until they determined if the wild elephant was injured, a bull in musth, or something else.

Immediately, Daphne wondered if it could be Lewa or Imenti, but John didn't know. The lodge was twenty miles from where they were released, and neither had been seen since. She asked John to measure the elephant's footprint, to determine if it could be one of theirs. Dr. David Western, the former head of the Kenya Wildlife Service, had discovered that the length of the hind foot is directly related to an elephant's shoulder height, therefore offering an approximation of its age. Yet, when the print was measured, it revealed that the culprit was much older and larger than either of the two.

Daphne consulted with the management at the lodge and instructed them to use firecrackers to scare the elephant away. Luckily, the strategy worked, and it disappeared. However, several days later, a trunk reached over the top of a guest's outdoor shower searching for a much-needed drink. The same guest was then seen running frantically—naked and screaming—across the resort's grounds.

Then John received a second call, this time from a different driver who shared yet another concerning incident. When the young man turned onto the entrance road of Kilaguni to drop off his group of tourists, a large, enraged elephant suddenly emerged and chased them through the front gate. Much to everyone's relief, no one was harmed.

"What color was the van that dropped off the guests?" Daphne asked John.

"I believe it was white. Why?"

"Were there any other vans nearby, in different colors?"

"Yes," said John, including his own olive-green one.

"Did the elephant chase any of them? Or just the white one?"

"I don't know," he replied. "Once word spread that an elephant chased one van, all the other drivers were told to head back to their lodges until they got the all-clear."

Though far from definitive, it offered the strongest clue. Mishak and Joseph, along with a set of backup keepers, were dispatched to Kilaguni. Since they could easily identify any orphan they raised, Daphne knew they could quickly tell if the rogue was one of theirs or gather insight into why it refused to leave.

A hotel worker on the roof waved at them, gesturing toward the angry elephant, just below, and out of sight. Mishak nodded, then tapped Joseph on the shoulder. He pointed at a nearby side building, suggesting potential cover, then directed his gaze to a distant fence, silently outlining his own escape in case things took a scary turn.

They walked around a corner and stopped in full view of a large elephant. It didn't notice them at first since it was preoccupied with a magnificent wooden pillar on the side of the main building, as if contemplating just how hard he would have to hit it to bring it crashing down.

Mishak and Joseph froze. Within moments, the elephant noticed their presence, turned his head, and stared right at them. Then he raised his trunk and spread his ears. Suddenly, he charged. A gasp echoed from one of the viewing platforms, and voices rang out in heightened alarm as the massive creature closed in with relentless speed. But Mishak and Joseph held their ground.

"Watch out!" someone yelled, but it was too late, and everyone knew it.

The crowd didn't notice the men exchanging a wide grin as the elephant barreled toward them. When they stretched out their arms, it wasn't a gesture of surrender, but rather a welcoming embrace for a friend neither thought they would ever see again.

"Imenti, my boy," Mishak said, watching as the large elephant squealed, trumpeted, and defecated like a dog happily reunited with his favorite companions.

Joseph laughed and shook his head, while Imenti spun around and trumpeted loudly toward the lodge, as if announcing to the world that he had finally found his missing family.

The tourists stood in stunned silence, hardly able to comprehend what was unfolding before them. Little did they realize that the rogue elephant they had feared and discussed for days was an orphan, lovingly nurtured by the very men they now watched in disbelief. They realized it was an experience they would never forget, and one they'd reflect on for years to come. Imenti wasn't mean or a rogue; he was just desperately unhappy being kept away from the only family he had ever known.

Once Imenti calmed, Joseph approached the hotel manager, who agreed to let the elephant have a drink from the swimming pool. Guests gathered on the roof and around the viewing deck, cameras in hand, their eyes brimming with emotion as they captured the extraordinary scene.

Outside the gate leading to the lodge entrance, several Kenya Wildlife Service officers, along with two extra keepers, readied the transport truck to load Imenti for the journey back to Voi. Once Mishak and Joseph said their goodbyes and the tourists had taken plenty of photographs of the remarkable moment, they walked back to their waiting vehicles. When they tried to lead Imenti inside his own truck, he refused. It soon became clear that the only way he would return to that rolling cage was if he were sedated. However, anesthetizing him again presented its own distinct challenges and risked causing further trauma, leaving them unsure of how much more he could take.

After contacting Daphne, they devised a new plan: rather than forcing Imenti into the truck against his will, they chose a different approach. Since it was clear, he had a deep attachment to Mishak and Joseph, never letting them out of his sight, they based their strategy on that connection.

The large transport truck was sent away, replaced by one loaded with food and supplies. If the men intended to walk Imenti back the entire seventy-five miles to their starting point in Voi, they would need all the provisions it could carry.

Mishak and Joseph flanked Imenti, followed by a large truck carrying the extra keepers and a cook, as they began their long walk home. Other than a few tour buses that stopped to photograph the keepers walking beside a massive elephant, they were left mostly alone while still inside the protected landscape of Tsavo West National Park. The men were uneasy about how people might react once they entered the heart of civilization, just a few miles away. And more importantly, how Imenti would respond to them.

They didn't have to wait long; their presence literally stopped traffic. Although thousands of people lived near the park entrance, few had ever ventured inside. The exorbitant entrance fee—equivalent to around three months' wages for the average Kenyan—deprived most from ever having the chance to see any of Kenya's iconic wildlife, including a living elephant.

Imenti, accompanied by the men, sparked a reaction similar to what would occur in any city across America. Large crowds lined the streets. Reporters converged on the scene. The Voice of Kenya ran nightly radio reports on the "Return of Imenti," warning everyone not to use their horns and to remain calm. Thousands of people witnessed the remarkable sight as the men walked Imenti home.

Overnight, he became one of Kenya's biggest sensations. And throughout it all, he behaved like a champion. When they reached a swollen river, too dangerous to walk or swim across, their only option was to take the bridge. Several volunteers rushed ahead to block traffic on both sides, allowing the group sole access. But true to elephant nature, Imenti was terrified of crossing it. Each time they tried, he backed away, refusing to move forward.

Mishak then spotted a large jeep waiting in the long line

of stopped vehicles when he had an idea. He approached the stranger and explained his plan. The man maneuvered his vehicle to the back of the procession: the first to lead the way was their truck carrying provisions, then Imenti with his two keepers walking on either side, and finally the stranger's jeep bringing up the rear. Mishak hoped that by surrounding Imenti, he would feel more secure and protected. To their surprise it worked, and he crossed the bridge, gently encouraged by the growing crowd with each step.

Temporin coated the sides of Imenti's face, and he defecated and urinated the entire way. As soon as he reached the other side, Imenti flared his ears and whipped around, trumpeting and squealing, having conquered yet another daunting challenge, prompting whistles and cheers from everyone who waited patiently in the traffic jam they had caused.

The keepers laughed, then shook hands with the volunteer driver, waved their goodbyes to the parade of vehicles, and continued on their way. With all the excitement, Imenti picked up the pace, forcing Mishak and Joseph to jog alongside until he finally slowed.

That night, the men huddled around a campfire while Imenti stood over them, perhaps drawn to the warmth and company.

"This is the same path," the cook said, studying a map. The others leaned in to see for themselves. "There's no other way Ndume could have come through here," he added, pointing at a line near their campsite.

Mishak gazed into the fire, lost in his own thoughts, as the keepers continued to puzzle over how Ndume had managed such an unbelievable feat. How had he walked through densely populated towns and regions without raising a single alarm, without anyone noticing? The men deliberated late into the night, struggling to comprehend the enormity of what he had accomplished.

Five days later, after crossing a substantial stretch of the country, attracting larger crowds than expected, they reached the main gate to Tsavo East in Voi. Thousands of people were captivated by the tale of "Imenti's Long Walk Home" which ended just before the New Year, at the peak of Kenya's summer season.

The story spread like wildfire, filling the pages of newspapers, magazines, and dominating radio broadcasts and television screens. It became the subject of countless discussions—an event that captured the attention of an entire nation.

The keepers in Voi were with the orphaned elephants when they noticed Emily lift her trunk toward the main gate. Soon after, Aitong joined her, as though they sensed Imenti's arrival was imminent. The men, of course, were already aware, having heard the news like everyone else.

When Imenti finally appeared, Emily and Aitong had been in the same position for over an hour. Aitong immediately squealed and rushed to greet him, but Emily hung back and stood still. She watched while the other orphans surged past her, eager to surround their friend.

It was only after all the elephants had showered Imenti with affection that Emily came forward. She walked between the rest of the herd, appearing to scrutinize him from a distance. Joseph wondered if she was reprimanding him for his behavior that led to his banishment in the first place. As Emily got closer, she extended her trunk, and with that, he was welcomed into the fold once again.

Later that afternoon, when Ndume arrived, Imenti surprised everyone by swiftly turning and walking in the opposite direction.

It seemed he wanted nothing to do with the elephant who had gotten him into trouble.

"I wonder if he's learned his lesson," Joseph chuckled at the sight of Imenti's cold shoulder.

"*Labda*," *Maybe*, Mishak ginned.

John kept a lookout for Lewa in Ngulia, but the young elephant was never seen again. He did, however, report encountering several bachelor herds with elephants of similar age and size, leading everyone to believe that Lewa was among them. At least one of the three had made a successful transition.

The authorities were alerted that two of the rebels were back. Though reluctant, the officials agreed to let the elephants stay but insisted on keeping a close eye on them in case further trouble arose. The media attention generated by Imenti's voyage had undoubtedly boosted revenue within the park. And the warden must have recognized the backlash he would face if they were to kill off one of the most famous elephants in Kenya.

Since Ndume's return two months earlier, he had avoided the garbage pits entirely, seemingly aware they were the cause of his expulsion. Everyone was relieved. As long as he stayed out of trouble, he was safe. But Imenti's grudge against Ndume seemed to last a lifetime, as they were never spotted together again.

Late one evening, several months after he returned, Imenti picked up the sound of a truck approaching from a road close to the stockades. Mishak heard it too and quickly grabbed Joseph's attention. It was against the rules for trucks to be driven in the park at night. When Imenti took off in that direction, Mishak and Joseph hopped into a jeep and followed. Their hearts sank as they witnessed yet another standoff unfold, but they were too far away to intervene.

Imenti positioned himself in front of the truck, blocking its path, rumbling gently to its occupant.

"Imenti no," the man said, waving. "Go back, get out of the way."

Mishak recognized Yusef, a KWS park official, who was already acquainted with Imenti and, fortunately, someone the elephant held in high regard. Imenti approached Yusef's driver-side door, extending his trunk and receiving a gentle pat in return. Then he pivoted, striding toward the front of the vehicle, and directly confronted Yusef. Anticipating the elephant's next move, he protested loudly. Imenti lowered his head and delicately pressed his tusks against the windshield, and with a subtle popping sound, he carefully shattered it.

The keepers arrived just in time to see the splash of broken glass.

"Wow," said Joseph, smiling as they observed the scene. "It looks like Imenti's giving him a soft telling-off for driving in the park at night."

"*Angejua vizuri zaidi,*" *He should know better,* Mishak remarked, leaving Joseph to wonder whether the comment was directed at Imenti or Yusef.

The next day, Daphne once again defended Imenti's actions in front of the head warden. He was more than displeased at the prospect of replacing yet another windshield, despite Daphne's offer to cover the expense. He voiced his concerns about Imenti, especially with the Minister of Wildlife, Newton Kulundu, scheduled to arrive soon. They could not afford to have an elephant interrupt his visit for any reason.

Daphne shuddered at the thought of Imenti acting out—he would be shot on the spot. With no other choice, she began preparing to relocate him again. As she moved through the motions, a gnawing sense of unease gripped her. Something in the air felt different this time. If he showed up again, he wouldn't be given a third chance.

Even though Imenti was raised by men, he had passed every test so far. But now, everyone knew this would be his last. If he failed, they failed. All they could do was hope she had selected the right place to relocate him, and that Imenti understood the stakes. Not just for his own future, but for theirs.

CHAPTER 31

The door to Leslie's hospital room opened and several members of her family poured in. Luckily, she had gotten a good night's sleep and had more energy than the day before. Once the lawyer arrived and I transferred her medical power of attorney back to her daughters, I got up to leave.

Leslie grabbed my hand and pulled me close. "You need to write that down."

"Write what down?"

"Your story ... the elephants ... all of it."

"What—like a book? But I don't know how—"

"You're Debbie-fucking-Ethell. You'll find a way."

"I'll keep trying," I smiled.

She'd previously encouraged me to consider how my story, intertwined with that of the elephants, could become a fascinating book. I'd written multiple drafts but had thrown them all away. I didn't know how to begin to write an entire manuscript. Research papers in college had been hard enough.

"I've never heard elephant stories told like you do—woven together with science," Leslie continued. "And the way you compare how elephants care for each other like we do in recovery—that's really powerful. We need more stories like that. You have the courage of Imenti. You'll find your way."

After a moment, she closed her eyes. As I got up to leave, she squeezed my hand and opened them again.

"I love you Debbie Ethell." She caught me by surprise. "I'll see you soon," she said, with an unmistakable finality in her voice.

"I love you too. See you soon," I whispered, before I left.

I drove home in silence—numb. Unable to imagine a world without her. *You have the courage of Imenti. You'll find your way.* Leslie's words replayed in my mind. We'd finished his story the night before and, surprisingly, she'd stayed awake until the end. I found solace in knowing that his was the last one she heard. That in her final hours, it provided the courage she needed to embark on her own long walk home.

∞

Arrangements were made to move Imenti to an area near the Tiva River, a region much farther north than the Ngulia Valley, where he'd been taken before. Once known for its herds of wild elephants and big tuskers, it had been drastically affected by the poaching crisis of the 1960s and '70s, leaving a scattered few that were anxious and afraid.

Years earlier, David Sheldrick dedicated himself to restoring stability to the region, creating a safe refuge for elephants. He worked with and fought against hunting tribes and poachers until his sudden death in 1977. His dedication had a lasting impact. The wardens who succeeded him not only apprehended fewer criminals, but saw a significant drop in poaching incidents. Over time, David's conservation plan took effect, and the wild elephants slowly returned, though most still preferred to venture out under the veil of darkness.

The specific location Daphne chose was well over one hundred miles from Voi and contained far fewer lodges and people. Imenti's pathway home would be obstructed by rivers, human settlements, and a vast desert—a multitude of barriers she hoped would be enough to prevent his return, ensuring his safety. Rangers reported evidence of small bachelor herds often led by larger, older bulls, offering Imenti ample company if they could just get him to stay.

To avoid any mishaps, Imenti was sedated and moved on the day of Minister Kulundu's arrival. For the second time, Mishak and Joseph accompanied the elephant to his new home. They stayed with him that first night to help ease the transition. To their surprise, Imenti seemed less anxious than they expected. When they left, he stood still, flared his ears, and watched as the men drove away.

Daphne had assigned a group of KWS rangers to monitor Imenti and provide regular updates on his movements. Shortly after Mishak and Joseph headed out, reports were already coming in: Imenti was on the move.

After several hours, it was clear—he was heading in the direction of Voi. But sitting between them and the Tiva River was a massive, arid desert, a formidable barrier that Daphne prayed would prevent him from advancing any farther.

A short time later, a message crackled over their radio, making their blood run cold. Mishak pulled the jeep to the side of the road as they listened to the incoming reports.

"He's got company," a ranger said. "Lions ... several lions are following him."

"How many?" Joseph asked into the radio.

"A large pride, maybe fifteen or more."

Without hesitation, Mishak turned the vehicle sharply, retracing their path in a desperate attempt to protect their precious elephant—even though, deep down, he knew they would never make it in time.

"*Msaidie! Tafadhali msaidie!*" *Help him! Please help him!* shouted Mishak into the handset.

In Nairobi, Daphne and several keepers, crowded around her radio, listening closely as the situation unfolded. Her thoughts matched the urgency in Mishak's voice. But the rangers were powerless to intervene. All they could do was watch through long-range binoculars from a rocky outcrop overlooking the scene below. The harsh terrain prevented them from getting any closer.

Imenti stood motionless, on high alert, adopting a defensive stance as he watched the large pride close in. The last thing they saw was Imenti lower his massive head and charge.

Suddenly, the ranger yelled. "The lions ... they've attacked!"

"Tell us what you see," Daphne replied frantically, as more men gathered around her radio.

"They're behind a huge cloud of dust, we can't see anything."

Mishak yanked the jeep to the side of the road again while he and Joseph listened intently.

"There are more lions jumping in, but we—we still can't see what's happening—just screaming."

Everyone fell silent, praying for a quick end to whatever was about to happen. Mishak closed his eyes and pressed his head into the steering wheel while Joseph laid a hand on his shoulder.

Then a ranger shouted, "One lion is flying! Wow! Another landed in a bush." He paused as they waited anxiously. "It just got quiet," he said. "There is still too much dust to see anything."

The tense silence stretched on, broken only by the faint crackle of static as everyone held their breath. The rangers frantically scanned the horizon, waiting for the cloud to clear, searching for any sign of movement.

Finally, a voice interrupted the stillness.

"The lions are leaving. They're going away. Wait—"

More silence. Static sputtered, then the ranger's voice exploded over the radio.

"He did it! Imenti … he won the fight … he beat the lions!"

A triumphant roar erupted as pandemonium swept the keepers—wild, euphoric, and deafening as a last-minute goal in a World Cup final. Tears streamed down Daphne's face.

Mishak slumped into his seat, letting out a long, shaky breath. Joseph took a moment to gather his own composure before he grabbed the radio.

"Je yuko sawa?" Is he OK?

"He seems just fine," said the ranger, watching Imenti through his binoculars. "Other than a big scratch on his back, but it doesn't look that bad. He's picked up his pace and is still heading in your direction. The lions have retreated."

A heavy silence settled in the jeep, thick with unspoken relief. For several minutes, as their surge of adrenaline receded, Mishak and Joseph sat in disbelief. Imenti had done it. An elephant they'd raised from birth had survived one of nature's greatest threats. Again.

"My goodness," Joseph finally said. "That's why he's called *Imenti the Brave.*"

Mishak shook his head, still too overwhelmed to speak. The two exchanged a glance, before he turned the jeep around once more and headed home.

With each mile, the radio sputtered with reports: Imenti was pressing on, his pace brisk despite the unforgiving desert landscape—until one update caught everyone's attention.

"He's stopped. He's standing in front of a rusted-out minibus on the side of an abandoned road. Just staring."

Laughter rang out from the keepers listening in, knowing what he was about to do, although the KWS rangers had no idea. True to form, Imenti took out his rage on that broken down van, pummeling it and trumpeting wildly. He lifted it with his tusks, smashed its frame against the rocks, charged at it, kicked it, and then pooped all over it, much to everyone's amusement.

Once the vehicle had been sufficiently obliterated, Imenti maintained his fast-paced trek across the desert. In a staggering feat, he covered over *sixty miles* in just fourteen hours. Daphne could hardly believe it as she listened. As his journey continued, the keepers sat glued to their radios as Imenti inched closer to the compound, until he came face-to-face with the raging Galana River, less than forty miles outside Voi.

The river was far too swollen for him to cross, much to everyone's relief. Many elephants died by falling in and accidentally drowning. Instead, he quenched his thirst and took off again in search of an alternative route.

It was the same area where one of the first elephants Daphne had rescued, Olmeg, had last been seen years earlier. She silently wished the two would find each other, that Imenti would choose to remain in that region, abundant with food, water, and the company of previous orphans.

Instead, Imenti turned and walked back in the direction he came. He retraced his steps all the way through the desert, by the smashed-to-smithereens minibus—though he did pause briefly contemplating whether to have another go at it—before continuing on. Then he stopped at the Tiva River, near where Mishak and Joseph had first left him. After quenching his thirst once more, he kept on walking.

This time, Imenti covered a staggering span of over *one hundred miles* by the next day, astonishing absolutely everyone. His was a feat unlike anything ever seen before. No elephant in Kenya—or anywhere—had crossed such a vast distance in so little time.

Imenti eventually found a place to cross the Tiva River and headed east until he finally disappeared, too far for the rangers to track. All they could do was wait. As the radio transmissions went silent, the keepers bet on how long it would take for Imenti to end up back where he started—in Voi. Daphne shuddered at the thought of explaining his return to the authorities again, wondering how or if she could convince them to spare his life.

Several days later, a man on a bicycle arrived at a KWS station in the northern Wakamba territory. He urgently reported that an elephant was seen wandering close to his village—something that had never happened before. The Wakamba were some of the most skilled elephant hunters, and likely the reason wild herds typically avoided the area.

David had concentrated his efforts there long ago, educating local leaders on the importance of elephants. He believed that convincing the most prominent hunters to cease their activities would significantly impact the elephants' survival. And he was not wrong. David's endeavors were so successful that several men from that region, including Mishak himself, became some of the greatest elephant rescuers he had ever known.

Daphne dispatched Mishak to the area immediately, but he was still hours away in Voi. Without delay, she contacted Wambua Kikwatha, the head of the de-snaring unit who was already stationed at their northern office. Like Mishak, he was also from the same Wakamba tribe. Luckily, he was a short drive from the location where the elephant, believed to be Imenti, had been spotted.

As Wambua cautiously approached, he saw people scattering in panic. Some had scrambled into trees while others hid beneath vehicles or sought refuge in their huts. No one had ever seen an elephant venture so close to their village before. The elephant extended his trunk to anyone within reach, but when met with nothing but fear, he trumpeted in disappointment.

While Wambua knew of Imenti, their relationship was not well-established. Daphne instructed him to call out by name and watch the elephant's response.

"Imenti," he spoke softly, positioning his truck near the elephant.

Recognition was instant. Imenti rushed toward Wambua, reaching out his trunk for reassurance while the villagers looked on in astonishment.

After finishing a box of treats Wambua had brought with him, he followed David's example, introducing Imenti to anyone brave enough to approach. He was surprised by how many did, realizing it was a moment that would stay with them for the rest of their lives, just as his first encounter had lingered with him. He hoped it might give them pause if they ever found themselves, gun in hand, face-to-face with another wild elephant.

With Wambua carefully driving the truck, Imenti stayed loyally by his side, plodding along as they made their slow journey back to his office. When they arrived, Mishak was already waiting to greet them, and Imenti erupted with excitement at the sight of being reunited once again with his oldest friend.

Daphne had often contemplated establishing a second reintegration point, once the young elephants outgrew the orphanage in Nairobi. While Voi suffered from prolonged droughts, the northern region of Ithumba, close to Wambua's office, remained lush year-round and provided all the essentials for the orphans to thrive in the wild. Though elephant herds were still scarce, and mostly came out only at night, they were there. Daphne hoped that the regular presence of keepers, combined with an influx of younger elephants, would be enough to enhance their sense of security. She moved ahead with her plan, with Imenti in mind as its primary resident.

Mishak set up a temporary camp until another group of men arrived to help build elephant stockades, keeper dormitories, milk stations, housing, and a repair shop for the vehicles. Then they got to work constructing a beautiful guest lodge for visitors.

During those first few months, Imenti remained inseparable from Mishak. Each day, they visited his favorite waterhole, where he splashed and played. As time passed, his confidence blossomed, and he began venturing farther afield, sometimes disappearing for several days on end. Once, he was even spotted in the company of a much larger bull—a connection to the local elephants everyone had hoped for.

An especially difficult poaching case summoned Mishak to Nairobi. A young rescue had lost its will to live, and nothing anyone did could save it. In a last-ditch effort, he was flown in to offer something no one else could—*magic*. With his gentle touch and quiet presence, Mishak worked his unique healing craft. Like a wilted flower revived by rain, he brought the little poaching victim back to life.

Once it became clear that the calf would survive, Mishak checked in on Emily and Aitong. While out in the bush with the orphans, he observed them occasionally lifting their trunks in the direction of Ithumba. He wondered if they were searching for their friend.

When Mishak returned to check on Imenti, he saw him one

last time. By then, he had discovered other bulls like him—nomads who traveled by night—and together he formed a new band of brothers.

Daphne dedicated herself to selecting which rescues to move from the orphanage to their newest outpost. But there were no older, experienced elephants in the region to mentor the younger ones, they were all in Voi. A plan was devised to permanently relocate four six-year-old bonded females: Yatta, Kinna, Mulika, and Nasalot. Daphne considered them to be ideal leaders and scheduled their early arrival to allow time to settle in before the first group of orphans was transferred to their care.

Yatta and Kinna had crossed paths with eight-year-old Imenti before, during their stay in Voi, though their interactions had been brief. Daphne hoped that their familiarity would be a comfort to Imenti in his new surroundings. When the mini-matriarchs finally reached Ithumba, Mishak had already returned to his permanent residence in Voi. Six months later, when the first rescues arrived, Imenti had fully transitioned into the wild.

Over the next few years, a large bull elephant continued to visit the orphans in their night stockades. None of the keepers stationed at Ithumba were able to recognize Imenti, having not raised him, but there were other signs. Elephants in the area were still afraid of people, yet not far from where the men slept, one lone bull regularly whispered quietly to Yatta, sometimes to Kinna, within earshot of the men, his low rumbles carrying through the stillness beneath a bright full moon.

With each passing month, more bulls began roaming closer to the compound and—just as Daphne had envisioned—a small miracle unfolded. Wild herds, both males and females, started visiting Ithumba during the day—and a page had turned in the violent history of that territory. Elephants made an official comeback, all thanks to the one brave elephant who led them there.

The orphans played in what was now called "Imenti's Waterhole," as it had always been his favorite. Occasionally, he was spotted there among his wild friends, lying in the water to allow the younger elephants to crawl all over his massive body, just as he had done in Voi. Pictures were sent to Mishak, Joseph, and Daphne and they confirmed it was definitely him. *Imenti the Brave* proved himself to be an extraordinary individual, and though his journey took longer than most, he had reached his freedom at last.

∞

I paced across my apartment for hours until finally, at 1:00 a.m., I received the text. Leslie was gone. Surrounded by a sudden, peaceful calm, I had an overwhelming urge to go outside, to walk and blend in with the night. I grabbed my coat and navigated my favorite trail in the darkness until I found my bench by the river.

Consumed by thoughts of her, I closed my eyes. I could almost feel Leslie's presence beside me. Earlier that afternoon, a text from her daughter called me back to the hospital. Despite being unconscious for the past two days, Leslie clung to life with fierce determination. I sat on the edge of her bed, clasped her hand, and began recounting tales of our shared adventures to her girls. Soon, the three of us were laughing uncontrollably.

All of a sudden Leslie's fingers gripped mine, and in an instant, her daughters and I froze, staring at each other in shock. After days with no hint of response, there she was. We encouraged her to cross over, to make the final journey, and we cheered her on. We sensed her awareness and knew she could hear us. And we continued to laugh, filling the room with a bittersweet mixture of joy and sorrow.

Shortly before the sun rose, I lifted myself off the bench and walked back to my apartment. Instead of going to bed, I felt compelled to sit at my desk. I turned on my computer and opened a blank document. Suddenly, I was consumed with a desire to write.

"Thank you, Leslie," I said, as my fingers flew across the keyboard.

Over the next seven days, I barely moved from that chair as my story, and that of the elephants, poured out. I must have eaten at some point, and showered, though I don't remember. When I had written it all down, when there were no more words left, I stopped—realizing I had typed over three hundred pages.

On the eighth day, as I held my book manuscript, *The Will of Heaven*, for the very first time, I felt the first crack in my steel armor. For months, I'd stayed strong, convinced that I was fine. Part of me even believed that I was. But in that instant, the tightly woven threads of my composure unraveled, and like a ball of string, I came undone.

CHAPTER 32

The entire mountain was draped in a soft blanket of early-morning fog. From the large picture window, I looked across the expansive forest. The valley below was hidden behind a cloud, while the trees above appeared enchanting and peaceful, softened by a gentle mist that blurred its edges. I yawned and stretched.

I was roused from a restless sleep by the familiar voice of Eloise. She had never visited my dreams until recently. Now she made regular appearances. Buddha continued nagging me, too. Sometimes he showed me a moment in his life: an intricate detail of his past. I felt like I was missing something, yet I couldn't figure out what. Drained by their nightly visits, I decided to make the trip for myself and go where this story began: Elephant Mountain. I wanted to see what they saw, walk where they walked, and search for any clue that might reveal what they wanted me to know. Maybe then I would understand why they persisted in their haunting presence.

Unable to quiet my mind, I got dressed, made coffee, and sat on the front porch, absorbing the stillness as the steam from my mug vanished like a ghost in the wind.

A slight movement caught my attention. I stared into the fog, willing whatever hid behind the thin veil to reveal itself. The dark silhouette of a buck with huge antlers slowly emerged. It held my gaze. Then another came into focus—a younger male. Through a narrow break in the mist, the faint outline of a doe appeared, her twin fawns pressed close to her legs.

Suddenly, the echo of a gunshot disrupted the tranquility. In an instant, the deer vanished. It was difficult to pinpoint the origin, but it seemed far away. Then I heard Eloise's voice, only this time I was wide awake. Its softness sounded as if it too had traveled a great distance before reaching my ears.

"Move up, come on ... up, foot up!"

Without thinking, I stood and walked toward it. Soon, I found myself standing before the memory of the original, massive barn. The structure burned down shortly after Morgan died, leaving only a small cement slab. I'd spent the previous day marking out each section, using old photographs and topography maps, but those hardly did it any justice. It was simply massive.

"Good. Now back foot up! Up, Up!"

Four distinctive pear trees in the background, much larger than they appeared in an old photograph, confirmed I was standing in the middle of the outdoor performance ring. It was now a large field of well-manicured grass, posing as someone's backyard. The family that lived there had invited me to stay in a guesthouse and granted me permission to wander wherever I chose.

Morgan's original eighty-acre farm had been broken up into smaller plots, and the mountain itself had undergone a massive transformation. Once filled with some of the oldest growth forest in the Pacific Northwest, most of it was logged after a lumber company sold it all to housing developers. In its place now stood mansions and expansive lawns of rolling grass, with tiny strips of timber woven between.

Over the past several months, I'd met many of the neighbors who owned plots of Morgan's former property, and gotten to know them. They graciously invited me into their homes, and I was surprised to learn that most knew very little about what had happened there. I eased into those conversations carefully, gauging their interest in the events that had occurred. To my surprise, they welcomed the history—the good and the bad—and gave me complete access anytime I wanted to visit.

I zipped my jacket against the chilly fall morning. As I cradled a warm cup of coffee in my hands, I looked closely at my surroundings. I pictured Eloise directly in front of me working with the Tuskers. Nearby stood a massive tub filled with concrete, topped by a large metal loop used for chaining the elephants during their outdoor stays. It was here that Buddha mastered all his tricks, including the one-foot stand balancing on a ball. In an ironic twist, I found that very same object hidden in the forest the day before.

A neighbor had discovered the weathered artifact, and led me to its final location. The ball was deceptively heavy and impossible to lift without a tractor. It was made of thick metal coated in rubber and lined in dense, bright, circus-colored sandpaper. I hadn't ever thought about the balls elephants balanced on in circuses—it never occurred to me they didn't actually move. By then, I had uncovered so many photographs that captured Buddha's various poses on that same ball, it felt as if he had quietly guided me to one of his earliest memories.

I never could have imagined, the first time I came to the mountain, how much history I would uncover. While filming interviews for the Woodland Historical Society's Oral History Project to preserve the legacy of Elephant Mountain, I spoke with everyone I could find who had direct knowledge of the events that occurred back then. Much of the access I was given was possible due to the society's president, Erin Thoeny, who introduced me to several people I never would have found on my own. As a child, she often visited Elephant Mountain with her father, a local farmer who sold the elephants their favorite treat—sweet pea hay. Morgan had given her a treasured set of ceramic elephants from Thailand, a gift she allowed me to see and hold myself.

None of the over twenty people I spoke with had ever been interviewed about the events that occurred there, despite being quoted in numerous articles. No one had sought them out to hear their stories or learn the truth of what happened. I was the only one. The laziness of those early reporters was stunning.

By the time I wandered back to my guesthouse lost in thought, the morning sun had melted through most of the fog and I needed a hot refresh for my cold coffee. I pulled on a cable-knit sweater and a pair of heavy boots, then headed out again, following the old access road, flanked by forest on both sides. It stretched from where the large barn once stood to Morgan's original home, at the top of the mountain.

It was my final visit, and I wanted to walk the grounds one last time before leaving for good. I hoped to show Buddha that, although I didn't fully understand what he wanted, I had done all I could. I wished for him to know I was at the place where his story began, retracing his past and searching for answers. Maybe then he would finally let me go.

I walked up a short hill, admiring the changing color of the leaves. The overgrown road led to a large, flat piece of granite with commanding views of the mighty Columbia and Lewis Rivers below. The beach of Martin Island, splitting the two waterways, was clearly visible to the naked eye. The Chinook people who approached the famous explorers Lewis, Clark, and their female guide, Sacagawea, likely stood in the same spot. It would have been quite easy to remain concealed in the surrounding vegetation.

Morgan spread Eloise's ashes across Elephant Mountain after she died, and I imagined he saved some for this peaceful outlook located just below his house. Over my shoulder, its expansive two-story windows faced the brilliant view.

I'd spent several afternoons with the current inhabitants of Morgan's home. We chatted beside the same fireplace Morgan had built with his sons and admired a wooden sculpture he had carved of Belle and Packy embedded in its hearth. We looked through old photographs of him sitting in the same spot with a baby elephant curled up in his lap. So much was still the same. At the end of their private driveway hung the original sign, "Welcome to the Elephant Farm," made by the man himself.

I followed an overgrown trail until it disappeared into the forest. Though the precise location of Buddha's fatal encounter with Morgan was lost to history, the surrounding evidence suggested I was in the right place.

While working in the area, the current owner discovered a portable weight concealed in the dense undergrowth. Its position—twenty feet from a dirt road mentioned in the coroner's report—corresponded with the location of two distinctive species of trees to which Buddha was tethered. There was little doubt: this was where they each met their fateful end. I took a moment to reflect on the tragedy.

A few paces down a short hill was the peaceful stream they buried Buddha next to. I sat on the bank, listening to a small trickle of water for a few minutes. It was just as tranquil as described. I hoped he had found peace during the four years he was buried there.

I continued walking further only to end up where I started, at the guesthouse. After packing for the long drive home, I took one final detour, hiking down a short embankment to the remnants of the last remaining structure.

When I was initially shown it several weeks earlier, no one knew its purpose or what had once occupied the space. Three crumbling, cement walls were all that remained, clinging to the hillside. Metal brackets, rusted and weathered with time, still clung to the opening that once held a large wooden door. The absent roof left the interior exposed to the elements.

Standing there, I thought about the people who had once worked inside this building. Two of the elephant keepers hired by Eloise lived nearby: Carl Mowry and Cliff Bozarth. Although barely teenagers at the time, they recalled their experiences with great clarity when I interviewed them for the Oral History Project. Later, I invited both men to join me one afternoon, along with several neighbors who were just as intrigued, to show us around the property and help pinpoint the original locations and purposes of each building.

They immediately recognized the last surviving structure as the smaller of the two barns. The larger was located a short distance away, on the far side of a dirt road. They confirmed that the smaller barn housed The African Trio, which surprised us all.

Crammed together inside, we listened as Cliff recounted his daily task of dumping enormous piles of elephant manure off an embankment just a few feet outside the missing door.

"See how big those blackberry bushes are?" he pointed. "That's because they're full of the best fertilizer known to man."

Until then, we hadn't noticed, but the prickly canes were thick and huge, standing so tall that the steep hill below was completely obscured. The neighbors had always wondered why the berries grew as large as apples. Now that the mystery was solved, it prompted a round of giggles.

Carl walked over to one of the cement walls and used his cane to part a dense tangle of vines.

"There's an elephant hook right there," he said, touching it.

Beneath the twisted green labyrinth lay a corroded iron metal loop anchored to the concrete. We soon uncovered four more—things we never would have noticed without Carl's guidance. The ground was lumpy and uneven, blanketed in thick, soft moss. At first, I mistook the lumps as old tree roots, not realizing the flat cement floor was still intact. Cliff bent down and tugged at something hidden underneath the emerald carpet.

We all gathered around, as he wiped away the mud and sludge, exposing the lower leg bone of a large animal. In a flurry of excitement, we each began tugging at the mounds beneath our feet, revealing a towering pile of partial skeletons.

I took photos of several sacra—triangular bones at the base of the spine with a winged-like appearance—to compare against a bone chart later. A part of me wished Violet was there with us. She would have been ecstatic to be surrounded by pieces of so many unsolved mysteries.

I discovered that most of the sacra belonged to cows, understandable since the land was home to a cattle dairy before Morgan bought it. However, one sacrum stood out. Its shape was more triangular than the others and had no wings. The bone chart revealed it was from the felid family—a lion, tiger, or most likely a jaguar—animals not native to this neck of the woods.

Shortly after Eloise's death, while Morgan was still in Canada, the ASPCA launched an investigation. Animal welfare officers converged on Elephant Mountain to address the care and well-being of Eloise's remaining animals. They determined that the big cats and bears she'd left behind, cramped in spaces so tight, they could hardly turn around, were at risk of starvation and too dangerous for untrained caretakers to handle. Unable to find a viable solution, they ordered them all to be put down.

Back then, performing animals, such as those with large claws and sharp teeth, were nearly always kept in small cages. The only time they were released was when they were in a performance ring. There had never been a larger enclosure for them to roam when not working. With zoos already overflowing with lions, tigers, and bears there were no suitable homes to place Eloise's animals, despite the ASPCA's efforts. Ending their life was the most humane option. Luckily, Morgan was able to rehome the surviving Peace in the Jungle animals Eloise had with her on the night she was killed, sending them to a female trainer in Florida.

"Huh, look at this," Cliff said, as we gathered in a tight circle.

He peeled back layers of moss from what looked like a long section of thick, black fabric. Then Carl realized he was standing on a chunky piece of metal. Together, the men pulled on the contraption until it was finally free, although nobody was sure what it was.

"This is what Buddha wore!" Cliff said excitedly. "When we logged the forest with Morgan, this was his harness!"

"How do you know it was his specifically?" I asked.

"Because Buddha is the only elephant ever known to log a forest here, or anywhere in North America. None of the others did—it was just him."

We huddled around the newfound treasure. Cliff explained how Morgan taught him to attach the large contraption to Buddha, though given the elephant's violent nature, he wasn't permitted to do so alone. He didn't realize he was making history as the elephant logged a small section behind Morgan's house—until a television crew arrived and revealed just that.

Each of us took turns holding the harness. It was surreal to touch something that had once laid across Buddha's skin.

Carl and Cliff recounted Morgan's warning to stay away from Buddha, pointing to the noticeable dent in his head as the likely cause of his unpredictable aggression. The revelation made me shudder. All the way back then, Morgan suspected the reason, yet never thought to investigate further.

On Cliff's final day working on the mountain, he parked his truck next to where Buddha was chained, while Morgan's attention was drawn to a large cargo ship on the river below. He could see that two of the elephant's legs were secured to the ground by heavy portable weights. With the chain pulled tight, he felt safe. Unbeknownst to him, however, Buddha had concealed the excess length by standing on it, giving the impression it was taut when it wasn't. The elephant waited patiently for Cliff to get close enough to reach and then he attacked, sending the young boy flying.

That was Cliff's last encounter with Buddha's violent nature, though it was far from his first. Following the terrifying incident, he quit, as it was simply too dangerous to continue. Neither he nor Carl knew about the infection, and we gathered around my phone as I showed them all pictures of his deformed skull.

The two shared many stories about Eloise, who remained an enigma to them even after all this time. Though she was a tiny woman, they were both still deeply impressed by her sheer physical strength. Despite their years in the logging industry, surrounded by the toughest men, neither had ever seen a work ethic like hers. Eloise never asked them to do anything she wouldn't do herself, and they would say, routinely outworked them all.

While doing chores in the barn on a slow afternoon, Carl once made the mistake of switching the music from classical to hard rock. Suddenly, all the animals began roaring and screeching. He didn't realize what he had done until Eloise came running. Before he could speak, she switched the station back to where it was. The commotion ceased instantly.

"Never change the music again!" she barked. "They like classical, that's why we only play that."

Carl had learned his lesson. Like Cliff, he was shaken when he was informed of Eloise's death. Following his dismissal, along with the rest of the keepers once she was gone, he visited Morgan on the mountain.

"He looked awful, frail and old," recalled Carl. "He told me he was feeding all nine of his elephants, including himself, off nothing more than his social security check, which wasn't much. Luckily, he had plenty of pasture where the elephants could graze so at least they could eat. But since he quit trading exotic animals, he was broke. Without Eloise, he lost the will for nearly everything."

Carl offered to help, lending his services for free, but Morgan refused.

"I'm going to stay right here and die with my elephants," he said.

Two months later, he did.

I stepped into the barn, surprised that it seemed larger than I remembered. The floor was still covered with the bones we'd unearthed weeks earlier. I carefully gathered each one and placed them together with care in the corner. Buddha's harness had already been taken to the Cowlitz County Museum. Even if it never went on exhibit, they had experts who could try to preserve the artifacts recovered.

The soft, mossy floor cushioned me as I took a seat and leaned against the crumbling cement wall, looping my finger through one of the old original elephant rings. Fragments of conversations drifted back, snippets from all of the people I'd interviewed.

I had learned that Buddha was also electrocuted while he was in musth, or whenever he stepped out of line. Carl and Cliff each described the long, strange stick with protruding transformers as Morgan laid it against his squirming body. They didn't know he had already perfected the technique with Thonglaw.

A faint recollection stirred. Dunda. The elephant at the heart of California's largest elephant court case, and immortalized in R.J. Ryan's *Keepers of the Ark*. My mind caught on something as I leaned forward. I'd always been puzzled by the legislation passed as the result of her injuries, which included banning the use of electricity on elephants, even though there was no evidence whatsoever Dunda had been electrocuted. The cruelty she'd suffered was undeniable, but that was not among the methods used against her. So, why was it included in the law? At the time, it leapt off the page. The question lingered, sharper now.

Then I recalled something that Dr. Schmidt, the Oregon Zoo veterinarian, wrote in his memoir, *Jumbo Ghosts*, regarding Thonglaw's treatment. He validated what R.J. claimed in his book when elephants were subject to the most horrific abuse: the barn was full of men during those late-night sessions after the zoo closed, but none who dared report it.

For years, stories of Thonglaw's electrocutions were dismissed as nothing more than rumors spread by animal activists. I'd often wondered why keepers denied such cruelty so vehemently. Now it all made perfect sense. Because they hadn't actually seen anything. Once their shifts ended, their watch was over. Whatever happened after that remained in the dark and unspoken.

I laughed and shook my head, almost admiring the strategy. By keeping compassionate keepers and experts away from those afterhours sessions, the zoo ensured that those most likely to object were never present. Unwittingly, the regular daytime staff became public defenders, while the real brutality remained hidden.

Dr. Schmidt believed the dark history of electrocuting elephants had ended with Thonglaw. It was a striking admission from the only person legally required to notify authorities of "the abuse"—his words, not mine, though on this we agree. However, California's law—passed nearly two decades after Thonglaw died—suggested it hadn't ended there. Because why pass legislation against something that no longer existed? Why include it in a law if the practice was confined to just one elephant twenty years earlier in another state. The answer seemed clear.

A heavy pit formed in my stomach as I wondered how many more Thonglaws there were. I couldn't help but think of Imenti and how vastly different his life was compared to Buddha's: bull elephants with potential far beyond what anyone realized. It was only luck that separated the two. One faced the misfortune of capture, while the other was granted his freedom.

Yet their stories are intertwined, because both need our help. I knew then that focusing solely on wild elephants was no longer an option. I couldn't pretend I didn't know what I did. Playing it safe wasn't possible anymore, no matter what future threats may come. Working only to help those in the wild, or sharing just their stories without addressing the plight of elephants in captivity, felt like building a monument to freedom while turning a blind eye to those still in chains.

A cold chill swept over me as the pieces finally began to fall into place. Had it not been for Morgan and his elephants, we would not be in the troubling situation we find ourselves in today. Without the breeding program at the Oregon Zoo, the nationwide fixation on producing as many elephants as humanly possible—with no intention of returning any to the wild—might never have taken hold. And with no plan for managing the high number of bulls being born in captivity compared to females, I fear their fate remains largely the same as it was forty years ago.

I lifted myself off the ground using the iron elephant ring. Just then, I realized whose home I was standing in. The barn that once housed The African Trio—who, I had learned by then, broke two historic records.

Not only were they the first troupe of performing African elephants in the world but after Morgan's death, they would also become the only three in U.S. history to ever be released back into the wild. Remarkably, they were returned to South Africa, where Arthur Jones had captured them.

The two females, Durga and Owalla, went on to become matriarchs of their own separate wild herds, raising several calves of their own. And they would spend decades living entirely free of human contact after their release. Just like the orphans in Tsavo. Just like Eleanor.

Their story rewrote the laws of wildlife conservation and opened an entirely new field studying the elephant brain. Most importantly, they shattered the long-held belief that once-captive elephants could never be released back into the wild, proving not only that it is possible, but they can flourish as a result. This directly

ELEPHANT MOUNTAIN

challenged one of the zoo industry's core tenets and the justification for keeping them in captivity.

I paced restlessly across the soft floor. The African Trio's story was a clear challenge to the deliberate narrative used to shield and defend its practices. To recount their remarkable journey was both an obligation and a delicate endeavor, its significance weighed heavily.

Suddenly I stopped. *This* was where it had all started. *Elephant Mountain*. It was where the breeding wars had begun, condemning thousands to a lifetime in a cage, and where the first captive elephants found their freedom. And right here, was the beginning of an awful chapter in American history. With a gust of the fall breeze, I felt Buddha's presence retreat as if his mission was now complete and I finally understood.

"Oh my God," I whispered.

This was what he wanted me to know and why he brought me here. While wild elephants faced grave challenges, their plight was nothing compared to the unimaginable suffering by those in captivity. Given back their autonomy, whether released to a sanctuary or the wild, they could—*and did*—thrive.

"Hey!" a familiar voice echoed.

I whipped around to find the image of my catcher, Deana, in full gear on the wall next to me. She winked, kneeled into position, and nodded at the batter's feet.

I followed her gaze. Our opponent was trying to direct our attention one way while their feet were pointed in the other—the false motive, the hidden intent. It mirrored everything I now realized about how the captive elephant industry kept their secrets.

A wide smile spread across her face as she gave me the signal: a giant middle finger. I smiled back, it was time for me to get my head in the game. There were no nerves and no more fear. Finally, I was ready. I looked up at the sky and silently thanked Buddha, my elephant teacher. Regardless of what my future held, I had learned one thing along the way with absolute certainty—the truth would set me free.

EPILOGUE

Between the release of my last book *The Will of Heaven* and this, the world has changed. The COVID-19 pandemic forced us all inside, killed millions of people worldwide, and compelled me to focus on the things that matter most. Honestly, it took a moment to steady myself. But from that stillness came a renewed sense of clarity.

Experts feared poaching would surge during that period, yet recent data from the Tsavo Trust in collaboration with the Kenya Wildlife Service reveal that wild elephant populations in parts of Kenya have actually grown. However, there is still much work to do.

In 2023, Tanzania lifted its hunting ban on elephants, which ended a thirty-year moratorium. Since then, the last few big tuskers (of which there are estimated to be less than ten) in the Amboseli region of southern Kenya are being killed one by one. At least one rich American has taken part in these hunts. And worse, Botswana—the country with the largest population of wild elephants in Africa—lifted its ban in 2019.

Wealthy, white trophy hunters are once again depriving African countries of their greatest national treasures, even as tourism remains the backbone of their economies. Few travelers would pay thousands of dollars and travel halfway across the world to go on a safari to see nothing more than baboons and warthogs.

Older, bull elephants are crucial to wild herds. Their prime breeding age spans well into their fifties and sixties. Unlike human males—whose libido typically wanes with age—a bull elephant's testosterone actually rises as he gets older, making him even more vital for breeding and passing on his genes.

Yet hunters persist in their claim that they target only individuals that are "past their prime in their forties." That may be true for themselves, but the science is clear: bull elephants are just getting started at that age. By removing them we—descendants of the original colonizers—are stripping these countries of their most valuable resources.

As elephants continue to die at alarming rates in American zoos, they have turned, once again, to the importation of wild elephants to replenish their stocks. Eswatini (formerly Swaziland), a country nestled within South Africa, is governed by the continent's last absolute monarch, a man who rules without the inconvenience of oversight or dissent. Unsurprisingly, the king has found considerable profit in selling his elephants to us, amassing a large fortune in the process.

Twice in the past twenty years, the AZA has exported elephants from his kingdom to the United States: eleven in 2003 and another seventeen in 2016 due to a rather generous loophole in the Endangered Species Act—legislation originally intended to prohibit this sort of trade. The lawsuits that followed revealed just how effortlessly this flaw could be exploited. I was involved in the latter case and witnessed the entire process from beginning to end. Given just how smoothly these transactions have proceeded, I have little doubt this will become the norm rather than the exception. Yet the success of this scheme hinges entirely on keeping the public in the dark—and that is what I hope to change.

In 2005, the AZA hired a massive crisis-management firm. According to an article in *The Seattle Times*, journalist Michael Berens described how they intended to "fight back" against mounting negative publicity. At their annual meeting that January, AZA-accredited facilities agreed to pick up the pace and "aggressively breed elephants."

Based on the documents and reports compiled by Mr. Berens, facilities nationwide also vowed to present a united front, insisting that elephants were "thriving" in zoos—even as an avalanche of evidence suggested otherwise. They also embraced a PR strategy that has become all too familiar in today's political climate known as DARVO—Deny, Attack, Reverse Victim, and Offender. This classic media manipulation tactic works like this: The accused viciously denies any wrongdoing, then they attack the accuser, and finally they portray themselves as the "real victims," flipping the roles to avoid responsibility. Over time, it has worked, effectively muting criticism.

Much of the negative coverage about captive elephants seems to have vanished from the internet, though a determined researcher can still uncover the truth. It resembles a different take on the same strategy used with the deaths of Morgan and Eloise, only new and improved.

While zoos prefer to showcase elephants enjoying pumpkins on Halloween or celebrating with birthday cakes, all is not quite as it seems. The numbers still speak for themselves: elephants are not thriving in captivity.

Sanctuaries are the best, *and only*, alternative to zoos. They provide elephants with a vastly improved quality of life, offering over a hundred times the space available in even the largest elephant exhibit in the world. Currently, there are only three true sanctuaries in the United States: PAWS in California, TES in Tennessee, and ERNA in Georgia.

Unlike zoos, legitimate sanctuaries do not breed elephants, are closed to the public though they offer live video feeds, and the elephants are not confined to either chains or small stalls. Although sanctuaries must use fencing for safety, the scale is incomparable—a sanctuary enclosure can be so vast that it would take a person several hours on foot, walking non-stop, to reach the other side. No zoo in the world comes anywhere close to providing that much space.

The power to end breeding programs for endangered species—*especially* when the solution is merely to capture more from the wild rather than restore them to it—also rests, in the hands of the people. There are numerous examples where this type of advocacy has succeeded, such as the Oakland, Detroit, and Toronto Zoos, where community campaigns led to the retirement of elephants to sanctuaries. Legal action at the city, town, and state levels brought an end to elephants performing in circuses like Ringling Bros., proving that collective voices drive meaningful change.

The countries that still harbor wild herds are among the poorest in the world. A $100 donation from the United States is worth over 3,300 Thai baht, more than 2.5 million Vietnamese dong, and nearly 13,000 Kenyan shillings—because a single U.S. dollar is more than a hundred times more valuable in these local communities, allowing donations to stretch far beyond what most people realize.

The cost of upgrading a single zoo exhibit—such the $57 million spent on the Oregon Zoo's Elephant Lands for just seven elephants—equates to billions of dollars in local currency in elephant range countries. That kind of funding could support anti-poaching efforts, habitat protection, and community programs that save thousands of elephants and support some of the world's poorest people who live alongside them. Not only could you stack rangers boot to boot around their entire countries but you could also dress every last living elephant in Prada. If saving the elephants were truly the goal, the solution isn't all that complicated: directing our resources to where they make the greatest difference could change the future for elephants and people alike.

Ultimately, since most zoos across the United States are managed by public charities, nonprofits, and city councils, we have the power. As members of the public, we can speak up by contacting our local city council members, attending public meetings, or writing to government officials to make our voices heard. Whether it's advocating for elephants to be released to sanctuaries, demanding transparency in zoo operations, or urging outside, independent oversight, we all have a role to play. We have influence over the decisions made by these taxpayer-funded organizations. The future of captive elephants depends not just on those who manage zoos, but on all of us to hold them accountable.

∞

The KOTA Foundation for Elephants thrived for many years and allowed me the opportunity to visit Kenya several times. We worked on conservation issues in local communities and built desks for nearly 900 students across six remote schools. Everything we did was driven by the belief that *you can't save the elephants if you don't help the people.* I gave more presentations, taught classes, and spoke to groups all around the world. And it's still clear—education is the key.

Unfortunately, KOTA became another casualty of the pandemic. Yet it taught me invaluable lessons and opened doors that continue to forge the road ahead. Letting go has allowed me more time to focus on writing books, blogs, podcasts and continuing to educate everyone I can about the magic of elephants.

Jason, KOTA's founding president and my mentor, passed away after a brief battle with cancer. Even in his final days, he remained the elephants' greatest champion. Not long after we celebrated his forty-second year of sobriety, he was gone. I have no doubt he continues to watch over the elephants—a species he knew little about when we first met, but one he grew to love above all others.

∞

Sightings of Imenti grew less frequent over the years, but since his release and reintegration into Ithumba, hundreds of elephants have returned to the area. What was once considered an elephant wasteland is now thriving. His favorite waterhole is filled with orphans learning how to live wild again, and large bulls are now also regularly seen there—in broad daylight.

Imenti is one of the most famous elephants to have ever lived in Kenya, thanks to his extraordinary "Long Walk Home." He is still perhaps the only wild elephant many Kenyans have ever seen in person. His story captured the imagination of a nation and was featured in countless newspapers, magazines, films and documentaries, ensuring his legacy continues.

Emily and Aitong remained co-matriarchs even after returning to the wild, forming their own makeshift herd—a blend of orphans and solitary elephants collected along the way seeking a new family. Each had babies of their own and, in a touching tradition, brought them back to meet the men who raised them. Over the years, they were often spotted, standing side by side with their trunks raised, pointed toward Ithumba. I like to think they were still looking for their friend. I hope, in some way, they knew he had built a beautiful life of his own.

∞

The rise of fentanyl has devastated communities, claiming countless lives among both addicts and friends alike. Yet, alcoholism looms in the background like a deadly predator waiting for just the right moment to strike. Still, those of us in recovery stand stronger together, echoing the powerful force of Emily, Aitong, Imenti, and the resilience of Buddha. It is only when we're tucked safely into the middle of our herd that we have the best chance of defying the odds stacked against us.

For the elephants and for the alcoholics and addicts still suffering, I am constantly reminded—as long as there is breath, there is always *hope*.

HOW YOU CAN HELP

*L*earn about what these organizations do, visit their websites, tell your friends, follow them on social media, and if you are able—donate. I am not affiliated with, nor do I receive compensation from, any of the organizations listed. These are simply causes I believe in and that can benefit from additional support.

In the U.S., a $100 might buy dinner for you and a friend. In Kenya, that same amount can fund weeks of fieldwork for a Kenyan elephant scientist, supply a classroom with materials for an entire year, or fully cover the cost of school uniforms for several children. In Thailand, it can cover nearly one-half of an elephant keeper's monthly salary, buy up to twenty rolls of bandages for multiple wound dressings, or feed a full grown elephant for several days.

ElephantVoices, California, Washington D.C.

ElephantVoices is dedicated to the research, protection, and ethical treatment of elephants, with a special focus on their complex communication and social lives. Co-founded and led by Dr. Joyce Poole, a world authority on elephant behavior, and Dr. Petter Granli, ElephantVoices has spent decades advancing our understanding of wild elephants across Africa. Their groundbreaking work includes developing the world's first comprehensive Elephant Ethogram—a detailed "elephant vocabulary" cataloguing over 300 distinct elephant behaviors and vocalizations. To view this extensive publicly accessible library or make a much-appreciated donation please visit elephantvoices.org.

Amboseli Trust for Elephants, Kajiado County, Kenya

Founded by Cynthia Moss in 2001, ATE operates the world's longest-running study of wild elephants, monitoring more than 3,500 individuals in the Amboseli ecosystem since 1972. The organization trains local Kenyan scientists, supports scholarships for Maasai women and men, and partners with communities to promote coexistence between people and elephants. To learn more about their remarkable work or to donate please visit their website at elephanttrust.org.

Reteti Elephant Sanctuary, Samburu County, Kenya

Located in northern Kenya, Reteti is Africa's first Indigenous community-owned and operated elephant sanctuary. Established by the Samburu people, Reteti rescues orphaned and abandoned elephant calves—often victims of poaching, drought, or human-wildlife conflict—with the goal of rehabilitating and returning them to the wild herds of the region. Everyone who works there is recruited from the local Samburu community, and it is the only rescue that hires women as elephant keepers reflecting a powerful model of community-driven conservation and empowerment. Reteti not only protects wildlife, but also transforms local livelihoods and inspires coexistence between people and elephants by demonstrating that conservation can benefit both nature and communities. To learn more, plan a visit, or donate please visit reteti.org.

Elephant Nature Park, Chaing Mai, Thailand

Located near Chiang Mai, Thailand, ENP is a pioneering elephant rescue and rehabilitation sanctuary founded by Saengduean "Lek" Chailert, known as the "Elephant Whisperer" of Asia. As the first ethical elephant sanctuary of its kind in Asia, the park provides a safe haven for Asian elephants rescued from street begging, logging, circuses, and riding camps—many of whom arrive with physical and psychological injuries. Elephants at ENP are free to live in natural herds, roam spacious grounds, and receive ongoing care and support. Devastated by recent floods they are in need of donations or volunteers that can travel there to help. To learn more please visit elephantnaturepark.org.

ACKNOWLEDGMENTS

*F*irst, I would like to extend my deepest gratitude to my team at Alberta Pearl Publishing and everyone who contributed to the editing, proofreading, design, marketing, and publicity processes. Katherine Lloyd, for your keen eye for design, Josh Millman, my audio engineer/director, and my audio producer Michelle Stolberg of Digital One Studios. Each of your efforts helped transform this into the beautiful book it is, and for that, I am truly grateful.

I'd like to give my heartfelt thanks to my attorneys, my fact checkers, as well as the Portland, Cowlitz County, and Woodland Historical Societies. Most especially, Erin Thoeny—your meticulous research and expertise were invaluable to this story. Thank you for your generosity, sharing your memories of Morgan, and for always coming so well prepared to our meetings. I also want to express my sincere appreciation to Joseph Govednik, Director of the Cowlitz County Historical Museum, and Curator Bill Watson. Your gracious hospitality, patience with my endless emails, and enthusiastic support have been a true gift to this project.

I am deeply grateful to Dr. Dana Tucker, Cowlitz County Coroner, for patiently guiding me through the complex medical terminology and investigative processes, and for unearthing long-forgotten boxes of crucial information. And to the Cowlitz

County Sheriff's Department for your invaluable assistance in locating retired law enforcement personnel whose insights helped me piece together the events surrounding Morgan's disappearance and death with accuracy and care.

I'd like to extend my profound appreciation to the National Archives of Quebec in Montreal and Sherbrooke, the Bibliothèque et Archives nationales du Québec (BAnQ), and France Monty. Your tireless help navigating an avalanche of news articles, police reports, and Eloise Berchtold's coroner's investigation was essential to reconstructing the most accurate timeline leading to her unfortunate passing. *Merci beaucoup.*

I owe Cliff Bozarth and Carl Mowry a most brilliant tip of the hat. The countless hours you spent with me filling in the gaps and sharing endless stories about Morgan and Eloise, the elephants who once roamed the mountain, and what life up there was like back then, were truly invaluable. I consider you both dear friends and feel incredibly fortunate to have gotten to know each of you.

To all the neighbors who now live on parcels of the original Elephant Mountain farm, I am deeply grateful for your kindness and generosity in allowing me to explore your lands at any time, and for inviting me into your homes for tea and hot chocolate. Your willingness to share stories, artifacts, and memories enriched this book in ways I never could have imagined.

I want to thank my friends, those who stood by me through every challenge—who listened, encouraged, and helped me maintain my strength, sanity, and sobriety. And everyone who helped me turn this project from a vision to reality. A most special thanks to: Dave Lutz, Sarah B., Stephanie M., Justine Light, Thelma P., Anna W., Tina W., Phil E., Kirsten Milliken, Lara N., Lisa W., Deana "Sally" Sallee, Steve W., Steve R., Hugh L., Debra L.,

ACKNOWLEDGMENTS

Aimee H., Julie Frost, Bobbi Pilip, Meg Goodwin, Heidi and Ben Porter, Ashley and Josh Porter, Sandra Garrison, Jan and George Abbott, Esther and Rodger Rast, Tom Golick, Brad Bright, Tom Hudson, Robin and Priscilla Berry, Dana Simms, Megan Seaver, and finally, Sam Sam, Charlie McBride, my sister Carrie, and my parents Ray and Sandra. Your support of my dreams amazes me every single day.

Throughout much of my time exploring Elephant Mountain, I was fortunate to be accompanied by one remarkable individual: Gina Scavera. Your laughter, sharp eye for detail, and invaluable help with research and documentation made this journey not only possible, but truly enjoyable. This story might have been told without you, but it wouldn't have been nearly as much fun. Thank you for offering me a welcoming place to stay during my many trips up the mountain and for standing by my side through most of it.

To the many scientists and experts who generously shared their knowledge and time to help me understand the complex scientific details behind this story, I thank you. Your guidance and support were essential in ensuring the accuracy and integrity of your research, and I truly appreciate your contributions, including Dr. Joyce Poole, Dr. Angela Stöeger-Horwath, and Dr. Mickey Pardo. And the valuable insights into dolphins and whales from the great whale/elephant scientist Katy Payne, Dr. Lori Marino, author/biologist Tom Mustill, and the lovely Violet—whose brilliant passion for bones became the inspiration for this story. You taught me how to find the secrets hidden within and introduced me to a world I didn't even know existed. For that, I will always be grateful.

Lastly, to everyone who read my first book *The Will of Heaven*, shared it with friends, requested it at your local libraries, and took the time to write reviews ... you have my deepest thanks. What began as a small ripple has grown into a powerful wave. You've reminded me, in the most moving way, that the strongest force behind any book is word of mouth—the genuine, heartfelt sharing from one reader to another.

As always,
For the elephants ...

BEHIND THE STORY

This is a partial bibliography. For the complete list—including videos, photographs, live links, and downloadable files—please visit my website at debbieethell.com.

Morgan Berry's History

Alexander, Shana. "Portland Has an Elephant Baby Boom." *Kansas City Star,* April 18, 1967, p. 24.

Alexander, Shana. "Belle's Baby 225 Pounds and All Elephant." *Life Magazine,* May 11, 1962, pp. 104-120.

Alexander, Shana. *The Astonishing Elephant.* New York: Random House, 2000.

"Animal Farm to Hold Open House." *The Lewis River News* (Woodland, Washington), July 20, 1967.

Berry, Morgan. Letter to Ted Reed, Director of National Park Zoo, regarding the transfer of Thonglaw and other elephants for breeding purposes. November 8, 1963. *Smithsonian Institutional Archives,* Washington DC.

"Berry and Friend (a Camel)." *The Lewis River News* (Woodland, Washington), January 26, 1967.

Bruns, Emlyn. "Elephant Mountain." *McMenamins Blog,* March 21, 2018. https://blog.mcmenamins.com/elephant-mountain/

Federman, Stan. "Did you Know? Facts and Figures about the Washington Park Zoo." *The Sunday Oregonian,* June 14, 1987, p. 160.

Iliff, Warren. "Morgan Berry Obituary." Wayne State University Archives, Article 18, December 15, 1980, p. 178.

Lang, Don. "Six Musicians Killed in Crash on One Nighter." *DownBeat,* November 1, 1941.

Lewis, George "Slim," and Byron Fish. *I Loved Rogues: The Life of an Elephant Tramp.* Seattle: Superior Publishing Company, 1978.

Luck, Marissa. "Through Famed Trainer Packy Had a Link to Cowlitz County." *The Daily News* (Longview, Washington), February 14, 2017. https://tdn.com/news/local/through-famed-trainer-packy-had-a-link-to-cowlitz-county/article_0c8e95d4-47da-51b9-a12a-e2d61e785565.html

"Morgan Berry and Bride Will Live in Minneapolis." *Minneapolis Star-Journal,* Sept 10, 1939, p. 28.

Moore, Randall Jay, and Christopher Munnion. *Back to Africa.* Johannesburg: Southern Book Publishers, 1989.

Moore, Randall Jay, and Christopher Munnion. *Elephants for Africa.* Auckland Park, South Africa: Abu Publications, 2000.

"Portland Takes Its New Baby Elephant Very Big." *St. Cloud Times* (St. Cloud, Minnesota), April 19, 1962, p. 11.

Richards, Leverett. "Dream For Sale ... If You Want Elephants." *The Oregonian,* February 6, 1980, p. 28.

Richards, Leveritt. "Herd of Wild Elephants Roams Through Tall Firs." *The Sunday Oregonian,* April 23, 1967.

Richards, Leverett. *Elephants Don't Snore.* Vancouver, Washington: Rose Wind Press, 1996.

"10 Baby Elephants Under One-Year Old Expected to Arrive at Elephant Farm." *The Lewis River News* (Woodland, Washington), January 26, 1967.

Ullman, Darren. "The Elephant, the Photographer, and the Sheriff." *Cowlitz Historical Quarterly* (Kelso, Washington), December, 2011. pp. 36-41.

Ullmann, Darren. "The Elephant, the Photographer, and the Sheriff." Cowlitz County Law Enforcement History Project

(Kelso, Washington), October 23, 2009. http://cclehistory.blogspot.com/2009_10_23_archive.html

Morgan Berry's Death

Alexander, Shana. *The Astonishing Elephant.* New York: Random House, 2000.

"Body of Trainer Recovered from Guard of Bull Elephant." *The Daily News* (Longview, Washington), June 29, 1979.

Bozarth, Cliff. "Everybody Has a Story: Working on Woodland Elephant Farm was Unusual Job." *The Columbian News* (Vancouver, Washington), April 2, 2023. https://www.columbian.com/news/2023/apr/02/everybody-has-a-story-working-on-elephant-farm-was-unusual-job/

Bozarth, Cliff. Interview. Conducted by Debbie Ethell. Woodland Historical Society Oral History Project. (October 8, 2023, and November 18, 2023).

Bright, Brad. Interview. Conducted by Debbie Ethell. Woodland Historical Society Oral History Project. (October 8, 2023, and November 18, 2023).

Bundy, Don. "Body of Trainer Found Next to Elephant." *The Oregonian*, June 28, 1979, p. 17.

Detzel, Helen M. "You Don't 'Tame' Lions." *Cincinnati Magazine*, December, 1973.

Elton, William. Autopsy and Pathology Report for Morgan Berry. Cowlitz County Medical Examiner's Office, June 28, 1979.

"Elephant Tramples Trainer." *The Spokesman Review* (Spokane, Washington), June 28, 1979, pp. 1-3.

"Elephant Walk Signals Trainer's Tragic End." *The Spokesman Review* (Spokane, Washington), July, 1979.

"He Died Amidst His Animal Family." *The Daily News* (Longview, Washington), June 28, 1979.

Hudson, Tom. Interview. Conducted by Debbie Ethell, Woodland Historical Society Oral History Project. (October 8, 2023, and November 18, 2023).

Maberry, Matthew, Patricia Maberry, and Michelle Trappen. *Packy & Me*. Beaverton, Oregon: Maberry Press, 2011.

McIntosh, Jay. "Lethal Elephant Episode Over." *The Daily News* (Longview, Washington), June 28, 1979, pp. 1-2.

Moore, Randall Jay, and Christopher Munnion. *Back to Africa*. Johannesburg: Southern Book Publishers, 1989.

Moore, Randall Jay, and Christopher Munnion. *Elephants for Africa*. Auckland Park, South Africa: Abu Publications, 2000.

Mowry, Carl. Interview. Conducted by Debbie Ethell, Woodland Historical Society Oral History Project. (October 8, 2023, and November 18, 2023).

Sternfeld, Joel. "Exhausted Elephant Renegade." Photograph, June 26, 1979. https://www.joelsternfeld.net/search?q=exhausted+elephant+renegade

Sullivan, Ann. "Death Came to Berry Among Beloved Giants." *The Oregonian*, June 28, 1979, p. 21.

"Trampling Listed as Killing Berry." *The Oregonian*, July 4. 1979.

Ullman, Darren. "The Elephant, the Photographer, and the Sheriff." *Cowlitz Historical Quarterly* (Kelso, Washington), December, 2011. pp. 36-41.

Ullmann, Darren. "The Elephant, the Photographer, and the Sheriff." Cowlitz County Law Enforcement History Project (Kelso, Washington), October 23, 2009. http://cclehistory.blogspot.com/2009_10_23_archive.html

Winebrenner, D.F. Coroner's Report for Morgan Berry. Case No. A 108-79, Cowlitz County Coroner's Office, June 27, 1979.

"Woodland Trainer Found Dead Next to Elephant." *The Daily News* (Longview, Washington), June 27, 1979.

BEHIND THE STORY

Sources with Conflicting Accounts and 'Heart Attack' Claims (surrounding Morgan Berry's death)

"Body of Trainer Recovered from Guard of Bull Elephant." *The Daily News* (Longview, Washington), June 29, 1979.

Bundy, Don. "Body of Trainer Found Next to Elephant." *The Oregonian*, June 28, 1979, p. 17.

Burner, Dell. "Up From the Grave." *The Daily News* (Longview, Washington), August 19, 1983.

"Elephant Walk Signals Trainer's Tragic End." *The Spokesman Review* (Spokane, Washington), July, 1979.

Hamilton, Donald. "Coroner Can't Tell if Berry Victim of Heart or Elephant." *Oregon Journal*, June 28, 1979, p. 35.

Maberry, Matthew, Patricia Maberry, and Michelle Trappen. *Packy & Me*. Beaverton, Oregon: Maberry Press, 2011.

McIntosh, Jay. "Lethal Elephant Episode Over." *The Daily News* (Longview, Washington), June 28, 1979, pp. 1-2.

Moore, Randall Jay, and Christopher Munnion. *Back to Africa*. Johannesburg: Southern Book Publishers, 1989.

Moore, Randall Jay, and Christopher Munnion. *Elephants for Africa*. Auckland Park, South Africa: Abu Publications, 2000.

Richards, Leverett. *Elephants Don't Snore*. Vancouver, Washington: Rose Wind Press, 1996.

Schmidt, Michael, DVM. *Jumbo Ghosts: The Dangerous Life of Elephants in the Zoo*. Chicago: Xlibris Corp, 2002.

Sullivan, Ann. "Death Came to Berry Among Beloved Giants." *The Oregonian*, June 28, 1979, p. 21.

"3 Elephants Retrained for Wilds." *The Oregonian*, March 17, 1980, p. A15.

Sources that Misidentified Elephant (Tunga/ Tonga) as Morgan's Killer

"Body of Trainer Recovered from Guard of Bull Elephant." *The Daily News* (Longview, Washington), June 29, 1979.

Bundy, Don. "Body of Trainer Found Next to Elephant." *The Oregonian*, June 28, 1979, p. 17.

"He Died Amidst His Animal Family." *The Daily News* (Longview, Washington), June 28, 1979.

McIntosh, Jay. "Lethal Elephant Episode Over." *The Daily News* (Longview, Washington), June 28, 1979, pp. 1-2.

Sullivan, Ann. "Death Came to Berry Among Beloved Giants." *The Oregonian*, June 28, 1979, p. 21.

Ullman, Darren. "The Elephant, the Photographer, and the Sheriff." *Cowlitz Historical Quarterly* (Kelso, Washington), December, 2011. pp. 36-41.

Ullmann, Darren. "The Elephant, the Photographer, and the Sheriff." Cowlitz County Law Enforcement History Project (Kelso, Washington), October 23, 2009. http://cclehistory.blogspot.com/2009_10_23_archive.html

"Woodland Trainer Found Dead Next to Elephant." *The Daily News* (Longview, Washington), June 27, 1979.

Sources that Correctly Identified the Elephant (Buddha) as Morgan's Killer

"Elephant Walk Signals Trainer's Tragic End." *The Spokesman Review* (Spokane, Washington), July, 1979.

Hamilton, Donald. "Coroner Can't Tell if Berry Victim of Heart or Elephant." *Oregon Journal*, June 28, 1979, p. 35.

Macpherson, Malcolm. *The Cowboy and His Elephant*. New York: St. Martin's Griffin, 2002.

Moore, Randall Jay, and Christopher Munnion. *Back to Africa*. Johannesburg: Southern Book Publishers, 1989.

Moore, Randall Jay, and Christopher Munnion. *Elephants for Africa*. Auckland Park, South Africa: Abu Publications, 2000.

Schmidt, Michael, DVM. *Jumbo Ghosts: The Dangerous Life of Elephants in the Zoo*. Chicago: Xlibris Corp, 2002.

Eloise Berchtold's History

Alexander, Shana. *The Astonishing Elephant*. New York: Random House, 2000.

Bordez, Claude, and Giovanni Iuliani. *Dernier Tour de Piste*. Paris: JCL, 2002.

"Cuneo Heir is Married to Woman Lion Tamer." *The Cincinnati Enquirer*, February 29, 1956, p. 3.

Detzel, Helen M. "You Don't 'Tame' Lions." *Cincinnati Magazine*, December, 1973.

"Elephant Returns to Portland with Damaged Eye." *The Oregonian*, February 14, 1976, p. 15.

Foster, Joan. "She Calls Those Big Cats' Bluff." *St. Louis Globe-Democrat*, May 2, 1958, p. 9.

"John Cuneo Weds." *The Holland Evening Sentinel* (Holland, Michigan), February 29, 1956, p. 2.

Laidman, Jenni. "Zoo Chimps Cope with Death in the Family Keeper Becomes One with Dwindling Troop Members." *The Blade* (Toledo, Ohio), April 2, 2000, pp. A1-5.

Macpherson, Malcolm. *The Cowboy and His Elephant*. New York: St. Martin's Griffin, 2002.

Moore, Randall Jay, and Christopher Munnion. *Back to Africa*. Johannesburg: Southern Book Publishers, 1989.

Moore, Randall Jay, and Christopher Munnion. *Elephants for Africa*. Auckland Park, South Africa: Abu Publications, 2000.

Richards, Leverett. "In the Center Ring...The Only Woman Animal Trainer in the United States." *The Oregonian*, February 4, 1973.

Sharp, Nancy. "She's Boss in Big Cage." *Oakland Tribune*, June 10, 1966, p. 49.

Warnick, Charles. "She's Fearless! This Teen-Age Animal Trainer When Spiders Are Absent." *The Cincinnati Enquirer,* June 17, 1951, p. 80.

Eloise Berchtold's Death

Beard, Marvin. "Former Cincinnatian Killed by Elephant During Circus." *The Cincinnati Enquirer*, May 7, 1978, p. 1.

Bordez, Claude, and Giovanni Iuliani. *Dernier Tour de Piste*. Paris: JCL, 2002.

Bosse, Madeleine. "A Rivalry Between Elephants." *La Tribune* (Sherbrooke, Quebec), May 8, 1978.

Bosse, Madeleine. "They Mourn a Sister." *La Tribune* (Sherbrooke, Quebec), May 8, 1978.

Bozarth, Cliff. "Everybody Has a Story: Working on Woodland Elephant Farm was Unusual Job." *The Columbian News* (Vancouver, Washington), April 2, 2023. https://www.columbian.com/news/2023/apr/02/everybody-has-a-story-working-on-elephant-farm-was-unusual-job/

"Circus Animals Killed." *The Spokesman Review* (Spokane, Washington), May 9, 1978.

"Circus Owner Vows He Will Never Use Elephants Again." *The Expositor* (Ontario, Quebec), May 9, 1978, p 7.

"Elephant Shot After Trampling Trainer to Death." *The Oregonian*, May 7, 1978.

Forgues, Daniel. "An Elephant Kills Its Trainer in Rock Forest." *La Tribune* (Sherbrooke, Quebec), 2008, p. 7.

Fudakowska, Anna. "I'll Never Use Elephants Ever Again." *The Sherbrooke Record* (Sherbrooke, Quebec), May 8, 1978, p. 1.

Gagne, Jean-Jacques. "An Elephant That Has Already Killed Can Kill Again, Said the Circus Manager." *The Montreal Matin* (Montreal, Quebec), May 8, 1978, p. 8.

"The Gatini Circus Presents An Entirely New Show." *L' Ècho de Frontenac* (Lac-Mégantic, Quebec), May 2, 1978.
Iuliani, Giovanni. "Eloise Berchtold's Last Performance." *Bandwagon* (Columbus, Ohio), Nov-Dec 2003, pp. 36-39.
Maberry, Matthew, Patricia Maberry, and Michelle Trappen. *Packy & Me*. Beaverton, Oregon: Maberry Press, 2011.
Marcus, Wendy. "Wild Animal Owner On Way Home From Canada." *The Columbian* (Vancouver, Washington), May 10, 1978.
Moore, Randall Jay, and Christopher Munnion. *Back to Africa*. Johannesburg: Southern Book Publishers, 1989.
Moore, Randall Jay, and Christopher Munnion. *Elephants for Africa*. Auckland Park, South Africa: Abu Publications, 2000.
Noles, B.J. "One More Tale..." *The Sunday Oregonian*, May 28, 1978, p. 22.
Pole, Corinna. "Don't Go to the Circus." *The Record* (Sherbrooke, Quebec), August 19, 2009, p. 2.
Rivard, Jean-Pierre. Coroner's Report in Case of Investigations: Eloise Berchtold. Magog, Quebec, Canada. Coroner's Office of Magog, Judicial District of St. Francois, May 5, 1978.
"Savage Animals Treated Savagely: SPA." *The Record* (Sherbrooke, Quebec), August 27, 2008, p. 3.
Saint-Jacques, Pierre. "Cost $40,000 and 30,000 Pounds." *La Tribune* (Sherbrooke, Quebec), May 8, 1978, p. 26.
Schmidt, Michael, DVM. *Jumbo Ghosts: The Dangerous Life of Elephants in the Zoo*. Chicago: Xlibris Corp, 2002.
Talburt, Lane. "From Frying Pan to Fire: Ruffin Switches to Vargas." *Bandwagon* (Columbus, Ohio), Sept-Oct 2007, pp. 25-27.

Inaccurate Reports of Eloise Berchtold's Death

Beard, Marvin. "Former Cincinnatian Killed by Elephant During Circus." *The Cincinnati Enquirer*, May 7, 1978, p. 1.
"Elephant Shot After Trampling Trainer to Death." *The Oregonian*, May 7, 1978.

Fudakowska, Anna. "I'll Never Use Elephants Ever Again." *The Sherbrooke Record* (Sherbrooke, Quebec), May 8, 1978, p. 1.

Maberry, Matthew, Patricia Maberry, and Michelle Trappen. *Packy & Me*. Beaverton, Oregon: Maberry Press, 2011.

Moore, Randall Jay, and Christopher Munnion. *Back to Africa*. Johannesburg: Southern Book Publishers, 1989.

Moore, Randall Jay, and Christopher Munnion. *Elephants for Africa*. Auckland Park, South Africa: Abu Publications, 2000.

Richards, Leverett. *Elephants Don't Snore*. Vancouver, Washington: Rose Wind Press, 1996.

The Elephant Packy

Alexander, Shana. "Belle's Baby 225 Pounds and All Elephant." *Life Magazine*, May 11, 1962, pp. 104-120.

Alexander, Shana. *The Astonishing Elephant*. New York: Random House, 2000.

ArnicaCreative. "Packy and Me." *YouTube* video, 3:00. February 28, 2011. https://www.youtube.com/watch?v=vWpfwSJvAdo

"Belle and Her Baby Set New Record at Portland Zoo." *Skagit Valley Herald* (Mt. Vernon, Washington), April 23, 1962, p. 1.

Bozarth, Cliff. "Everybody Has a Story: Working on Woodland Elephant Farm was Unusual Job." *The Columbian News* (Vancouver, Washington), April 2, 2023. https://www.columbian.com/news/2023/apr/02/everybody-has-a-story-working-on-elephant-farm-was-unusual-job/

"Elephant Gives Birth in Oregon Zoo." *The New York Times*, April 15, 1962, p. 52.

Federman, Stan. "Packy Comes of Age for Grand Birthday Party." *The Oregonian*, April 7, 1983, p. C1.

Maberry, Matthew, Patricia Maberry, and Michelle Trappen. *Packy & Me*. Beaverton, Oregon: Maberry Press, 2011.

Muldoon, Katy. "Oregon Zoo Prepares to Celebrate Half a Century with its Most Beloved Elephant, Packy." *OregonLive*, April

9, 2012. https://www.oregonlive.com/portland/2012/04/packy_oregons_renowned_elephan.html

Patterson, Rod. "Formal Dedication of New Elephant Facilities at Washington Park Zoo." *The Sunday Oregonian,* May 4, 1980, p. 2.

"Portland Belle Fund Passes Goal." *Skagit Valley Herald* (Mt. Vernon, Washington), May 17, 1962, p. 1.

"Portland Takes Its New Baby Elephant Very Big." *St. Cloud Times* (St. Cloud, Minnesota), April 19, 1962, p. 11.

"Precocious Pachyderm Puts Portland on Map." *The Oregonian*, April 13, 1963, p. 16.

"Reluctant Belle Puts on Weight." *Skagit Valley Herald* (Mt. Vernon, Washington), March 9, 1962, p. 1.

Richards, Leverett. "Elephant in Waiting Getting Mail…Across the Nation." *The Oregonian*, January 23, 1962, p. 1.

Richards, Leverett. *Elephants Don't Snore.* Vancouver, Washington: Rose Wind Press, 1996.

Richards, Leveret. "Belle Loses Her Temper." *The Oregonian*, January 23, 1962, p. 1.

"Stork on Way for Elephant." *Skagit Valley Herald* (Mt. Vernon, Washington), January 15, 1962, p. 1.

The Elephant Buddha

Alexander, Shana. *The Astonishing Elephant.* New York: Random House, 2000.

Bozarth, Cliff. "Everybody Has a Story: Working on Woodland Elephant Farm was Unusual Job." *The Columbian News* (Vancouver, Washington), April 2, 2023. https://www.columbian.com/news/2023/apr/02/everybody-has-a-story-working-on-elephant-farm-was-unusual-job/

Bozarth, Cliff. "Comment on McMenamins Blog," *McMenamins Blog*, June 25, 2022. https://blog.mcmenamins.com/elephant-mountain/

McIntosh, Jay. "Elephants: Ken Berry had Tough Job Finding Home for Beasts." *The Daily News* (Longview, Washington), November 21, 1979.

Moore, Randall Jay, and Christopher Munnion. *Back to Africa.* Johannesburg: Southern Book Publishers, 1989.

Moore, Randall Jay, and Christopher Munnion. *Elephants for Africa.* Auckland Park, South Africa: Abu Publications, 2000.

Excavation of Buddha by Lewis & Clark College Students

Burner, Dell. "Up From the Grave." *The Daily News* (Longview, Washington), August 19, 1983.

Miller, J., December 4, 2012. "Comment on The Elephant, Photographer and Sheriff Blog," *Cowlitz County Law Enforcement History Blog.* http://cclehistory.blogspot.com/2009/10/elephant-photographer-and-sheriff.html#comment

Ruble, Web. "Students Excavate Elephant Bones." *The Oregonian*, August 22, 1983, p. B4.

The Electrocution Sessions on Thonglaw

Bozarth, Cliff. "Everybody Has a Story: Working on Woodland Elephant Farm was Unusual Job." *The Columbian News* (Vancouver, Washington), April 2, 2023. https://www.columbian.com/news/2023/apr/02/everybody-has-a-story-working-on-elephant-farm-was-unusual-job/

Crandall, Melissa. *Elephant Speak: A Devoted Keeper's Life Among the Herd.* Portland, Oregon: Ooligan Press, 2020.

Maberry, Matthew, Patricia Maberry, and Michelle Trappen. *Packy & Me.* Beaverton, Oregon: Maberry Press, 2011.

Richards, Leverett. *Elephants Don't Snore.* Vancouver, Washington: Rose Wind Press, 1996.

Schmidt, Michael, DVM. *Jumbo Ghosts: The Dangerous Life of Elephants in the Zoo.* Chicago: Xlibris Corp, 2002.

BEHIND THE STORY

Electrocution of Other Elephants

"Interim Hearing on San Diego Zoological Society: The Care and Handling of Animals and Other Management Issues." Hearing before the California Legislature, Senate Committee on Natural Resources and Wildlife, Senator Dan McCorquodale, Chairman. Escondido, CA. July 19, 1989.

Frammolino, Ralph. "Elephant-Abuse Bill, Sparked by Dunda Incident, Advances." *Los Angeles Times*, June 9, 1989. https://www.latimes.com/archives/la-xpm-1989-06-09-me-1539-story.html

Montgomery, David. "Ex-Trainer Accuses Circus of Elephant Cruelty." *NBC News*, December 16, 2009. https://www.nbcnews.com/id/wbna34442605

"Riddle's Elephant and Wildlife Sanctuary." *Encyclopedia of Arkansas*. https://encyclopediaofarkansas.net/entries/riddles-elephant-and-wildlife-sanctuary-4060/

"South Africa Elephant Park Accused of Horrific Cruelty." *Phys.org*, May 20, 2014. https://phys.org/news/2014-05-south-africa-elephant-accused-horrific.html?form=MG0AV3

"Zoo Admits Using Illegal Animal Prods." *BBC News*, December 12, 1999. http://news.bbc.co.uk/2/hi/uk_news/561671.stm?form=MG0AV3

The Elephant Tyke

Lambert, Susan, and Stefan Moore, directors. *Tyke: Elephant Outlaw*. Media Stockade, 2014. 78 min.

Schmidt, Michael, DVM. *Jumbo Ghosts: The Dangerous Life of Elephants in the Zoo*. Chicago: Xlibris Corp, 2002.

"Tyke Elephant Outlaw Clip." *YouTube* video, 3:53. American Film Institute, June 8, 2015. https://www.youtube.com/watch?v=amAGD6q U7Ms

The Elephant Gunda

"Bronx Zoo Elephant Chained for 2 Years." *The New York Times*, June 23, 1914, p. 3.

"Bullet Ends Gunda Bronx Zoo Elephant." *The New York Times*, June 23, 1915, p. 8.

"Elephant Attacks Keeper." *The New York Times,* July 29, 1907, p. 1.

"Gunda Breaks Tusk in Fight to be Free." *The New York Times*, July 14, 1914, p. 1.

"Gunda Must Submit to Shackles Again." *The New York Times*, July 13, 1914, p. 9.

"Gunda's Exercise is the One-Step." *The New York Times*, June 25, 1914, p. 6.

"It's Now Up to Gunda." *The New York Times*, August 14, 1914, p. 12.

"Open Door to Loose Big Gunda's Chains." *The New York Times*, July 2, 1914, p. 6.

Schmidt, Michael, DVM. *Jumbo Ghosts: The Dangerous Life of Elephants in the Zoo*. Chicago: Xlibris Corp, 2002.

"Times Readers Protest Against Gunda's Imprisonment." *The New York Times*, July 19, 1914, p. SM6.

"Vetoes $1000 Plan for Relief for Gunda: Dr. Hornaday Says He Would Rather Kill Beast Than Rebuild Zoo." *The New York Times*, July 1, 1014, p. 5.

Shana Alexander

Alexander, Shana. "Belle's Baby 225 Pounds and All Elephant." *Life Magazine*, May 11, 1962, pp. 104-120.

Alexander, Shana. "For the Love of Elephants: An Inquiry into the Violent Death of an Old Friend." *Life Magazine*, March 1980, pp. 79-92.

Alexander, Shana. *The Astonishing Elephant*. New York: Random House, 2000.

Maberry, Matthew, Patricia Maberry, and Michelle Trappen. *Packy & Me*. Beaverton, Oregon: Maberry Press, 2011.

Melson, Foggy. "Shana Alexander Interview (November 27, 1976)." Interview by Quentin Melson. *YouTube* video, 9:15. March 30, 2023. https://www.youtube.com/watch?v=b-YrQKGGQGE

The Media Hoarder. "60 Minutes: Point Counterpoint." *YouTube* video, 3:28. January 1, 1978. https://www.youtube.com/watch?v=cESACuuh6kM&t=18s

Saturday Night Live. "Weekend Update: Jane, You Ignorant Slut." *YouTube* video, 2:16. August 7, 2017. 1979. https://www.youtube.com/watch?v=c91XUyg9iWM

George "Slim" Lewis

Alexander, Shana. *The Astonishing Elephant*. New York: Random House, 2000.

Bordez, Claude, and Giovanni Iuliani. *Dernier Tour de Piste*. Paris: JCL, 2002.

Lewis, George "Slim," and Byron Fish. *I Loved Rogues: The Life of an Elephant Tramp*. Seattle: Superior Publishing Company, 1978.

Lewis, George "Slim." "Not Protective." *The Oregonian*, July 16, 1979, p. 14.

Arthur Jones

Cundiff, Rick, and Austin L. Miller. "Jumbolair Founder Arthur Jones Dies." *Ocala StarBanner* (Ocala, Florida), August 29, 2007. https://www.ocala.com/story/news/2007/08/29/jumbolair-founder-arthur-jones-dies/31216563007/

Hess, Jennie. "Inventor of Nautilus Exercises Right to Tell It How He Thinks." *The Chicago Tribune*, September 7, 1986.

Medina, Carlos. "Jumbolair Sells for $9.5 Million." *Ocala Gazette* (Ocala, Florida), March 2, 2021.

Moore, Randall Jay, and Christopher Munnion. *Back to Africa*. Johannesburg: Southern Book Publishers, 1989.

Moore, Randall Jay, and Christopher Munnion. *Elephants for Africa*. Auckland Park, South Africa: Abu Publications, 2000.

Pohlman, Katie. "Former Trump Attorney Cohen Has Tie to Marion County." *Ocala StarBanner* (Ocala, Florida), August 31, 2018. https://www.ocala.com/story/news/local/2018/08/31/former-trump-attorney-cohen-has-tie-to-marion-county/10875187007/

Television Obscurities. "Wild Cargo." March 9, 2009, https://www.tvobscurities.com/spotlight/wild-cargo/

Television Obscurities. "Wild Cargo Opening Credits." *YouTube* video, 1:03. January 29, 2019. https://www.youtube.com/watch?v=rQAZOA_mNK0

Michelle McNamara

I'll Be Gone in the Dark. Directed by Liz Garbus, Myles Kane, Josh Koury, and Elizabeth Wolff. HBO Max, 2020. https://www.max.com/shows/ill-be-gone-in-the-dark/a823014d-fa0b-4bbe-ab98-14ea00e551bb

Legacy. "Michelle McNamara Obituary." April 23, 2016. https://www.legacy.com/news/celebrity-deaths/michelle-mcnamara-1969-2016/

McNamara, Michelle, Paul Haynes, and Billy Jensen. *I'll Be Gone in the Dark: One Woman's Obsessive Search for the Golden State Killer*. New York: Harper Perennial, 2019.

Elephant Births at the Oregon Zoo Between 1962 - 1980

Berens, Michael. "Elephants are Dying Out in Zoos." *The Seattle Times*, December 1, 2012. https://special.seattletimes.com/o/html/nationworld/2019809167_elephants02m.html

Bordez, Claude, and Giovanni Iuliani. *Dernier Tour de Piste*. Paris: JCL, 2002.

BEHIND THE STORY

Crandall, Melissa. *Elephant Speak: A Devoted Keeper's Life Among the Herd*. Portland, Oregon: Ooligan Press, 2020.

Ethell, Debbie. "Captive Elephant Births/Histories Between 1962 and 1980." PDF 2024.

Ethell, Debbie. "Rosy's Birth Records and Pregnancies." PDF 2023.

Federman, Stan. "Elephant Bite Not Sans Bright Side." *The Sunday Oregonian*, July 15, 1984, p. 56.

O'Rourke, Ciara. "A Closer Look at the Oregon Zoo's Elephant Breeding Program." *Portland Monthly*, April 1, 2020.

Patterson, Rod. "Formal Dedication of New Elephant Facilities at Washington Park Zoo. *The Sunday Oregonian*, May 4, 1980, p. 2.

Richards, Leverett. "Dream For Sale ... If You Want Elephants." *The Oregonian*, February 6, 1980, p. 28.

Schmidt, Michael, DVM. *Jumbo Ghosts: The Dangerous Life of Elephants in the Zoo*. Chicago: Xlibris Corp, 2002.

History of Oregon Zoo Elephant Inbreeding

Castano, Carla. "Elephants Part 2: Elephant Breeding." Part 2 of a 3-part KOIN 6 News Investigations series. *YouTube* video, 9:41. August 7, 2015. https://www.youtube.com/watch?v=3qcRPLOWdMk

Federman, Stan. "Portland's Zoo Helping to Fulfill Noah's Ark Plan." *The Oregonian*, October 24, 1984, p. 32.

Maberry, Matthew, Patricia Maberry, and Michelle Trappen. *Packy & Me*. Beaverton, Oregon: Maberry Press, 2011.

O'Rourke, Ciara. "Elephant in the Room: A Closer Look at the Oregon Zoo's Elephant Breeding Program." *Portland Monthly*, April 1, 2020. https://www.pdxmonthly.com/travel-and-outdoors/2020/04/a-closer-look-at-the-oregon-zoo-s-elephant-breeding-program

Webster, Bayard. "Inbreeding Called Peril in Zoos." *The New York Times*, November 27, 1979, p. C3.

Outcome of the Oregon Zoo's Original Elephants (including Morgan's Herd)

Alexander, Shana. *The Astonishing Elephant*. New York: Random House, 2000.

Castano, Carla. "Elephants Part 3: The Bullhook: Insurance, Weapon or Both." Part 3 of a 3-part KOIN 6 News Investigations series. *YouTube* video, 8:16. August 12, 2015. https://www.youtube.com/watch?v=WQh5mqqApME

Classen, Allan. "Zoo Director Says All is Well in Elephant Lands." *NW Examiner* (Portland, Oregon), March 2014, p. 1.

Crandall, Melissa. *Elephant Speak: A Devoted Keeper's Life Among the Herd*. Portland, Oregon: Ooligan Press, 2020.

Fowler, Murray E, DVM. *Hummingbirds to Elephants and Other Tales: Autobiography of Murray E. Fowler, DVM*. Jackson, California: Clay Press Inc, 1999.

Maberry, Matthew, Patricia Maberry, and Michelle Trappen. *Packy & Me*. Beaverton, Oregon: Maberry Press, 2011.

Markowitz, Hal, Michael Schmidt, Leonie Nadal, and Leslie Squier. "Do Elephants Ever Forget?" *Journal of Applied Behavior Analysis* 8 (1975): 333-335.

Richards, Leverett. *Elephants Don't Snore*. Vancouver, Washington: Rose Wind Press, 1996.

Schmidt, Michael, DVM. *Jumbo Ghosts: The Dangerous Life of Elephants in the Zoo*. Chicago: Xlibris Corp, 2002.

Schmidt, M.J. "Antagonism of Xylazine Sedation by Yohimbine and 4-Aminopyridine in an Adult Elephant (Elephas maximus)." *The Journal of Zoo Animal Medicine* 14, No. 3 (September 1983): 94-97.

BEHIND THE STORY

Rose-Tu Beating Incident at the Oregon Zoo, April 2000

ASPCA v. Feld Entertainment, Inc. No. 03-2006. United States District Court for the District of Columbia, April 24, 2009.

Castano, Carla. "Elephants Part 3: The Bullhook: Insurance, Weapon or Both." Part 3 of a 3-part KOIN 6 News Investigations series. *YouTube* video, 8:16. August 12, 2015. https://www.youtube.com/watch?v=WQh5mqqApME

Classen, Allan. "Zoo Director Says All is Well in Elephant Lands." *NW Examiner* (Portland, Oregon), March 2014, p. 1.

Laborers' International Union of North America, Local 483 and Metro. Collective Bargaining Agreement, July 1, 2018 - June 30, 2023. https://www.laborers483.org

The Firestorm Surrounding the Oregon Zoo Bond in 2008

ASPCA v. Feld Entertainment, Inc. No. 03-2006. United States District Court for the District of Columbia, April 24, 2009.

Berens, Michael. "Elephants are Dying Out in Zoos." *The Seattle Times*, December 1, 2012. https://special.seattletimes.com/o/html/nationworld/2019809167_elephants02m.html

Binder, Melissa. "Oregon Zoo Firings." *OregonLive*, May 17, 2014. https://www.oregonlive.com/portland/2014/05/oregon_zoo_firings_few_red_fla_1.html

Casey, Jerry. "Elephants Take Lead in Zoo's Bond Hopes." *OregonLive*, November 8, 2008. https://www.oregonlive.com/elections/2008/11/elephants_take_lead_in_zoos_bo.html

Casey, Jerry. "Metro's Zoo Bond Passes." *OregonLive*, November 5, 2008. https://www-oregonlive-com.translate.goog/elections/2008/11/zoobond.html?_x_tr_sl=auto&_x_tr_tl=en&_x_tr_hl=en-US

Crandall, Melissa. *Elephant Speak: A Devoted Keeper's Life Among the Herd.* Portland, Oregon: Ooligan Press, 2020.

Evans, Brian, Angela Owens, and Simone Rede. *Oregon Zoo Audit: Clarify Vision, Prioritize Actions, and Learn from*

Change to Improve Organizational Culture. Portland, OR: Metro, February 2017. https://www.oregonmetro.gov/oregon-zoo-audit

Free the Oregon Zoo Elephants. "Metro Final Vote on the Offsite Preserve 2-18-16." *YouTube* video, 18:17. March 1, 2016. https://www.youtube.com/watch?v=EZl_9aC2Mj8

Flynn, Suzanne, Elizabeth Wager, Kristin Lieber, and Kathryn Nichols. *Oregon Zoo Capital Construction Audit.* Portland, OR: Metro, November 2009. https://www.oregonmetro.gov/news/oregon-zoo-capital-construction-audit

"Going Rogue Each Week." *Willamette Week*, November 17, 2009. https://www.wweek.com/portland/article-11327-going-rogue-each-week.html

Jaquiss, Nigel. "Zoo Audit Due Tomorrow: Two Staffers Scram." *Willamette Week*, November 11, 2009. https://www.wweek.com/portland/blog-3011-zoo-audit-due-tomorrow-two-staffers-scram.html

Jaquiss, Nigel. "Metro is About to Dump its Plans for an Off-Site Elephant Reserve." *Willamette Week*, January 19, 2016. https://www.wweek.com/uncategorized/2016/01/20/metro-is-about-to-dump-its-plans-for-an-offsite-elephant-reserve/

Jaquiss, Nigel. "Oregon Zoo Audit Shows Employee Discontent, Stagnant Attendance." *Willamette Week*, February 23, 2017. https://www.wweek.com/news/2017/02/23/oregon-zoo-audit-shows-employee-discontent-stagnant-attendance/

KOIN 6 News. "After Years, Oregon Zoo's Elephant Lands Opens." *YouTube* video, 2:44. December 15, 2015. https://www.youtube.com/watch?v=qMxjD-OI9d0

KOIN 6 News. "The Elephant in the Room with Oregon Zoo Bond." *YouTube* video, 6:30. March 12, 2015. https://www.youtube.com/watch?v=6vzsxSppP7E

KOIN 6 News. "Oregon Zoo Defends Bond Money Expenditures." *YouTube* video, 2:49. February 5, 2014. https://www.youtube.com/watch?v=69l1gLJRx74

"Last Call for Hippos: Poppy and Bubbles Move to Texas." *OregonLive*, March 13, 2018. https://www.oregonzoo.org/news/last-call-hippos-poppy-and-bubbles-move-texas

Mesh, Aaron. "12 Mammals that Matter to the Oregon Zoo." *Willamette Week*, May 28, 2014, pp. 12-19.

Mesh, Aaron. "Tusk, But Verify." *Willamette Week*, December 11, 2012. https://www.wweek.com/portland/article-20023-tusk-but-verify.html

"Metro: Off-Site Elephant Range Never Promised in Bond Measure." *KGW News*, January 22, 2016. https://www.kgw.com/article/news/local/metro-off-site-elephant-range-never-promised-in-bond-measure/283-20061550

Mortensen, Eric. "Audit Shows Cost Overruns and Mangled Management of Oregon Zoo Projects." *Oregon Live*. November 13, 2009. https://www.oregonlive.com/news/2009/11/audit_shows_cost_overruns_and.html

Muldoon, Katy. "Oregon Zoo Prepares to Celebrate Half a Century with its Most Beloved Elephant, Packy." *OregonLive*. April 8, 2012. https://www.oregonlive.com/portland/2012/04/packy_oregons_renowned_elephan.html

Muldoon, Katy. "Oregon Zoo Goes to Work on Elephant Lands, it's New $53 Million Exhibit." *OregonLive*, June 10, 2013. https://www.oregonlive.com/portland/2013/06/oregon_zoo_goes_to_work_on_ele.html

Muldoon, Katy. "Oregon Zoo Sees High Staff Turnover, Culture Shift." *OregonLive*, June 18, 2012. https://www.oregonlive.com/portland/2012/06/oregon_zoo_sees_high_staff_tur.html

Multnomah County Elections Division. November, 4 2008. *Measure No. 26-96: Shall Zoo Protect Animal Health and Safety; Conserve, Recycle Water; Issue $125 million in General Obligation Bonds; Require Independent Audits?* https://multco.us/info/november-4-2008-measure-no-26-96

"Oregon Zoo Director Vecchio Leaving for FL Job." *KGW News*, September 17, 2009. https://www.kgw.com/article/entertainment/oregon-zoo-director-vecchio-leaving-for-fl-job/283-90341849

Scottwork47 "Metro Hearing on the Offsite Elephant Preserve" *YouTube* video, 8:58. January 29, 2016. https://www.youtube.com/watch?v=qILVeBtGbxY

"Oregon Zoo Polar Bear Tasul Dead at Age 31." *OregonLive*, November 18, 2016. https://www-oregonlive.com.translate.goog/portland/2016/11/tasul_oregon_zoos_elderly_pola.html?_x_tr_sl=auto&_x_tr_tl=en&_x_tr_hl=en-US

O'Rourke, Ciara. "A Closer Look at the Oregon Zoo's Elephant Breeding Program." *Portland Monthly*, April 1, 2020. https://www.pdxmonthly.com/travel-and-outdoors/2020/04/a-closer-look-at-the-oregon-zoo-s-elephant-breeding-program

Preusch, Matthew. "Metro Names New Director of Oregon Zoo." *OregonLive*. December 29, 2009. https://www.oregonlive.com/news/2009/12/metro_names_new_zoo_director.html

"Two Senior OZ Employees Step Down." *Willamette Week*, November 1, 2009. https://issuu.com/willametteweek/docs/36.02_willamette_week__november_1

Training Points on an Elephant's Body

ASPCA v. Feld Entertainment, Inc. No. 03-2006. United States District Court for the District of Columbia, April 24, 2009.

Berens, Michael. "Elephants are Dying Out in Zoos." *The Seattle Times*, December 1, 2012. https://special.seattletimes.com/o/html/nationworld/2019809167_elephants02m.html.

Jacobsen, Gary. Deposition, October 24, 2007. ASPCA v. Feld Entertainment, Inc., No. 03-2006: United States District Court for the District of Columbia, April 24, 2009.

Moore, Randall Jay, and Christopher Munnion. *Back to Africa*. Johannesburg: Southern Book Publishers, 1989.

Moore, Randall Jay, and Christopher Munnion. *Elephants for Africa*. Auckland Park, South Africa: Abu Publications, 2000.

Tuy Hoa's (actual) Final Moments
* Tuy Hoa is not mentioned by name in the following scientific paper. However, I identified her based on the details provided in the paper: the elephant described was a 28-year-old female Asian elephant with chronic foot pain, euthanized in 1983. Tuy Hoa died on April 20, 1983, at age 28, and records confirm she was the only elephant of that age and circumstance at the Oregon Zoo that year.

Schmidt, M.J. "Antagonism of Xylazine Sedation by Yohimbine and 4-Aminopyridine in an Adult Elephant (Elephas maximus)." *The Journal of Zoo Animal Medicine* 14, No. 3 (September 1983): 94-97.

Medical Experiments Conducted on Other Elephants
Brown, Janine L., Ravi Corea, Ashoka Dangolla, E.K. Easwaran, Susan Mikota, Zaw Min Oo, Kushal Sarma, and Chatchote Thitaram. "Management and Care of Captive Asian Elephant Bulls in Musth." *IUCN SSC Asian Elephant Specialist Group* (2020): 60-63.

Fowler, Murray E. "Castration of an Elephant." *The Journal of Zoo Animal Medicine* 4, No. 3 (September 1973): 25-27.

Fowler, Murray E, DVM. *Hummingbirds to Elephants and Other Tales: Autobiography of Murray E. Fowler, DVM*. Jackson, California: Clay Press Inc, 1999.

Foerner, Joseph J., Richard I. Houck, John F. Copeland, Michael J. Schmidt, H.T. Byron, and John H. Olsen. "Surgical Castration of the Elephant *(Elephas maximus and Loxodonta africana)*." *Journal of Zoo and Wildlife Medicine* 25, No. 3 (September 1994): 355-359.

Schmidt, Michael, DVM. *Jumbo Ghosts: The Dangerous Life of Elephants in the Zoo*. Chicago: Xlibris Corp, 2002.

Kari and Gary Johnson, Owners of Have Trunk Will Travel

Animal Defenders International. "Elephant Training at Have Trunk Will Travel." *YouTube* video, 9:54. March 21, 2013. https://www.youtube.com/watch?v=L1AvNGWAkCY&list=PL8816EFB830EF16AC

Cole, Jim. "Miller-Johnson Circus 1972." *Buckles Blog*, March 31, 2008. https://bucklesw.blogspot.com/search?q=smokey

Lewis, George "Slim," and Byron Fish. *I Loved Rogues: The Life of an Elephant Tramp*. Seattle: Superior Publishing Company, 1978.

Mesh, Aaron. "12 Mammals that Matter to the Oregon Zoo." *Willamette Week*, May 28, 2014, pp. 12-19.

Protect All Wildlife. "Animal Trainers Abuse at Have Trunk Will Travel." *YouTube* video, 1:00. July 3, 2017. https://www.youtube.com/watch?v=jwB5xU66ODc

Sheridan, Tom. "The Elephants Not in the Room: As Culture Shifts from Using the Creatures in Circuses and Elsewhere, Family's Livelihood Uncertain." *The Orange County Register*, May 15, 2015. https://www.ocregister.com/2015/05/15/the-elephants-not-in-the-room-as-culture-shifts-from-using-the-creatures-in-circuses-and-elsewhere-familys-livelihood-uncertain/

Elephant Leasing and Sales Contracts

Alexander, Shana. *The Astonishing Elephant*. New York: Random House, 2000.

Berens, Michael. "Portland's Baby Elephant Belongs to Traveling Show." *The Seattle Times*, December 4, 2012. https://www.seattletimes.com/seattle-news/portlands-baby-elephant-belongs-to-traveling-show/

Berens, Michael. "Portland Zoo Vows Elephant Calf Will Stay Put - Even if They Have to Buy Her." *The Seattle Times*, December 4, 2012. https://special.seattletimes.com/o/html/localnews/2019829395_elephant05m.html

Berens, Michael. "Elephants are Dying Out in Zoos." *The Seattle Times*, December 1, 2012. https://special.seattletimes.com/o/html/nationworld/2019809167_elephants02m.html

"Elephant Might Go to Portland." *The Columbian* (Vancouver, Washington), August 14, 1979, p. 10.

Federman, Stan. "Elephant Bite Not Sans Bright Side." *The Sunday Oregonian*, July 15, 1984, p. 56.

"Oregon Zoo Buys Elephants for $400K." *Oregon Business*, February 11, 2013. https://oregonbusiness.com/8825-oregon-zoo-buys-elephants-for-400k/

McIntosh, Jay. "Elephants: Ken Berry had Tough Job Finding Home for Beasts." *The Daily News* (Longview, Washington), November 21, 1979.

Mesh, Aaron. "12 Mammals That Matter to the Oregon Zoo." *Willamette Week*, May 28, 2014, pp. 12-19.

Richards, Leverett. "Zoo's New Elephant Pen Opens." *The Sunday Oregonian*, April 27, 1980, p. 53.

"Newborn Male Elephant Fine." *The Oregonian*, October 3, 1982, p. 23.

Richards, Leverett. "Dream For Sale ... If You Want Elephants." *The Oregonian*, February 6, 1980, p. 28.

Richards, Leverett. "Tonga Joins Elephant Herd at Washington Park Zoo." *The Oregonian*, November 20, 1979, p. 54.

Richards, Leverett. "New Bull Takes Charge at Zoo." *The Oregonian*, December 6, 1979, p. 33.

Schmidt, Michael, DVM. *Jumbo Ghosts: The Dangerous Life of Elephants in the Zoo*. Chicago: Xlibris Corp, 2002.

Sheridan, Tom. "The Elephants Not in the Room: As Culture Shifts from Using the Creatures in Circuses and Elsewhere, Family's Livelihood Uncertain." *The Orange County Register*

(Santa Ana, California), May 15, 2015. https://www.oc
register.com/2015/05/15/the-elephants-not-in-the-room
-as-culture-shifts-from-using-the-creatures-in-circuses
-and-elsewhere-familys-livelihood-uncertain/

History of Killing Young Male Elephants in Captivity

Alexander, Shana. "Belle's Baby 225 Pounds and All Elephant." *Life Magazine*, May 11, 1962, pp. 104-120.

Alexander, Shana. *The Astonishing Elephant*. New York: Random House, 2000.

Foerner, Joseph J., Richard I. Houck, John F. Copeland, Michael J. Schmidt, H.T. Byron, and John H. Olsen. "Surgical Castration of the Elephant *(Elephas maximus and Loxodonta africana)*." *Journal of Zoo and Wildlife Medicine* 25, No. 3 (September 1994): 355-359.

Fowler, Murray E. "Castration of an Elephant." *The Journal of Zoo Animal Medicine* 4, No. 3 (September 1973): 25-27.

Fowler, Murray E, DVM. *Hummingbirds to Elephants and Other Tales: Autobiography of Murray E. Fowler, DVM*. Jackson, California: Clay Press Inc, 1999.

Lewis, George "Slim," and Byron Fish. *I Loved Rogues: The Life of an Elephant Tramp*. Seattle: Superior Publishing Company, 1978.

Maberry, Matthew, Patricia Maberry, and Michelle Trappen. *Packy & Me*. Beaverton, Oregon: Maberry Press, 2011.

Crandall, Melissa. *Elephant Speak: A Devoted Keeper's Life Among the Herd*. Portland, Oregon: Ooligan Press, 2020.

McIntosh, Jay. "Elephants: Ken Berry had Tough Job Finding Home for Beasts." *The Daily News* (Longview, Washington), November 21, 1979.

Schmidt, Michael, DVM. *Jumbo Ghosts: The Dangerous Life of Elephants in the Zoo*. Chicago: Xlibris Corp, 2002.

Sukumar, Raman. *The Living Elephants*. New York: Oxford University Press, Inc, 2003.

Elephant Vocal Mimicry & Human Speech

"Elephants Learn Through Copying." *BBC News*, March 23, 2005. http://news.bbc.co.uk/2/hi/science/nature/4377297.stm

Beeston, Richard. "Asian Elephant Can Say Human Phrases." *The Telegraph*, April 9, 1980.

"Batyr" *Bionity Encyclopedia*. https://www.bionity.com/en/encyclopedia/Batyr.html

Choi, Charles. "Say What?! This Elephant Can Speak Korean - Out Loud." *NBC News*, November 1, 2012. https://www.nbcnews.com/id/wbna49643352

"Forest Elephants and Infrasound." *Elephant Listening Project*. https://www.elephantlisteningproject.org/all-about-infrasound/

"Meet Koshik, A Male Elephant Who Mimics the Sound of Human Speech." *The Guardian*, November 1, 2012.

Herman, Steve. "Researchers Verify Elephant Mimics Human Speech." *VOA News*, November 1, 2022. https://www.voanews.com/a/south-korean-zoo-elephant-mimics-human-speech/1537520.html

Poole, Joyce, Peter L. Tyack, Angela S. Stöeger-Horwath, and Stephanie Watwood. "Elephants are Capable of Vocal Learning." *Nature* 434 (March 24, 2025): 434-456.

Milius, Susan. "Big Mimics: African Elephants Can Learn to Copy Sounds." *Science News*, March 23, 2005. https://www.sciencenews.org/article/big-mimics-african-elephants-can-learn-copy-sounds

Madin, Kate. "To Decipher Odd Elephant Calls, Call in a Whale Expert." *Oceanus Magazine*, 2005, p. 10.

Pardo, Michael A., Kurt Fristrup, David Lolchuragi, Joyce Poole, Petter Granli, Cynthia Moss, Iain Douglas-Hamilton, and George Wittemyer. "African Elephants Address One Another with Individually Specific Calls." *bioRxiv*, (August 27, 2023) 1-38. Published online 2024. https://www.biorxiv.org/content/10.1101/2023.08.25.554872v1

Stöeger, Angela S., Daniel Mietchen, Sukhum Oh, Shermin de Silva, Christian T. Herbst, Soowhan Kwon, and W. Tecumeseh Fitch. "An Asian Elephant Imitates Human Speech." *Current Biology* 22 (November 1, 2012): 2144-2148.

Stöeger, Angela S. "An Elephant that Speaks Korean." *Eurekalet! AAAS*, 2012. Audio Recording. https://www.eurekalert.org/multimedia/595931

Stöeger, Angela S. "An Elephant that Speaks Korean." *Eurekalet! AAAS*, 2012. Video Recording. https://www.eurekalert.org/multimedia/595928

Stromberg, Joseph. "This Elephant Learned to Speak Korean: Koshik, an Asian Elephant at a South Korean Zoo, Learned to Uncannily Mimic Five Korean Words by Stuffing His Trunk in his Mouth." *Smithsonian Magazine*, November 1, 2012. https://www.smithsonianmag.com/science-nature/video-this-elephant-learned-to-speak-korean-104813016/

Dolphins and Whales

AppleTV. "Fathom – Official Trailer | Apple TV+." *YouTube* video, 2:36. April 22, 2021. https://www.youtube.com/watch?v=Y-Mmnk0LZLU

Armstrong, Brian, and Andy Mitchell, directors, writers, and creators. *Secrets of the Whales*. Produced by James Cameron. Narrated by Sigourney Weaver. *National Geographic*. Disney+. April 22, 2021.

Deecke, V. B., J.K.B. Ford, and P. Spong. "Dialect Change in Resident Killer Whales: Implications for Vocal Learning and Cultural Transmission." *Animal Behaviour* 60 (April 4, 2000): 629-638.

Ford, John K.B. "Vocal Traditions Among Resident Killer Whales (*Orcinus orca*) in Coastal Waters of British

Columbia." *Canadian Journal of Zoology* (June 1991): 1454-1483.

Herman, Louis M. "Can Dolphins Understand Sentences?" *JSTOR, ResearchGate* (January 2009): 3-20.

Hamilton, Philip, director and producer. *Ocean Souls*. Produced by Scott Wilson. Narrated by Flora Clark. *Journeyman Pictures*, May 16, 2020. https://www.journeyman.tv/film/8669

Iacoboni, Marco. "Imitation, Empathy, and Mirror Neurons." *Annual Review of Psychology* 60 (January 2009): 653-670.

MacDonald, James. "The Cultural Differences in Humpback Whale Songs." *JSTOR Daily*, October 3, 2019. https://daily.jstor.org/cultural-differences-humpback-whale-songs/

McDonald, Mark A., Sarah L. Mesnick, and John A. Hildebrand. "Biogeographic Characterisation of Blue Whale Song Worldwide: Using Song to Identify Populations." *Journal of Cetacean Research and Management* 8 (July 2005): 55-65.

Miller, Patrick J.O., and David E. Bain. "Within-Pod Variation in the Sound Production of a Pod of Killer Whales, *Orcinus orca*." *Animal Behavior* 60, Issue 5 (December 2000): 617-628.

Miller, Patrick James O'Malley. "Maintaining Contact: Design and Use of Acoustic Signals in Killer Whales, *Orcinus Orca*." PhD diss., *Massachusetts Institute of Technology/Woods Hole Oceanographic Institution*, 2000. https://apps.dtic.mil/sti/tr/pdf/ADA384341.pdf

Mustill, Tom. *How to Speak Whale: A Voyage into the Future of Animal Communication*. New York: Grand Central Publishing, 2022.

National Geographic. "Secrets of the Whales | Official Trailer | Disney+." *YouTube* video, 0:59. March 10, 2021. https://www.youtube.com/watch?v=xOySOlB78dM

Payne, Katy. *Silent Thunder*. New York: Penguin Publishing Group, 1999.

Payne, Katy, and Roger Payne, producers. *Songs of the Humpback Whale.* CRM Records, 1979.

Prochazkova, Eliska, and Mariska E. Kret. "Connecting Minds and Sharing Emotions Through Mimicry: A Neurocognitive Model of Emotional Contagion." *Neuroscience and Behavioral Reviews* 80 (2017): 99-114.

Stromberg, Joseph. "Dolphins Can Remember Their Friends After Twenty Years Apart." *Smithsonian Magazine*, August 6, 2013. https://www.smithsonianmag.com/science-nature/dolphins-can-remember-their-friends-after-twenty-years-apart-24490888/?itm_source=related-content&itm_medium=parsely-api

Stromberg, Joseph. "Do Dolphins Use Whistles to Call Themselves by Unique Name?" *Smithsonian Magazine*, July 22, 2013. https://www.smithsonianmag.com/science-nature/do-dolphins-use-whistles-to-call-themselves-by-unique-names-16005708/?itm_source=related-content&itm_medium=parsely-api

Xanthopoulos, Drew, director. *Fathom.* Produced by Megan Gilbride. Starring Dr. Michelle Fournet and Dr. Ellen Garland. *AppleTV,* June 25, 2021. https://tv.apple.com/us/movie/fathom/umc.cmc.5dba56sgwst50iuh5h9uqpdsq

YouTube Movies and TV. *Ocean Souls.* Directed and produced by Philip Hamilton. Produced by Scott Wilson. Narrated by Flora Clark. *YouTube* film, 57:46. (2020). https://www.youtube.com/watch?v=AfSE51HVWbA

Zandberg, L., Lachlan RF, Lamoni L., and Garland EC. "Global Cultural Evolutionary Model of Humpback Whale Song." *The Royal Society Publishing Journal,* (May 29, 2021): 1-12.

BEHIND THE STORY

Ota Benga: Former Congolese Slave Put on Display at the Bronx Zoo

"Ota Benga Attacks Keeper." *The New York Times,* September 25, 1906, p. 1.

"Ota Benga Having a Fine Time: Zoo Visitor Finds No Reason for Protests Over Pygmy." *The New York Times,* September 13, 1906, p. 6.

"Ota Benga, Pygmy, Tired of America." *The New York Times,* July 16, 1916, p. 12.

"Wants to Buy the Pigmy: An Elderly French Woman Writes to Inquire About Ota Benga." *The New York Times,* October 2, 1906. p. 9.

"What is Ota Benga: One Who Has Explored Suggests that the Supposed Pigmy is a Hottenhot." *The New York Times,* September 24, 1906, p. 7.

Washington, Harriet A. "In Captivity: In the Early 1900s, Americans Flocked to See the 'African Pygmy'." *The New York Times,* June 7, 2015, p. A26.

The Downfall of John Cuneo's Hawthorn Corp.

"McHenry County Elephant Linked to TB." *Chicago Tribune,* August 11, 2021. https://www.chicagotribune.com/1997/02/06/mchenry-county-elephant-linked-to-tb/

Schmidt, Michael, DVM. *Jumbo Ghosts: The Dangerous Life of Elephants in the Zoo.* Chicago: Xlibris Corp, 2002.

"The Suffering is Over at the Hawthorn Corporation!" *People for the Ethical Treatment of Animals,* November 30, 2017. https://www.peta.org/blog/hideous-hawthorn-corporation-history/

Thomas, Rob. "Feds Suspend License of Animal Compound." *Northwest Herald* (Crystal Lake, Illinois), February 8, 1997.

U.S. Department of Agriculture, Animal and Plant Health Inspection Service. *Animal Care Inspection Report: The Hawthorn Corp, John F. Cuneo, Jr.* License 33-C-053. April 10, 1997.

Musth in Bull Elephants

Moss, Cynthia. *Elephant Memories.* Chicago: The University of Chicago Press, 2012.

Poole, Joyce H. "Announcing Intent: The Aggressive State of Musth in African Elephants." *Animal Behavior* 37 (1989): 140-152.

Poole, Joyce. *Coming of Age with Elephants: A Memoir.* New York: Hyperion, 1997.

Poole, Joyce. H. "Rutting Behavior in African Elephants: The Phenomenon of Musth." *Behaviour* 102, No.3-4, (September 1987): 283-316.

Rasmussen, H.B. "Reproductive Tactics of Male African Savannah Elephants (*Loxodonta africana*)." DPhil Thesis. *University of Oxford, UK.*

Sukumar, Raman. *The Living Elephants.* New York: Oxford University Press, Inc, 2003.

Taylor, LA., F. Vollrath, B. Lambert, D.Lunn, I. Douglas-Hamilton, and G. Wittemyer. "Movement Reveals Reproductive Tactics in Male Elephants." *Journal of Animal Ecology* 89 (March 30, 2019): 57-67. https://besjournals.onlinelibrary.wiley.com/doi/10.1111/1365-2656.13035

Learned Helplessness

Ackerman, Courtney. "Learned Helplessness: Seligman's Theory of Depression." *Positive Psychology*, March 2, 2018. https://positivepsychology.com/learned-helplessness-seligman-theory-depression-cure/.

Bradshaw, Gay. 2010. *Elephants on the Edge.* New Haven, CT: Yale University Press.

Santos, Cristiano Valerio dos, Tuane Gehm, and Maira Helena Leite Hunziker. "Learned Helplessness in the Rat: Effect of Response Topography in a Within-Subject Design." *Behavioral Processes* 86 (2011): 178-183.

Seligman M.E., G. Beagley. "Learned Helplessness in the Rat." *Journal of Comparative Psychology* 88, No.2 (1975): 534-541. https://psycnet.apa.org/doiLanding?doi=10.1037%2Fh0076430

Seligman, Martin E.P., and Steven F. Maier. *Learned Helplessness: A Theory for the Age of Personal Control.* New York: Oxford University Press, 1993.

To Learn More About the Wild Elephants in this Book Please Visit:

Films:

Bloody Ivory, Wanted Dead or Alive, Elephants of Tsavo: Love and Betrayal, and *The Keepers Diaries* (Directed by Simon Trevor)
The Elephants of Tsavo (NBC Wild Kingdom)
Born to Be Wild (IMAX Pictures)
Elephants: Back to the Wild (Hoferichter & Jacobs)

Websites:

African Environmental Film Foundation (aeff.org)
Sheldrick Wildlife Trust (sheldrickwildlifetrust.org)

Television Episodes/Series:

The Elephant Diaries (BBC Studios)
Noel's Christmas Presents (BBC Two)

IN THEIR OWN WORDS

(As Written by Zoo Veterinarians and PhDs)

Schmidt, Michael, DVM*. *Jumbo Ghosts: The Dangerous Life of Elephants in the Zoo.* **Chicago: Xlibris Corp, 2002.**

Pg. 75: "The traditional methods that are known to work well to control a dangerous bull elephant are not well tolerated by the public."

Pg. 53-54: "...these ancient traditional methods developed specifically for elephants in war became ingrained as the only way to properly train and manage elephants. Since these methods were unquestionably successful, no other well-established elephant training and management methods were ever developed by those who wanted to break and train a wild elephant from scratch. Many of these same ancient methods that were developed for war elephants are still being used—inappropriately—by our modern zoos."

Pg. 127: "Traditional elephant training techniques were perfected over 2000 years ago when elephants used to fight ancient wars and have changed remarkably little since then. The traditional techniques work but they have two major drawbacks that turn out to be very dangerous for elephants and people in zoos: 1) they require skilled application and 2) they can be unnecessarily cruel and abusive.

---

* Doctor of Veterinary Medicine

On why using physical force, beating, and inflicting pain is still common practice in most U.S. zoos today:

Pg. 136: "When a new young elephant arrives at the zoo it goes through the same breaking method as the timber elephants before it ever arrives at the zoo."

Pg. 65-66: "Elephants know quite clearly when they've done something wrong, and they do not resent physical punishment for such transgressions…The super-alpha humans can—and do—use the traditional elephant hook and physical punishment to maintain normal discipline."

Pg. 75: "Everyone who works with [elephants] is required to achieve super-alpha status [by inflicting pain, i.e., beating them into submission]. It was true in Jumbo's day [in the 1880s] and it's still true today."

Pg. 125: "Obviously, if the citizens of Portland had ever found out about this business [Thonglaw's repeated electrocution sessions] they would have stopped it, which is why it was done at night with no witnesses around. It was a woefully misguided attempt to maintain control over an adult bull elephant in a zoo."

How the lack of education affects elephants:

Pg. 142: "…the [elephant keepers] 'don't know what they don't know' meaning they aren't even aware of it. When you add that kind of elephant keeper ignorance about the zoos elephants in a free-contact [where the keepers and elephants are not separated by a barrier] situation to the more typical elephant ignorance of the zoo managers you can brew up some really dangerous situations."

IN THEIR OWN WORDS

Crandall, Melissa. *Elephant Speak: A Devoted Keeper's Life Among the Herd.* **Portland, Oregon: Ooligan Press, 2020.**

Pg. 81-83: "Each time [Thonglaw's] trunk came close, [the keeper] jabbed it with a blade...he asked what they were going to do about the cuts he inflicted on [Thonglaw's] trunk. 'Nothing,' said Tucker [the head keeper at the Oregon Zoo]. They'd keep watch to make sure the wounds didn't fester, but otherwise those cuts would be left to heal on their own. Any discomfort would serve to remind the bull that [the keeper] was no pushover."

Maberry, Matthew, DVM, Patricia Maberry and Michelle Trappen. *Packy & Me.* **Beaverton, Oregon: Maberry Press, 2011.**

eBook Loc 931: "Zoo animals were the test subjects of drug companies."

eBook Loc 1283: "The zoo is built and supported by taxpayers who want a place where they can enjoy and get to know animals. Tax money, I felt, should not be used to fund a private laboratory for professionals with special interests looking, perhaps for the same publicity Packy's birth had generated."

Fowler, Murray E, DVM. *Hummingbirds to Elephants and Other Tales: Autobiography of Murray E. Fowler, DVM.* **Jackson, California: Clay Press Inc, 1999.**

Pg. 268: "Often males [elephants] would have to be euthanized after repeated attempts to injure keepers."

Pg. 275: "Those who truly love elephants would not wish to force one to live out her life alone."

Alexander, Shana. *The Astonishing Elephant.*
New York: Random House, 2000.

Pg. 135: Quoted by George "Slim" Lewis, "The death of an...[elephant bull handler] could be readily hushed up. Often the party line was: 'We warned him not to treat the animal that way. You couldn't really blame the animal for striking back...' Switching sympathy to the elephant tended to avoid lawsuits or public outcry...After her death [that of an innocent housewife and bystander at a circus], says Lewis, circus owners redoubled their efforts to get rid of male elephants, 'selling or giving them to zoos if they could, or shooting them after the slightest misbehavior.'"

Bradshaw, G.A., (holds two PhDs in Ecology and Psychology) *Elephants on the Edge: What Animals Teach Us About Humanity.* **Brainard, Minnesota: Sheridan Books, 2009, pg. 42:**

"It is easy to forget that [elephant] 'violence' exists only because humans have manufactured an environment that leaves them few behavioral choices."

THE ELEPHANT WHO INSPIRED IT ALL

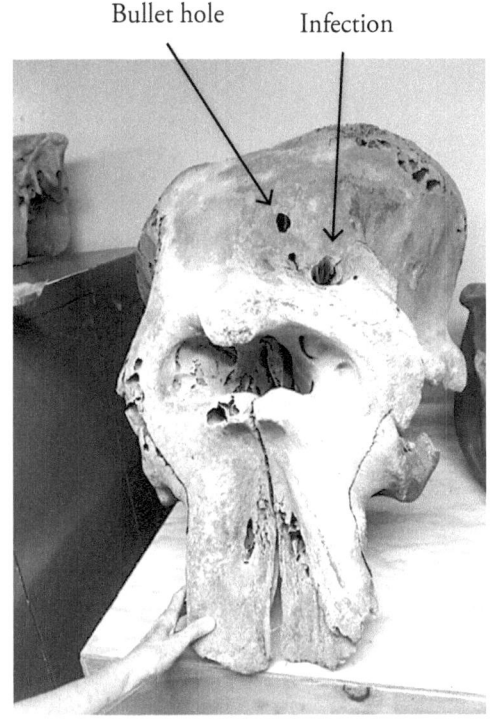

Buddha's Skull

Photo credit: Debbie Ethell

ABOUT THE AUTHOR

DEBBIE ETHELL is a conservation research scientist and former founder of The KOTA Foundation for Elephants, which was dedicated to increasing awareness about elephants. She has worked with organizations such as Friends of Animals, OneVoice (Association de Protection Animale) in France, and the Nonhuman Rights Project on important elephant-related court cases. Debbie's writing and research has appeared in various outlets around the world including *Africa Geographic, Mother Nature Network*, and several scientific journals. She enjoys public speaking and has traveled widely to share her passion for elephant protection and conservation. This is her second book in *The Will of Heaven* series.

Debbie lives in Portland, Oregon, with her dog Jax and a wild starling she raised, named Pip, who visits often but who remains beautifully untamed.

For more information about Debbie or elephants, please visit debbieethell.com.

Thank you for reading! If you enjoyed this book, please consider leaving a written review wherever you found it—whether at your local bookstore, online, or your library. This (greatly) helps increase the book's visibility and makes it easier for new readers to discover ...

the extraordinary lives of elephants.

—Debbie Ethell

www.ingramcontent.com/pod-product-compliance
Lightning Source LLC
Chambersburg PA
CBHW060546080526
44585CB00013B/459